Lecture Notes in Artificial Intelligence   1286

Subseries of Lecture Notes in Computer Science
Edited by J. G. Carbonell and J. Siekmann

Lecture Notes in Computer Science

Edited by G. Goos, J. Hartmanis and J. van Leeuwen

Springer

Berlin
Heidelberg
New York
Barcelona
Budapest
Hong Kong
London
Milan
Paris
Santa Clara
Singapore
Tokyo

Chengqi Zhang   Dickson Lukose (Eds.)

Multi-Agent Systems

Methodologies and Applications

Second Australian Workshop
on Distributed Artificial Intelligence
Cairns, QLD, Australia, August 27, 1996
Selected Papers

 Springer

Series Editors

Jaime G. Carbonell, Carnegie Mellon University, Pittsburgh, PA, USA
Jörg Siekmann, University of Saarland, Saarbrücken, Germany

Volume Editors

Chengqi Zhang
Dickson Lukose
School of Mathematical and Computer Sciences
University of New England
Armidale, NSW 2351, Australia
E-mail: chengqi@neumann.une.edu.au
        lukose@peirce.une.edu.au

Cataloging-in-Publication Data applied for

Die Deutsche Bibliothek - CIP-Einheitsaufnahme

Multi-agent systems : methodologies and applications ; selected
papers / Second Australian Workshop on Distributed Artificial
Intelligence, Cairns, QLD, Australia, August 27, 1996. Chengqi
Zhang ; Dickson Lukose (ed.). - Berlin ; Heidelberg ; New York ;
Barcelona ; Budapest ; Hong Kong ; London ; Milan ; Paris ; Santa
Clara ; Singapore ; Tokyo : Springer, 1997
  (Lecture notes in computer science ; Vol. 1286 : Lecture notes in
  artificial intelligence)
  ISBN 3-540-63412-6

CR Subject Classification (1991): I.2.11, C.2.4, I.2, D.1.3

ISBN 3-540-63412-6 Springer-Verlag Berlin Heidelberg New York

© Springer-Verlag Berlin Heidelberg 1997
Printed in Germany

Typesetting: Camera ready by author
SPIN 10547680   06/3142 – 5 4 3 2 1 0   Printed on acid-free paper

Preface

This volume of lecture notes contains revised versions of all accepted papers presented at the Second Australian Workshop on Distributed Artificial Intelligence (DAI'96), together with a set of invited papers. The workshop was held in Cairns, Queensland, Australia on August 27, 1996. The goal of the workshop was to promote research in distributed artificial intelligence, both nationally and internationally. The workshop covers a wide range of issues in the field of distributed artificial intelligence, such as methodology, cooperation, conflict resolution, and application.

Many people have contributed to the success of this workshop. We would like to thank all the authors who submitted papers to this workshop. Many thanks also to the members of the programme committee who diligently reviewed all the papers submitted for this workshop. Special thanks to our invited speaker Professor Jörg H. Siekmann from Universität des Saarlandes, German Research Center for AI (DFKI), Germany. Finally, we thank the editorial staff of Springer-Verlag for publishing this contribution to the Lecture Notes in Artificial Intelligence series.

August 1996   Chengqi Zhang and Dickson Lukose

Programme Committee

Dr Chengqi Zhang (Co-Chair)
School of Mathematical
and Computer Sciences
University of New England
Armidale, NSW 2351
AUSTRALIA
Email: chengqi@neumann.une.edu.au

Dr Dickson Lukose (Co-Chair)
School of Mathematical
and Computer Sciences
University of New England
Armidale, NSW 2351
AUSTRALIA
Email: lukose@peirce.une.edu.au

Professor Victor Lesser
Department of Computer Science
University of Massachusetts
Amherst, MA01003
U.S.A.
Email: lesser@cs.umass.edu

Dr Mark d'Inverno
School of Computer Science
University of Westminster
London, W1M 8JS
U.K.
Email: dinverm@westminster.ac.uk

Dr Toshiharu Sugawara
NTT Basic Research Labs
3-1 Wakamiya, Morinosato
Atsugi, Kanagawa 243-01
JAPAN
Email: sugawara@square.ntt.jp

Dr Jeffrey S. Rosenschein
Department of Computer Science
Hebrew University
Jerusalem
ISRAEL
Email: jeff@cs.huji.ac.il

Dr Nicholas Jennings
Department of Electronic Engineering
Queen Mary & Westfield College
University of London
Mile End Road, London E1 4NS
U.K.
Email: N.R.Jennings@qmw.ac.uk

Dr Keith S. Decker
Department of Computer and
Information Sciences
University of Delaware
Newark, DE 19716
U.S.A.
Email: decker@cis.udel.edu

Dr Norbert Glaser
CRIN-INRIA Lorraine
615, rue jardin Botanique, BP 101
F-54602 Villers-les-Nancy Cedex
FRANCE
Email: Norbert.Glaser@loria.fr

Dr Rose Dieng
ACACIA Project, INRIA
2004 Route des Lucioles, BP 93
06902 Sophia-antipolis Cedex
FRANCE
Email: dieng@sophia.inria.fr

Table of Contents

The CoMoMAS Methodology and Environment for Multi-Agent System Development

Norbert Glaser

CRIN/CNRS-INRIA Lorraine,
BP 239, F-54506 Vandœuvre-lès-Nancy
Fax: (+33) (0) 3 83.27.83.19 Tel: (+33) (0) 3 83.59.30.83
Email: Norbert.Glaser@loria.fr

Abstract. This paper presents the CoMoMAS[1] methodology and environment for the development of multi-agent systems. We use a conceptual model set to describe a multi-agent system under different views. These models are derived from the knowledge-engineering methodology CommonKADS. In contrast to CommonKADS, our approach takes several agent-specific aspects into consideration, in particular, the use of additional knowledge structures and their flexible representation to guarantee an agent's autonomy at execution time. A knowledge engineering environment has been conceived to demonstrate the feasibility of this conceptual approach. Conceptual models are represented in an extended version of the Conceptual Modeling Language (CML).

1 Introduction

The work in multi-agent systems (MAS) remains quite heterogeneous and varies from agent languages and agent architectures to agent theory [33]. Some methodological support seems to be interesting for the design of MAS systems and their implementation. A methodology can support both: on a formal side, the verification of particular properties of a MAS, and on an theoretical side, the design and development through a structured approach. Thereby, theory is a question of content and formalism a question of the form to represent this content.

We present a methodology which views the development of a MAS from a knowledge-engineering perspective: a set of conceptual models is proposed which were derived from the CommonKADS methodology [30]. We propose an extension of CommonKADS to the domain of MAS by including MAS-specific reactive, cognitive, cooperative and social knowledge; major updates needed to be made to the expertise and agent models. Other recent methodologies are inspired from practical programming experience (e.g., object-oriented language [23]); others propose a specification language [10] or are based on a business process approach [22]. A comparison is given in the related work section.

A benefit of our CommonKADS-based approach is the unified view of the construction of a MAS, with the support of a flexible structured library. This is

---

[1] Conceptual Modeling of Multi-Agent Systems (CoMoMAS).

of great advantage for the construction of a large range of applications. Indeed, applying the methodology to new domains extends the library through the integration of new or refined model templates. Our methodology and the proposed agent model respect the requirement for autonomy of an agent [13]. Autonomy means that each agent has its particular competencies and knowledge; it is able to act independently and make its decisions on its own. Autonomous agents may need to cooperate to solve complex problems. A methodology has to support both autonomy and cooperation, and should provide an agent model which encapsulates competencies and knowledge so that we can work with modular knowledge structures during modeling and implementation.

This paper is organized as follows: in the first two sections, we detail the Co-MoMAS approach, starting with the conceptual model set (Section 2), followed by the methodology (Section 3); Section 4 describes the knowledge engineering environment which we have realized; Section 5 illustrates our approach on an example and Section 6 discusses our contribution.

2 The CoMoMAS Model Set

2.1 CoMoMAS is derived from CommonKADS

Our methodology uses a conceptual model set for the description of a MAS, i.e. the various types of knowledge for MAS design and development. This model set is derived from the CommonKADS methodology [30], a quasi European standard for the development of knowledge-based systems (KBS). The development process is itself seen as a modeling activity, i.e. the construction of seven models representing the system at a conceptual level [27].

Within CommonKADS, the central position is occupied by the expertise model which reflects the problem-solving behavior of a multi-agent system for achieving the tasks assigned to it. Tasks are specified within the task model; it consists of a decomposition of real-life tasks which are necessary to achieve the function of the system to be built. Tasks are executed by agents having a role, a position and a certain type [32]. Transactions and transaction plans between agents are represented by the communication model.

The CommonKADS model set applies to the domain of distributed problem-solving rather than to multi-agent systems [17]: the CommonKADS agent model describes a task-solving entity, a specification which does not cover all aspects of an agent within a multi-agent society. We need to consider also agents which exhibit reactive and social behavior [4,5,11]. This observation requires the CommonKADS expertise and agent models to be modified and extended.

Previous attempts to extend CommonKADS for MAS modeling concern the modeling of multi-expert systems [9] and the proposition of an additional conceptual model [21]. The purpose of the first approach is to support knowledge acquisition from multiple experts. It puts forward a model for a cognitive agent including the individual and social aspects of human experts. The second approach introduces a global coordination model on top of the other models for handling the interaction of agents. This model is based on speech acts and is seen as extension to the CommonKADS communication model.

Our approach for MAS modeling is a compositional one: an agent model is built from the results of five analysis steps. Hereby, an agent is seen as an entity having social, cooperative, cognitive and reactive competencies.

2.2 Views and Models of a Multi-Agent System

Modeling a MAS from a knowledge-engineering perspective motivates the identification of different types of knowledge which can be represented within conceptual models. We introduce five different views of a multi-agent system inspired by the different types of competencies of an agent and by design and development aspects.

- The *functional view* describes the functional decomposition of the problem to be solved by the multi-agent system in terms of primitive and complex functional entities. An entity corresponds to a task to be solved either by the user or by the system.
- The *competence view* describes the cognitive and reactive competencies necessary to achieve the MAS tasks and goals. Cognitive competencies solve non trivial problems and are, among others, classical reasoning and planning methods [19]. Reactive competencies are stimulus-response relations [25].
- The *requirement view* describes the functional and non-functional requirements for the MAS design and implementation. Requirements can have a decisive influence on the clustering of tasks and the encapsulation of competencies; typical examples are efficiency and robustness.
- The *cooperative view* describes the competencies for cooperation and interaction between the agents to be composed. Reactive interaction can be used to simply and quickly solve problems [11]. Cooperative interaction can be used to jointly build plans [12].
- The *social view* describes the competencies for building and maintaining organizations which can be defined by a set of roles assigned to the agents. In our view, the purpose of social knowledge is to maintain an agent organization in an optimal state which reduces conflicts between agents [18].

Based on these views, we introduce a set of six conceptual models as illustrated in Figure 1. The cooperation model describes the cooperative view, the expertise model the competence view, and the system model the social view of a MAS, its organization and architecture. The task model describes the tasks that the multi-agent system is able to perform. The design model on the other side describes design guidelines and requirements. Agent models describe the agents of the MAS system. The development of conceptual models is related as illustrated in the figure by arcs labeled in italic for type dependencies and in normal for content dependencies. The development of the agent model, for example, depends on the knowledge represented in the model of expertise and in the model of cooperation. Model dependencies are reflected by relations between landmark states of different models [30,28].

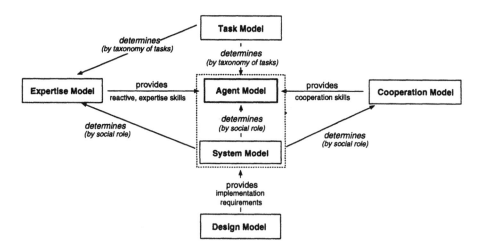

Fig. 1. The model set for MAS development

A multi-agent application corresponds now to a set of five conceptual models representing the views of the system and to one or several agent model constructed from this set of conceptual models. An application is represented by an application model as illustrated below. The model is given in CML syntax.

```
application ::= APPLICATION Application-name ;
               FUNCTIONAL-VIEW: task-model
               COMPETENCE-VIEW: expertise-model
               COOPERATIVE-VIEW: cooperation-model
               SOCIAL-VIEW: system-model
               REQUIREMENT-VIEW: design-model
               AGENTS: agent-model+
               END APPLICATION [ Application-name ; ] .
```

The major modifications and extensions which have been performed on the CommonKADS model set are detailed below:

- The *expertise model* was extended through the integration of strategies and reactive behaviors. A strategy describes a mechanism for the selection and application of problem-solving methods for a given goal. This was mainly motivated by the fact that an agent should have modular and flexible knowledge at execution time, i.e. a set of problem-solving methods and a set of strategies (see [17,16]). Reactive behaviors have been included as second source of knowledge — besides problem-solving methods — for solving goals on a event-driven basis. Reactive behaviors are a necessary ingredient for the design of real-time multi-agent systems.
- The *agent model* is structured according to four types of competencies, i.e. social, cooperative, cognitive and reactive knowledge (see [15]). Figure 2 summarizes the composition of the CoMoMAS agent model. In addition to the four types of competencies, an agent has control knowledge describing its internal control mechanisms, for example, how to make behaviors, problem-solving methods and strategies work together in order to achieve the agent's primitive goals or its more complex ones.

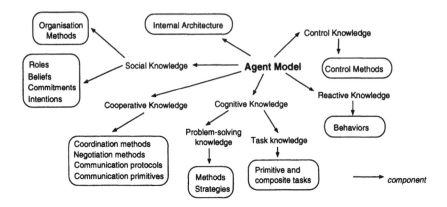

Fig. 2. Knowledge components of our agent model

2.3 Flexible Knowledge Structures

The description of an agent as an encapsulation of different types of competencies allows us to work with modular knowledge structures at the conceptual as well as at the implementation level. Figure 3, for example, illustrates the problem-solving and task knowledge of an agent.

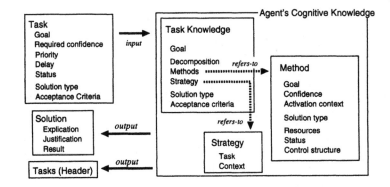

Fig. 3. Task and Problem-Solving Knowledge of an Agent

Task knowledge represents an agent's experience about previously solved tasks, i.e. previously applied problem-solving methods and possible task decompositions. Task knowledge evolves over time. Problem-solving knowledge, on the other hand, describes the problem-solving capacity of an agent in terms of strategies and methods: a strategy describes how to select and apply a method to solve a particular task. An agent returns either a list of subtasks or a solution containing a result, an explanation and a justification. The agent model contains other modular knowledge structures to describe, among others, the methods for cooperation, control, reorganization and the reactive behaviors.

2.4 Formalizing the Content of a Model with CML

We use the conceptual modeling language (CML) [29] for a structured and semi-formal description of a model's content, in particular, of the agent model. Originally introduced for the specification of CommonKADS expertise models, we needed to extend this language for our use, among others, we introduced additional language elements for the description of behaviors, control methods, cooperation and reorganization methods. Moreover, we extended the language to specify the content of the system, agent, cooperation and design models.

```
bhv-description ::= BHV Behavior-name ;
                        io-def
                        competence-spec
                        selection-info-bhv
                        control-info-bhv
                        decomposition
                        [ additional-roles ]
                        [ data-flow ]
                        control-structure
                    END-BHV [ Behavior-name ; ] .
```

Above is given a behavior in CML syntax which is very close to that of a problem-solving method. The CML descriptions of methods and behaviors contain attributes for the representation of the internal control and data flow.

3 The CoMoMAS Methodology

We define the development of a multi-agent system as a process which is composed of different phases: specification of the application, construction of conceptual models, validation of the models, implementation and testing. The construction of models is based on five different analysis steps as shown in Figure 4. Each analysis step results in one model of the previously introduced model set.

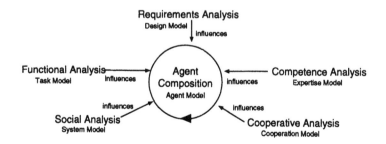

Fig. 4. Analysis steps during MAS construction

Results from functional analysis are stored in the task model, results from requirements analysis in the design model, results from competence analysis in the expertise model, results from cooperative analysis in the cooperation model, and finally, results from social analysis in the system model. The design model contains additional information including design guidelines and the design history [8]. The system model also includes architectural aspects, i.e. the system and agent architectures.

1. **Requirements Analysis:** The purpose of the requirements analysis is to determine the design requirements of the multi-agent system. This includes listing the requirements, determining their interdependencies and ranking them. The results obtained are represented in the design model.

   (a) Identify the design requirements.
   (b) Identify the interdependencies between requirements.
   (c) Rank the requirements.

   The results from requirements analysis have an impact on the identification of the agents to be built. Reliability, for example, may ask for the duplication of agents or communication by data sharing instead of message passing.

2. **Functional Analysis:** The purpose of functional analysis is to determine the set of tasks the multi-agent system has to solve. The result from functional analysis is a task hierarchy with user-solvable and agent-solvable tasks represented in the task model. We focus here on the agent-solvable tasks and assume that the task hierarchy represents agent-solvable tasks. A subsequent step is to identify the data and control dependencies between the tasks. Control dependencies are represented within the control structure of each task.

   (a) Analyze the application domain and problem space.
   (b) Determine goals, tasks and decompositions.
   (c) Determine data and control flow.
   (d) Build and validate the initial task model.

```
task-description ::= TASK Task-name;
                     TASK-DEFINITION
                         task-goal
                         control-info
                         io-def
                         [ task-specification ] .
                     TASK-BODY
                         task-type
                         decomposition
                         acceptance-criteria
                         solution-type
                         [ psm-ref ]
                         [ strategy-ref ]
                         [ additional-roles ]
                         [ data-flow ]
                         control-structure
                         [ assumptions ] .
                     END TASK [ Task-name ; ] .
```

3. **Competence Analysis:** The purpose of the competence analysis is to identify the competencies which the system should provide to solve the goals of the task model. As mentioned earlier, a task can be solved by a problem-solving method or by a set of primitive behaviors.

   (a) Determine the problem-solving methods.
   (b) Determine the resources.

(c) Determine the strategies.

(d) Determine the behaviors and the patterns of behavior.

The results of the competence analysis step are stored in the form of an expertise model. The expertise model provides at development time a global view on the different competencies which are encapsulated into distinct agent models in a subsequent development step.

```
expertise-model ::= EXPERTISE-MODEL Application-name ;
                    domain-knowledge
                    inference-knowledge
                    task-knowledge
                    [ psm-knowledge ]
                    [ reactive-knowledge ]
                    END EXPERTISE-MODEL [ Application-name ; ] .
```

4. **Social Analysis:** The purpose of social analysis is to identify social competencies required by agents. Social knowledge enables agents to act more smoothly during cooperation and interaction. This is a particular understanding of the usefulness of social knowledge and competencies. The result of the social analysis is the construction of the system model.

   (a) Identify conflicting actions and goals between agents.

   (b) Identify goal and data dependencies.

   (c) Determine the agent organization and associate roles to agents.

   (d) Determine and associate intentions to actions.

   (e) Determine and associate desires to goals.

   (f) Determine and associate commitments to goals.

   (g) Determine and associate beliefs to goals.

5. **Cooperative Analysis:** The purpose of cooperative analysis is to identify the cooperation protocols, cooperation methods and the conflict resolution methods for the agents. Cooperative analysis results in the elaboration of a cooperation model for the MAS.

   (a) Identify needs and levels of cooperation between agents:
       i. competence-driven: sharing of resources, methods, behaviors;
       ii. execution-driven: sharing of resources, methods, behaviors.

   (b) Identify conflict raising facts in agent interaction:
       execution-driven: conflicting goals and actions.

   (c) Determine coordination and negotiation strategies.

```
cooperation-model ::= COOPERATION-MODEL Application-name ;
                      domain-knowledge
                      inference-knowledge
                      cooperation-methods+
                      interaction-knowledge
                      END COOPERATION-MODEL [ Application-name ; ] .
```

The construction of agent models is based on the results of the five analysis steps. The starting point of this cyclic model construction process depends on the knowledge engineer. Moreover, an important question is if model templates are reused or not. An initial set of agent models can be based on the task model. This involves identifying subtrees or subsets of tasks within the task hierarchy and encapsulating the attached competencies into agent models. This first set of agent models is updated through the integration of reactive, cooperation and social knowledge and competencies. The information provided by the design model indicates if agent models need to be split or grouped together. The process of agent model construction can be described as follows:

1. Analysis of task model to build subtrees or subsets of tasks
2. Identification of agents based on categorization of tasks
3. Construction of agents with cognitive and/or reactive knowledge
4. Integration of cooperation knowledge into agent model(s)
5. Integration of social knowledge into agent model(s)

Resulting from the these five analysis steps are several conceptual agent models and a system model describing the overall organization and the architecture of the MAS. Below is illustrated the structure of the agent model.

```
agent-model ::= AGENT-MODEL Agent-name ;
                social-knowledge
                cooperation-knowledge
                task-knowledge
                psm-knowledge
                reactive-knowledge
                control-knowledge
                architecture
            END AGENT-MODEL [ Agent-name ; ] .
```

4 The CoMoMAS Environment

4.1 The Architecture

The CoMoMAS knowledge engineering environment has been developed to demonstrate the feasibility of our methodology. It is composed of four different modules to cover the whole knowledge engineering cycle. We give a short description of its architecture as illustrated in Figure 5.

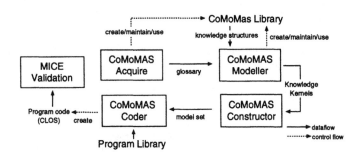

Fig. 5. The CoMoMAS architecture

A knowledge engineer interacts with the modules for knowledge acquisition and modeling to create the initial knowledge base to be used by the Constructor to build the model set. The acquired knowledge, in the form of transcription protocols and a glossary, is used to build the initial library containing domain hierarchies, semantic networks, inference structures, task hierarchies and other knowledge categories. Both modules are realized by KADSTOOL, a commercial knowledge engineering environment based on the CommonKADS methodology. As example is given the specification of a navigation method.

```
PSM Navigate-01;
    INPUT: World-model: SET-OF World-constraints;
           Goal-position: Position;
    OUTPUT: Navigation-plan: SET-OF Actions AND/OR SET-OF Subgoals;
    SELECTION
       GOAL : G12 "Determine navigation plan";
       COMPETENCE: "Navigation with no obstacles in the world; required
                    inputs are a world map and goal position.";
       CONFIDENCE : [1-5];
    ACTIVATION-CONTEXT : "Sensor data available";
    SOLUTION-TYPE : composite .
    CONTROL-INFO STATUS : text;
    RESOURCES : Sonar sensors; .
    SUBTASKS: Localisation, Planning;
    ADDITIONAL-ROLES: Start-position: Position;
    DATA-FLOW : INFERENCE "is-03-navigate";
    CONTROL-STRUCTURE : localise(World-model->Start-position);
       plan-path(Start-position+Goal-position+World-Model->Navigation-plan);
END PSM [Navigate-01] .
```

After knowledge modeling, the model components are exported in the form of knowledge kernels in CML syntax. The Constructor imports these knowledge kernels and guides the knowledge engineer for the composition of agent models by selecting knowledge structures from the previously introduced models. The Constructor is implemented in CLOS {citeBobrow88 and GINA [1], an additional package for interface construction. Resulting from this construction step are conceptual agent models represented in CML syntax.

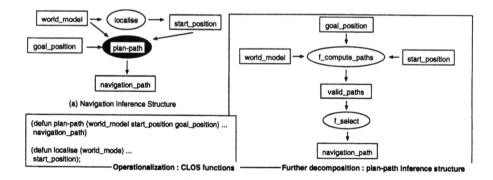

Fig. 6. Operationalising a problem-solving method

The Coder has the job of translating the conceptual agent models into an executable language, for example, CLOS. Translating our agent model means to translate the CML descriptions of its social, cooperative, cognitive and reactive competencies. The CML description of each competence holds two attributes which allow us to represent the internal control and data flow; they refer to inference structures which can be used as support for the identification of procedures from a program library during implementation. Such a program library provides procedures implementing, among others, reactive behaviors, planning methods and cooperation protocols. It is the task of the Coder to provide a set of program libraries with procedure which are linked to complete inference structures or pieces of them.The Coder is written in using Bison 1.24, a YACC compatible parser, and the fast scanner generator Flex 2.5.

Figure 6 illustrates this idea. The conceptual modeling delivers us an inference structure for a navigation method; this is shown on the left side. The inference structure is composed of two functions for localization and path-planning. The knowledge engineer has the choice between a more detailed decomposition of the inference steps of conceptual inference structure or an identification of procedures of the program library. On the right side of the figure is shown a more detailed decomposition of the path-planning inference step. The procedure selected from the program library are given in the lower side of the figure.

The developed agent models are validated within an extended version of the Michigan Intelligent Coordination Experiment (MICE) [26]. This environment provides evaluation mechanisms for the experimentation validation of agent architectures and systems in simulation. Agent-specific windows monitor the internal and external actions performed by each agent.

5   An Example Application

This example illustrates the application of our methodology for the modeling the AIbot agent model [20] which was applied for a surveillance application with several Nomad200 robots. The results of the analysis are given in natural language form:

- **Requirements analysis:** the functional behavior performed by the real robots should be efficient, and robust to perception and motion errors. Efficiency motivates implementing time-consuming computation off-board.
- **Social & system analysis:** the AIbot architecture is composed of a cognitive and a physical level. The cognitive level is implemented by the BB1 blackboard and the physical level is a simplified version of it. There is no social knowledge.
- **Functional analysis:** there are tasks for the cognitive and for the physical level (see Table 1). The cognitive level assesses communication (T1); it builds plans and determines locations (T2, T3); it builds navigation paths (T4) and monitors their execution (T5). The physical level executes the received navigation action (T6) and perceives the environment (T7).
- **Competence analysis:** task solving procedures are implemented as behaviors. At a conceptual level, we keep the separation between methods and

behaviors. There are message-driven assessment (T1); skeletal planning (T2); case-based planning and generative planning (T3); graph-search (T4); step-through (T5); dead-reckoning, feed-back control and mapping-navigation (T6); template-based perception (T7). The preconditions of a behavior describe its application context; its interface description the required resources and its accuracy.

– **Cooperative analysis:** internal communication is realized by data sharing and external by the exchange of messages. Cooperative methods would be necessary if several robots cooperate explicitly through the exchange of messages. The current implementation realizes only implicit interaction.

Task	Input	Output	Method
T1	new message received	new goal	message driven
T2	changed goal	new reasoning plan	skeletal planning
T3	new goal	new destination sequence	case-based planning generative planning
T4	new destination plan	new route plan	graph search-D/-U
T5	new perceived node	new physical command navigate [path] under [constraints]	step through
T6	new node perceived	at new node, new node perceived, other conditions	dead-reckoning feedback-control, mapping navigation
T7	new message/event	new perceived problem	template-based

Table 1. AIBOT: Tasks and Methods for Surveillance Application

Short pieces of the CML descriptions for the system model of the robot application and the agent models for the robot are given below. The system model refers to a specific application, i.e. the surveillance of floor B in a building by two mobile robots.

```
SYSTEM-MODEL Surveillance;
  AGENTS Nomad1 : Nomad200;
         Nomad2 : Nomad200;
  DEPENDENCY GOAL : "watch floor B" .
  ORGANISATION FLAT .
END SYSTEM-MODEL [Surveillance;] .
```

The conceptual agent model illustrates part of the tasks, the problem-solving methods and the behaviors which need to be implemented into the executable agent architecture. These components are obtained from functional and competence analysis.

```
AGENT-MODEL Nomad200;
  TASK-KNOWLEDGE
    TASK Plan-construction; ... END TASK [Plan-construction;] .
    ...
    TASK Perceive-environment; ... END TASK [Perceive-environment;] .
  PROBLEM-SOLVING-KNOWLEDGE
    PSM case-based-planning; ... END PSM [case-based-planning;] .
    PSM generative-planning; ... END PSM [generative-planning;] .
```

```
...
PSM graph-search; ... END PSM [graph-search;] .
REACTIVE-KNOWLEDGE
   BEHAVIOR dead-reckoning; ... END BEHAVIOR [dead-reckoning;] .
   ...
   BEHAVIOR identify-intruder; ... END BEHAVIOR [identify-intruder;] .
END AGENT-MODEL [Nomad200;] .
```

Based on the conceptual agent model an executable agent can be built as shown below. The executable agent is given in the CLOS programming language as it is implemented within an updated version of MICE [26,14].

```
(create-agent :NAME "ROBOT1" :TYPE :ROBOT
              :LOCATION (make-location :X 2 :Y 19)
              :ORIENTATION :NORTH
              :INVOCATION-FUNCTION 'surveillance-robot
              :DRAW-FUNCTION '(hero-icon :label "R1")
              :BLOCKED-BY-TYPES (list :SCREEN :ROBOT :BLOCK1 :BLOCK2)
              :METHODS '( '#'cb-planning '#'gen-planning '#'graph-search
                          '#'skel-planning '#'step-through)
              :BEHAVIORS '( '#'dead-reckoning '#'avoid-obstacle '#'wandering
                           '#'identify-intruder '#'inprete-pereception)
              :SENSORS (list *sensor-sonar*)
              :MOVE-DATA (make-move-data :NORTH 1 :SOUTH 1 :EAST 1 :WEST 1)
)
```

The agent model is implemented as a structure composed of different slots. Some of these slots have execution purpose (e.g. **draw-function**); others like the **behaviors** represent the functions which have been identified to implement the reactive knowledge of the conceptual agent model. The **invocation-function** implements the internal control of the agent.

6 Related Work

Methodologies for MAS development have become a very popular research topic. Noteworthy are the object-oriented methodology proposed by [23], the extension of the Z-specification language by [10,24] and the DESIRE framework [3,2] for the design and specification of complex compositional systems. Two approaches are based on the CommonKADS methodology: the work of [21] and the work of [9]. Interesting is also a comparison to the KSM [7] methodology originally introduced for KBS development.

The MAS methodology proposed by [23] views a MAS from an external and an internal viewpoint. On the external side an agent model and an interaction model are introduced to describe the decomposition of the system into abstract and concrete agent classes and their interaction. The internal viewpoint is represented by a belief, a goal and a plan model reflecting the BDI agent architecture. The introduction of libraries of abstract and modular agent classes could be interesting for the implementation of our conceptual agent models. In fact, we already use libraries of procedures.

A MAS system can also be within the Z language as advocated by [10,24]. They introduce a hierarchy of entities comprising autonomous agents, agents and objects as the most general one. An entity is specified by attributes, actions, goals and intentions. An object-based orientation is given in [31]. Their approach can be applied to obtain a description of the interaction and cooperation between agents which can be used as a basis for the elaboration of our cooperation model.

Noteworthy also is the DESIRE approach [3,2] which allows one to build task models including, among others, the sequencing and delegation of tasks between agents. Tasks can be specified at different levels of abstraction depending on the knowledge structures to be represented. In [3] a generic model is put forward for a knowledgeable agent. The elaboration of the task model during functional analysis and the identification of necessary cooperation methods could be supported through this compositional task-model framework.

[21] introduces a coordination model on top of the other models to coordinate tasks. This approach does not respect the autonomy principle of agents: there is one global expertise model which represents the knowledge of all agents. Our approach uses one expertise model at design time for having a global view on the system; it is clustered into distinct and flexible knowledge structures to be used by the agents at run-time.

Our work can also be compared to the KSM methodology [7]. It introduces three different views on an application: regarding knowledge, task and vocabulary. The knowledge view consists of a hierarchical collection of knowledge units; these units are linked to tasks which are associated to methods to solve them. The vocabularies are used to share concepts among different knowledge bases. The task view can be compared to our functional view and the knowledge view more or less to the competence one. The KSM methodology seems not to support explicitly the description of social and cooperative knowledge from a multi-agent system perspective. Nevertheless, the use of knowledge units may encapsulate knowledge to build autonomous agents.

7 Conclusion

This paper proposes a CommonKADS-based methodology for the development of multi-agent systems. Agent models are composed from knowledge structures which were obtained from five analysis steps. Each analysis step results in a conceptual model describing the multi-agent system from a from a different view point. We advocate a functional, a social, a cooperative, a competence-driven and a requirement-driven view.

Knowledge is represented in CML, a semi-formal language introduced by CommonKADS; CML has been extended by additional language constructs for the representation of our competence-based agent models. An argument for the use of a semi-formal language CML is the simplified but structured formalism for the description of knowledge. Simple verifications of CML descriptions, i.e. a static validation of input and output types of parameters, can be performed by the Cokace environment [6].

Inference structures have appeared to be a useful tool for guiding the implementation of our conceptual agent model. In fact, we use the data flow and the operators within an inference structure to select procedures from a program library implementing the competence related to the inference structure. Doing so, we built an executable agent architecture through a constructive process.

We have realized a knowledge engineering environment to validate our Co-MoMAS methodology; it integrates KADSTOOL for knowledge acquisition and MICE for the implementation of executable agent architectures. Moreover, we have illustrated the application of our approach for the modeling of mobile robots within a concrete problem, the surveillance of indoor environments.

8 Acknowledgments

The project was partly funded by the European Union as doctoral fellowship, contract ERB4001GT930339. The author is grateful to Philippe Morignot for critical comments on the paper and the presented example.

References

1. Thomas Berlage. *Object-oriented application frameworks for graphical user interfaces: the GINA perspective*. Gesellschaft für Mathematik und Datenverarbeitung, München, Wien, Oldenbourg, 1993.
2. F. Brazier, B. Dunin-Keplicz, N. Jennings, and J. Treur. Formal specification of multi-agent systems: a real-world case. In *Proc. 1 st ICMAS*, San Francisco, California, 1995.
3. F.M.T. Brazier, C.M. Jonker, and J. Treur. Formalisation of a cooperation model based on joint intentions. In *ECAI-96 workshop on ATAL*, pages 141–155, Budapest, Hungary, 1996. LNAI Series, 1193.
4. R.A. Brooks. Intelligence without reason. A.I. Memo 1293, MIT, AI Lab., 1991.
5. R. Conte and C. Castelfranchi. *Cognitive and Social Action*. UCL Press, 1995.
6. O. Corby and R. Dieng. COKACE: A centaur-based environment for commonkads conceptual modelling language. In *Proc. 12 th ECAI*, pages 418–422, Budapest, Hungary, 1996.
7. J. Cuena. Knowledge-oriented application development: Lessons learnt from real-time decision support systems. In *Proc. 12 th ECAI*, pages 711–714, Budapest, Hungary, 1996.
8. W. Van de Velde. Design model and process. Technical Report KADS-II/M7/VUB/RR/064/2.1, ESPRIT Project P5248 KADS-II, 1994.
9. R. Dieng. Agent-based knowledge acquisition. In *Proc. 8 th European Knowledge Acquisition Workshop*, pages 63–82, Hoegaarden, Belgium, 1994.
10. M. D'Inverno and M. Luck. Formalising the contract net as a goal-directed system. In *Proc. 7 th MAAMAW*, pages 72–85, Eindhoven (NL), 1996. LNAI Series, 1038.
11. J. Ferber and A. Drogoul. Using reactive multi-agent systems in simulation and problem solving. In N.M. Avouris and L. Gasser, editors, *Distributed Artificial Intelligence: Theory and Practise*, pages 52–80. Kluwer Academic Publishers, 1992.
12. K. Fischer, J.P. Müller, M. Pischel, and D. Schier. A model for cooperative transportation scheduling. In *Proc. 1 st ICMAS*, pages 109–116, San Francisco, California, 1995.
13. S. Franklin and A. Graesser. Is it an agent, or just a program?: A taxonomy for autonomous agents. In *ECAI-96 workshop on ATAL*, pages 21–36, Budapest, Hungary, 1996. LNAI Series, 1193.

14. N. Glaser. *Contribution to Knowledge Acquisition and Modelling in a Multi-Agent Framework - The CoMoMAS Approach.* PhD thesis, U. Henri Poincaré, Nancy I, 1996.

15. N. Glaser, V. Chevrier, and J.-P. Haton. Multi-agent modeling for autonomous but cooperative robots. In *Proc. 1 st DIMAS*, pages 175–182, Cracow, Poland, 1995.

16. N. Glaser and J.-P. Haton. Flexible and adaptive problem-solving in robot navigation. In *Proc. 1 st DIMAS*, pages 167–174, Cracow, Poland, 1995.

17. N. Glaser, M.-C. Haton, and J.-P. Haton. Models and knowledge acquisition cycles for multi-agent systems. In *Proc. of 9 th KAW*, pages 24/0–20, Banff (CAN), 1995.

18. N. Glaser and Ph. Morignot. The reorganization of societies of autonomous agents. In *Proc. 8 th MAAMAW*, Ronneby (S), 1997. LNAI Series. (forthcoming).

19. J.P. Haton, N. Bouzid, F. Charpillet, M.C. Haton, B. Lâasri, H. Lâasri, P. Marquis, T. Mondot, and A. Napoli. *Le raisonnement en intelligence Artificielle.* Interedition, 1991.

20. B. Hayes-Roth, K. Pfleger, Ph. Lalanda, Ph. Morignot, and M. Balabanovic. A domain-specific software architecture for adaptive intelligent systems. *IEEE Transactions on Software Engineering*, v(n), 1995.

21. C.A. Iglesias, M. Garijo, J.C. Gonzàlez, and J.R. Velasco. A methodological proposal for multiagent systems development extending commonkads. In *Proc. of 10 th KAW*, Banff (CAN), 1996.

22. E.A. Kendall, M.T. Malkoun, and C.H. Jiang. A methodology for developing agent based systems. In *Distributed Artificial Intelligence - First Australian Workshop on DAI*, pages 85–99, Canberra, November 1995. Lecture Notes in Computer Science.

23. D. Kinny and M. Georgeff. Modelling and design of multi-agent system. In *ECAI-96 workshop on ATAL*, pages 1–20, Budapest, Hungary, 1996. LNAI Series, 1193.

24. M. Luck and M. D'Inverno. A formal framework for agency and autonomy. In *Proc. 1 st ICMAS*, San Francisco, California, 1995.

25. M.J. Matarić. *Interaction and Intelligent Behavior.* PhD thesis, Massachusetts Institute of Technology, 1994.

26. T.A. Montgomery and E.H. Durfee. Using MICE to study intelligent dynamic coordination. In *Proc. 2 nd IEEE Conf. on Tools for AI*, pages 438–444, 1990.

27. A. Newell. The knowledge level. *Artificial Intelligence*, 18:87–127, 1982.

28. G. Schreiber, J. Breuker, B. Biedeweg, and B.J. Wielinga, editors. *KADS - A Principled Approach to Knowledge-Based System Development.* Academic Press, 1993.

29. G. Schreiber, B.J. Wielinga, J.M. Akkermans, W. Van de Velde, and A. Anjewierden. CML: The CommonKADS conceptual modelling language. In *Proc. 8 th European Knowledge Acquisition Workshop*, pages 1–25, Hoegaarden, Belgium, 1994. LNAI Series, 867.

30. G. Schreiber, B.J. Wielinga, R. de Hoog, H. Akkermans, and W. Van de Velde. Commonkads: A comprehensive methodology for KBS development. *IEEE Expert*, 9(6):28–37, 1994.

31. From Agent Theory to Agent Construction : A Case Study. M. luck and n. griffiths and m. d'inverno. In *ECAI-96 workshop on ATAL*, pages 50–63, Budapest, Hungary, 1996. LNAI Series, 1193.

32. A. Wærn and S. Gala. The CommonKADS agent model. Technical Report KADS-II/M4/TR/SICS/002/V.1.1, ESPRIT Project P5248 KADS-II, 1993.

33. M. Woolridge and N.R. Jennings. Agent theories, architectures, and languages: A survey. In *Proc. Workshop 7 at 11 th ECAI*, pages 1–32, Amsterdam (NL), 1994.

Design Patterns for the Development of Multiagent Systems

Elizabeth A. Kendall
kendall@rmit.edu.au

Margaret T. Malkoun
maggie@rmit.edu.au

Computer Systems Engineering
Royal Melbourne Institute of Technology
City Campus
GPO Box 2476V
Melbourne, VIC 3001 AUSTRALIA

Abstract

This paper focuses on the design of multiagent systems using object oriented design patterns. In earlier papers the distinctions and relationships between agents and objects were discussed; these findings are employed here as a foundation for a multiagent system architecture. Patterns are flexible, reusable, and effective object oriented designs. The role of design patterns for multiagent systems is discussed, and a design is proposed that addresses agent concurrency, virtual migration, collaboration, and reasoning. The paper yields a software architecture for multiagent systems and compares it to other approaches. Key software engineering issues for multiagent systems, such as reusability, testability, and maintainability, are addressed by the proposed design.

1 Introduction

Distributed problem solving is the cooperative sharing of information between work groups to produce a solution to a particular problem as a whole. Manufacturing enterprises often consist of many applications, databases and people across various departments. Intelligent agent systems are able to encapsulate applications and databases and facilitate the exchange of information and services through cooperation with other agents.

The term agent has various meanings in the literature. In this paper, we adopt the definitions of [20]. A weak agent is (i) autonomous (ii) social (iii) reactive and (iv) pro-active, and a strong agent, in addition to the above, has one or more of the following: (v) mentalistic notions (beliefs, goals, plans, and intentions) (vi) rationality (vii) veracity and (viii) adaptability. Within autonomous behaviour are the concepts of agent migration and transportability [19], and a social multiagent system must be open [1].

Relationships and distinctions between agents and objects are discussed in [11, 12]. Many commonalities between objects and agents are cited, along with relationships between agents and coexisting objects. An object is a software abstraction with behaviour, inheritance, encapsulation, compound, state, and identity. A strong agent is an object that is able to reason and to communicate via structured messages. Agents are also active objects, in that they have their own thread of control, and they are pro-active, which encompasses mobility. Passive objects without behaviour and encapsulation can coexist with agents as declarative knowledge or beliefs; additional objects, termed sensors and effectors, allow an agent to interact with coexisting objects that exhibit behaviour and encapsulation.

An agent system aims to be more flexible and adaptive than an object system through autonomous and pro-active behaviour. Part of the agent system's flexibility is in its openness, where agents can enter and/or exit a society, and in its ability to carry out opportunistic problem solving through various techniques, including plans, negotiation, and reasoning.

A multiagent system is complex and therefore must be carefully designed. A multiagent system architecture must address concurrency, synchronisation, and transportability, and it must also be flexible and reusable. Additional software engineering issues, such as testing and maintainability, must be considered. The present approach to object oriented design centers on design patterns [8]. Patterns are flexible and reusable object oriented designs with demonstrated effectiveness for particular application areas. A design pattern consists of a set of abstract objects and the interfaces between them, and catalogues of design patterns for various applications are now available [8], [6]. Whereas class/object descriptions can still be employed on their own for design, recurring practise has uncovered useful patterns or sets of objects that work together to effectively solve design problems.

Several object oriented design patterns have been found to be relevant to multiagent systems and are detailed below. In particular, the design patterns for active objects, brokers, mediators, sensors, adapters, and interpreters address the design problems of agent concurrency, virtual migration, negotiation, object-agent coexistence, and automated reasoning. These patterns and their applicability to multiagent systems are discussed in the following sections. The net result is a reusable, maintainable software architecture for multiagent systems that is compared and contrasted to other known approaches.

2 Object Oriented Design Patterns for Agents

2.1 Aspects of Agency

Strong agents reason to select a capability or plan that could achieve their stated goal(s). Declarative knowledge in reflective agent oriented systems has primarily been represented as beliefs in extensions to first order predicate calculus. Passive objects or object oriented databases should be used to represent agent knowledge in that they are more easily maintained [12].

Strong agent behaviour or capabilities are stored in a plan library. A plan is instantiated when a triggering event, such as a posted goal, occurs and when the context conditions are satisfied; an instantiated plan is an intention. The body of a plan is a set of tasks that can be subgoals, actions, assertions to and retractions from the beliefs, and messages to other agents. An intention executes in its own thread, and an agent may have several intentions executing concurrently. An intention can cause synchronous and asynchronous events; an intention is suspended when it gives rise to a synchronous event but not when it causes an asynchronous event.

Agents cooperate and negotiate with each other through tasks within plans that can be represented in conversations, and languages (such as KQML, COOL [2], and AgenTalk [13] have been developed to support this. Agents must be transportable and able to migrate to different processors in a distributed system [19]. With this, agents have the power to control their location. Migrating agents must be able to gain access to and share resources; they must also be able to enter and leave open systems.

These aspects of agency are summarised in Fig. 1. An agent is indicated, along with all the aspects of agency discussed above. The agent's reasoning are within its interpreter, beliefs, and plans. The agent's declarative knowledge (beliefs) may be impacted by a sensor interacting with external objects. Three intentions are shown for illustration. One intention involves an effector object that then interacts with external objects. The other two intentions feature collaboration with other agents, either within the original society or external to it. Each of the agent's intentions has its own thread of control. Additionally, agent collaboration, and interaction with effectors and sensors, must consider issues of synchronous communication.

The aspects of agency shown in Fig. 1 are analogous to those described elsewhere. [7] provides a generic internal architecture for an intelligent agent that has incoming and outgoing communication channels and queues, a central controller, and transient and persistent knowledge. Fig. 1 incorporates all of these features, with additional detail shown for threads of control, synchronous communication, and virtual migration. The agent's knowledge (beliefs, goals, and plans) may be persistent or transient, depending on the application. The ADEPT agent architecture [9] was also used in the ARCHON system, and it distinguishes between knowledge and capabilities used for self and acquaintance models, and interaction management. That is, the ADEPT architecture separates knowledge and capabilities that address the agent's own behaviour from those that address the agent's interactions with other agents.

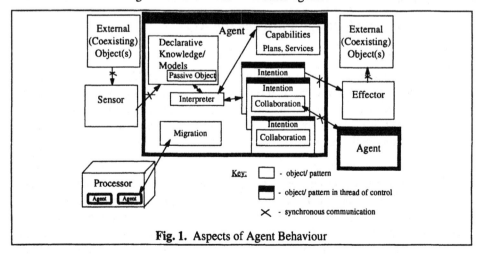

Fig. 1. Aspects of Agent Behaviour

2.2 Required Patterns

The fundamental approach in object oriented design patterns is one of teamwork and delegation. A problem is addressed by a team of well defined, cohesive objects that work together to solve the problem; each object on the team has a clearly defined responsibility. This approach promotes reusability and flexibility in that when a new capability is needed or requirements change, a new team player can be brought in to replace an existing one but the remainder of the team can usually be employed as is.

The second aspect of a pattern is the definition of the interfaces between the objects. Object interfaces must minimise dependency or coupling. Team members that are of the same class category, or expected to play the same role in the team, must maintain or subscribe to the same interface so that they are interchangeable [4].

Lastly, a pattern addresses object implementation. This includes static relationships between objects, such as containment or aggregation, and any required type information. With patterns for C++, type information is parameterized via templates whenever possible to make the pattern more abstract and reusable.

A design pattern has four essential aspects: (i) *a name*, (ii) *a problem and its context*, (iii) *the solution* - the objects, their responsibilities, interfaces, and implementation, and (iv) *results and tradeoffs*. Patterns for agent based systems can be identified by starting at item (ii); what are the design problems involved in the aspects of agency described in Section 2.1 ?

(1) Interaction with Coexisting Objects via Sensors and Effectors: A sensor must adapt to the interface of specific external objects, messaging it appropriately; it must also interact with the agents via structured messaging. An effector must be able to isolate an agent from platform or domain factors so that different types of objects can be addressed with the same interface.

(2) Collaboration with Other Agents: Agents collaboration is done via structured messages, such as KQML, COOL, or AgenTalk. The collaboration follows a conversation or coordination protocol that is itself a finite state machine.

(3) Synchronisation and Concurrency: Agents, intentions, and coexisting objects act in different threads of control and may require access to one or more shared resources. Agents and objects may themselves bezcome shared resources.

(4) Mobility: Agents must access each other and to other resources in a way that is transparent to location.

(5) Automated Reasoning: An agent selects a service or plan on the basis of their declarative knowledge.

(6) Interaction with external database: An agent must have direct access to relational or object oriented databases so that they can work with existing mainstream systems.

3 Relevant Patterns

3.1 Patterns for Synchronisation and Concurrency

Fig. 2 is a Booch object diagram (used in this section to indicate parameterized classes) based upon the active object pattern [14] and the ACE concurrency encapsulation pattern [16]. These patterns address synchronisation and concurrency. Four objects appear in the active object pattern: the Client Interface, the Scheduler, the Resource, and the Activation Queue. The Client Interface provides the interface to a client application. The invocation of a method triggers the construction of a Method Object which is then enqueued on the Activation Queue by the Scheduler. When the Resource is available, the Scheduler removes an activity from the queue and dispatches it to the Resource.

The additional two objects in Fig. 2 are the Thread and the Guard. The Thread is a thread of control, and this object encapsulates any operating system specific behaviour for thread creation, termination, and management. Thread is a parameterized class, parameterized by Resource Type, and the Resource's do() member function is what is executed in the Thread. The Resource may be shared; the Guard is responsible for managing shared or concurrent access to the resource by the (potentially) multiple Schedulers.

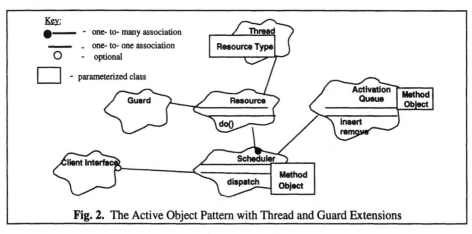

Fig. 2. The Active Object Pattern with Thread and Guard Extensions

In the active object pattern, the Client Interface decouples the interface *and the synchronisation behaviour* from the active object (Resource) itself. This is very significant in that it can be used to remove the inheritance anomaly [15, 16]. That is, subclasses of the active object Resource can be written to specialize the do() functionality but to directly inherit other behaviour of the class. If the subclass requires specialised synchronisation behaviour, this can be added through writing a new Client Interface class; it does not require additional changes to the Scheduler, Activation Queue, or Resource classes.

3.2 Patterns for Interaction and Collaboration

3.2.1 The Mediator, Sensor and Adaptor Patterns

Agent collaboration and interaction with objects give rise to similar design problems. Whereas delegation can enhance reusability, proliferating interconnections increase complexity and reduce reusability because every agent needs to know of every other object or agent. Additionally, if behaviour is distributed excessively any modification requires significant effort. The Mediator pattern [8] and its derivatives, Sensor and Adaptor [6], address these issues and are proposed here for aspects of agent interaction and collaboration.

A mediator is responsible for controlling and coordinating the interactions of a group of colleague objects; it is an intermediary so that the colleagues do not have to refer to each other explicitly. The pattern is made up of a Colleague class category and two Mediator classes: an abstract Mediator class that defines an interface for communicating with colleagues, and a concrete Mediator class that implements the cooperative behaviour by coordinating the colleagues. The Mediator pattern localises collaborative behaviour to one class. This is beneficial in that it replaces many-to-many interactions and removes the need for every colleague to have knowledge of every other colleague. It can be a drawback if communication bottlenecks occur.

A Mediator-Colleague structure with only two Colleagues is an Adapter pattern [6]. The Adapter transforms messages being sent from one Colleague into a form that is comprehensible by the other Colleague. The Adapter pattern is applicable to the Effectors in Fig. 1 that reformat the agent's actions into something that is recognisable by coexisting objects. The Sensor pattern [6] is a variant of the Adapter pattern when one of the Colleagues' interfaces is a generic (structured) interface and one is a specific or customised one. The Sensor pattern is relevant to the Sensors and the Effectors in Fig. 1 in that the agents follow structured messaging but the objects typically do not.

The roles of the Mediator, Adapter, and Sensor patterns in agent based systems are summarised in Fig. 3. Agent Colleague and Coexisting Object Colleague are subclasses of class Colleague. (The colleague nomenclature indicates cooperating, interacting agents and objects from Fig. 1.) Class Mediator has the behaviour that facilitates cooperation, and it is specialised to the subclasses Interagent Mediator, Effector (Adapter) Mediator, and Sensor Mediator. If the Agent Colleague interface is generic, the Effector Mediator and the Sensor Mediator understand this generic interface and the specific interfaces of the Coexisting Object Colleague(s).

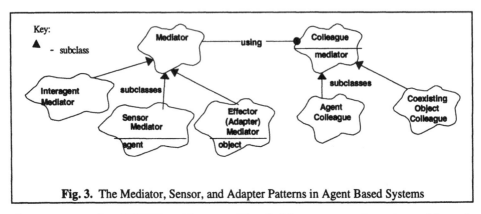

Fig. 3. The Mediator, Sensor, and Adapter Patterns in Agent Based Systems

In contrast to the ADEPT architecture, Fig. 3 delegates acquaintance models and aspects of interaction management to mediator objects. The Mediator pattern serves as an abstraction for collaborative behaviour and promotes object reusability in that Colleague classes do not have to be specialised to change only collaborative behaviour.

3.2.2 A Decentralised Collaboration Pattern

If communication bottlenecks become a problem, decentralised collaboration can be utilised. For this, each agent would require an instance of a Proxy for every interface that it supports, and it would have to maintain information or knowledge of every agent it wants to interact with. A Proxy [6, 8] controls access to the Real Subject; it can also provide a distinct interface. The KQML Proxy would support or subscribe to the KQML interface, while the COOL Proxy and the AgenTalk Proxy would subscribe to the COOL and AgenTalk interfaces, respectively.

In agent collaboration via coordination protocols the agent must be able to determine its behaviour based upon the state of the coordination protocol [13] that it is engaged in. One agent may be engaged in several conversations simultaneously, requiring that it be able to accomplish context switching. The Memento pattern [8] externalised an object's internal state so that the object can be restored to this state later. Agent proxies that support languages which involve conversations must store and recover their state. With the Memento pattern, they can delegate this to a companion Memento object. The Memento class is parameterized by Protocol, which gives the possible states and transitions.

The resulting pattern for decentralised agent collaboration is shown in Fig. 4. Each Agent Colleague must have an instance of an Agent Proxy for every interface that it needs to support. Each Proxy responds to messages from their own interface that would be sent by other agents via their proxies; they also know the corresponding messages that must be sent to the actual agent. To support the specific agent interface, the Agent Proxy class is parameterized by Agent Type.

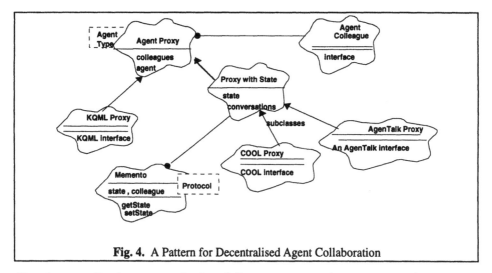

Fig. 4. A Pattern for Decentralised Agent Collaboration

For the coordination protocols that follow a conversation or a speech act state machine, companion Memento objects are shown. The Proxy is the originator of the Memento, and a Memento is instantiated whenever a conversation is engaged with another agent in the given language. The class State with Proxy therefore stores all conversations (instances of Memento) in a data member. When a collaboration is suspended, the Memento instance's state is set f

or storage so that when the conversation is subsequently resumed it can be recovered.

If Mediators were added to the pattern in Fig. 4, they would be responsible for determining which colleagues need to cooperate. The proxies would be responsible for intercepting messages for the agent in a given language, while the mementos would store the conversations that the agent is presently engaged in so that the proxy could recover them. As before, the benefit of employing this design or pattern is that agent behaviour for structured message passing and conversing in finite state machine protocols is abstracted and delegated to component objects. Other behaviour can be inherited, specialised, or delegated separately.

3.3 The Broker Pattern

Decentralising access to an open society, or making every agent responsible for the security and interactions within its open society, leads to the same possibly N-to-N connections described in Section 3.2.1. The Broker pattern [5], which led to CORBA [18], provides for communication and location transparency for objects and/or applications that wish to be clients and servers of one another. With this pattern, an agent can act as a client or a server to any agent or object that is registered. The agent (or its proxy) can become a virtual member of any open societies managed by the brokers. Bridges between societies are also supported.

In the Broker Pattern, agents who wish to be clients and servers for one another must use or employ a broker who is responsible for locating a server once a client has requested its services. Both the client and the server must have registered themselves with the broker.   Both the server and the client employ proxies who respond to the interface known by the broker; the proxies may also be located in a different (the broker's) address space.   In CORBA terms [17], the proxies subscribe to a certain interface, usually defined by an Interface Definition Language (IDL); the clients and the servers do not have to have direct knowledge of these interfaces.   The Broker pattern is depicted in Fig. 5, and brokers can also have a Bridge for forwarding requests and responses to another broker who manages another society of clients and/or servers.

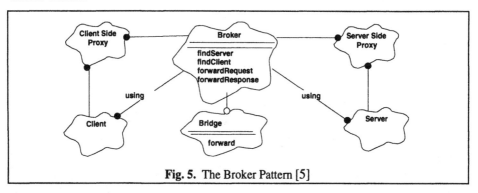

Fig. 5. The Broker Pattern [5]

3.4 Patterns for Automated Reasoning

Two patterns that are relevant to agent automated reasoning are the Interpreter and the Strategy patterns [8]. The Interpreter pattern defines objects for the grammar of a language. Composite objects are used to represent the syntax and the statements to be interpreted, and an Iterator is used to traverse the structures. Interpreters relevant to agent oriented reasoning, such as one that interprets beliefs, goals, plans, context conditions and invocation conditions, could be designed via this pattern. Plans would be instantiated into intentions when the beliefs, context, and invocation conditions are satisfied. This would provide the autonomous, reactive, and pro-active behaviour that is central to the definition of an agent; with a knowledge based representation.

The Strategy pattern encapsulates or objectifies algorithms or strategies for solving a problem. With this approach, each plan in the plan library can be an object, and each plan has its own invocation and context conditions. The key to the pattern is that each strategy has the same interface; each plan and each intention can also have the same interface.

The Interpreter and Strategy patterns represent object oriented designs for agent automated reasoning.   Performance issues are crucial to agent automated reasoning, especially for the Interpreter, so the designs must be refined to address this.

3.5 Pattern for Database Access

Agents require access to databases to be able to participate in an architecture where information is exchanged. As discussed above the commonalties between objects and agents, a persistent object stored in an object oriented database would be viewed by the agent as an external object. The Adapter pattern in Fig. 3 would transform messages being sent from an agent colleague into a form that is comprehensible by the coexisting object colleague, an object oriented database. Object adapters such as the one provided by CORBA encapsulate the object oriented databases with an access layer.

Relational database systems are far more complex. An agent must be able to transform records from the relational database into implementation objects and vice versa. Transition from objects to records is complex due to the mismatch in design methodologies. The Objects from Records [6] and Clerk's Files [10] are patterns which facilitate the exchange of information between relational databases and object oriented agent clients.

Fig. 6 illustrates the Clerk's Files pattern. For simplicity we will assume that the agent can only instantiate one transaction at a time therefore a singleton object is used as the DB Adapter. An agent is able to start, commit or rollback a transaction. Each transaction instantiates a view of the database. The view manager is a container of AgentView records (a relation). It acts as a caching mechanism by keeping track of whether an AgentView record has already been loaded during the current transaction. At the end of the transaction any AgentView records that have been marked as modified are written to the database. Data members of AgentView are objects, not database types. Map translates the data members of AgentView from objects into database types and vice versa. AccessDB encapsulates the database access functions and behaviour.

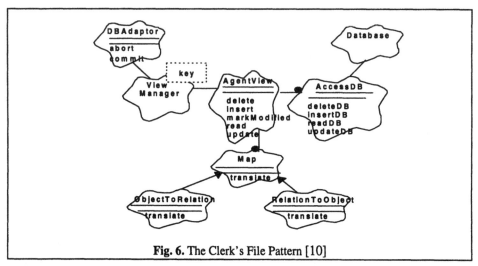

Fig. 6. The Clerk's File Pattern [10]

The complexity of mapping objects to relations and vice versa could not be adequately represented in Fig. 6. Map must provide the ability to a) assemble complex data types and objects from simple data types b) map object attributes to relation fields with respect to inheritance and relationships between objects c) give objects a unique identity and d) map associations using foreign keys and primary key fields in relations.

A wide variety of products are now available that provide object-oriented access to relational databases. Persistence from Persistence Software and DB.h++ from RogueWave provide C++ class libraries for object oriented access to relational databases.

4 An Agent Pattern

The patterns discussed in Section 3 must be integrated to formulate an agent pattern. As illustrated in the various patterns the internal structure of an agent can be quite complex. Each pattern dealt with a different aspect of the agent. The aspects of an agent make it sensible to use a layered pattern [5] in which to integrate the patterns. Each layer will deal with one specific aspect and uses the services of the layer direct below or above it. This is depicted in Fig. 7 and Fig. 8 where we have defined an agent as having four layers.

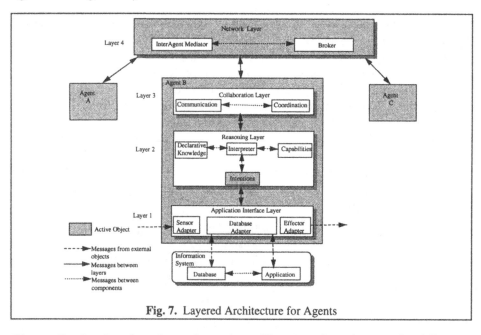

Fig. 7. Layered Architecture for Agents

The application interface layer, layer 1, will encapsulate the agent's ability to collaborate and interact with external objects, applications and databases through the use of the mediator, sensor and adaptor patterns in Fig. 3. The reasoning layer, layer 2, will encapsulate the interpreter and strategy patterns in Fig. 7 for automated reasoning and the instantiation of intentions in many threads using the active object pattern in Fig. 2. Layer 3, the collaborative layer models the agent's ability to communicate and coordinate to other agents through standard message passing and coordination protocols. Fig. 4 shows the linking of the communication and coordination functions through the use of the mediator and proxy patterns. The network layer, layer 4, provides the agent with the ability to physically transmit messages across threads and processes to other agents. It incorporates the mediator, active object and broker pattern (Fig. 5).

Fig. 7 illustrates a top-down and bottom-top approach to communication. Each layer deals with a specific aspect and uses the services of the next lower or higher layer. A top-down request may be issued from Agent A to Agent B's broker. The broker checks whether Agent A is registered with Agent B. If it is, the broker passes the request to the server proxy which inturn passes it to the collaboration layer. The collaboration layer initiates conversation with Agent A. Depending on the request Agent B may forward the request onto Agent C or seek the services of the reasoning layer to satisfy the request. The collaboration layer may send several requests to the reasoning layer. The reasoning layer may be able to satisfy the request or may seek the services of the API layer. From this example we can see that each layer has the ability to send requests down the line. Each layer may send one or many requests to a layer below (1:N relationship).

A request for services may flow from lower to higher levels, a bottom-up approach. An agent's intention may be triggered by input through the sensor (the application or database work in a similar manner). The sensor may report a change in the external environment to the reasoning layer. The reasoning layer may instantiate a plan to advise other agents requiring the services of the collaboration layer. The reasoning layer may instantiate many intentions to satisfy a particular request. Each intention is within it's own thread of control. One intention may require the services of other layers giving a cycling effect.

A facade [8] is used to encapsulate each layer and give a common interface between each layer. The double headed arrow in Fig. 7 represents the flow of services and requests between layers using the facade object. Complex layers such as the reasoning layer consist of different components (dashed, double headed arrow). The components in the reasoning layer are held together via the interpreter. The application interface layer and the collaboration layer use a mediator to link the different components. Fig. 7 also conveys the communication with external objects, databases and applications and the application interface layer (dotted lines).

The layered pattern provides an overall structure to a complicated system with many modules. Through this framework we are able to formulate the agent pattern in Fig. 8. Following the diagram from left to right we can see the association between the layers, a 1:N relationship. Each layer is encapsulated in a facade and inherits its services from its components. The network facade is responsible for concurrent behaviour. The collaboration facade is responsible for the collaboration with other agents through an agent communication language using particular coordination protocols. The API facade decouples the support for external objects from the other layers.

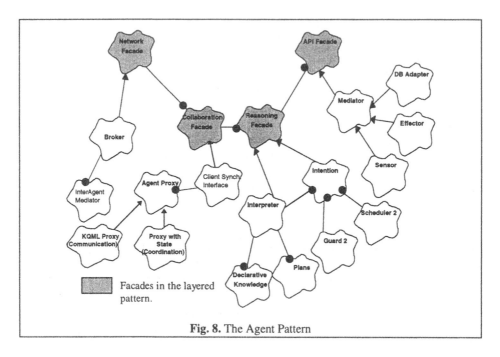

Fig. 8. The Agent Pattern

5 Summary

In summary, an agent pattern or architecture has been proposed. It is based upon the active object, mediator, proxy, and broker patterns, with additional features for automated reasoning, database access and thread encapsulation. The pattern was based on the layered pattern and has been described in terms of component objects with associations, messaging, class parameterization, and some inheritance. Some interfaces have been identified, but more work is needed. This should lead to further refinement of the pattern, especially in the areas of automated reasoning, agent mobility and security and data integrity issues related to database access.

This agent architecture is in use at RMIT and the CRC for Intelligent Manufacturing Systems and Technologies in Australia to develop an agent based system for an application in discrete parts manufacturing at the CRC-Intelligent Manufacturing Systems. C++ implementations have been carried out, and the merits of the pattern have been demonstrated, particularly in the removal of the inheritance anomaly, the delegation of coordination and interaction behaviour, and the centralised, CORBA compliant management of an open agent system.

Future work will concentrate on incorporating legacy systems and on the benefits and drawbacks of centralised and decentralised databases for agent based systems. Additionally, constraint technology [3] is being investigated as an alternative to the BDI (belief, desires, intentions) knowledge representation discussed here. Constraint technology is valuable for opportunistic problem solving where human expertise cannot really be formalised, such as in scheduling.

6 Ackowledgements

This project was partly funded by the CRC's for Intelligent Decision Systems and for Intelligent Manufacturing Systems and Technologies under the Australian Government's CRC Program.

7 References

1. Avouris, N.M. and L. Gasser, *Distributed Artificial Intelligence: Theory and Praxis.* 1991: Kluwer Academic Publishers.
2. Barbuceanu, M. and M.S. Fox. *COOL: A Language for Describing Coordination in Multi-Agent Systems.* in *First International Conference on Multi-Agent Systems.* 1995.
3. Baumgartel, H., S. Bussmann, and M. Klosterberg. *Combining Multi-Agent Systems and Constraint Techniques in Production Logistics.* in *Artificial Intelligence, Simulation and Planning in High Autonomy Systems.* 1996. La Jolla.
4. Booch, G., *Object Oriented Analysis and Design with Applications.* Second Edition ed. 1994: The Benjamin/Cummings Publishing Company.
5. Buschmann, F., *et al.*, *Pattern-Oriented Software Architecture: A System of Patterns.* 1996: Wiley and Sons.
6. Coplien, J. and D. Schmidt, *Pattern Languages of Program Design.* 1995: Addison-Wesley.
7. Farhoodi, F. and I. Graham. *A Practical Approach to Designing and Building Intelligent Software Agents.* in *First International Conference on the Practical Application of Intelligent Agents and Multiagent Technology.* 1996. London.
8. Gamma, E.R., *et al.*, *Design Patterns: Elements of Reusable Object-Oriented Software.* 1994: Addison-Wesley.
9. Jennings, N.R., *et al. Using Intelligent Agents to Manage Business Processes.* in *First International Conference on the Practical Application of Intelligent Agents and Multiagent Technology.* 1996. London.
10. Keller, W., *Clerk's Files,* Web site http://www.c2.com:80/ppr/clerks 1996.
11. Kendall, E.A., M.T. Malkoun, and C.H. Jiang. *A Methodology for Developing Agent Based Systems.* in *First Australian Workshop on Distributed Artificial Intelligence at the Eighth Australian Joint Conference on Artificial Intelligence.* 1995. Canberra.
12. Kendall, E.A., M.T. Malkoun, and C.H. Jiang. *A Methodology for Developing Agent Based Systems for Enterprise Integration.* in *EI '95, IFIP TC5 SIG Working Conference on Models and Methodologies for Enterprise Integration.* 1995. Heron Island, Australia.
13. Kuwabara, K., T. Ishida, and N. Osata. *AgenTalk: Describing Multiagent Coordination Protocols with Inheritance.* in *submitted to Tools for Artificial Intelligence.* 1995.
14. Lavender, R.G. and D.C. Schmidt. *Active Object: an Object Behavioral Pattern for Concurrent Programming.* in *Pattern Languages of Programming.* 1995. Illinois.

15. Matsuoka, S. and A. Yonezawa, *Analysis on Inheritance Anomaly in Object-Oriented Concurrent Programming Languages*, in *Research Directions in Concurrent Object-Oriented Programming*, G. Agha, P. Wegner, and A. Yonezawa, Editors. 1993, MIT Press: Cambridge, MA.

16. Schmidt, D.C., *The ACE Object-Oriented Encapsulation of Light Weight Concurrency Mechanisms*. 1995.

17. Schmidt, D.C. and S. Vinoski, *Object Interconnections: Comparing Alternative Client-Side Distributed Programming Techniques (Column 3)*. SIGS C++ Report Magazine, 1995(May).

18. Vinoski, S., *Distributed Object Computing with CORBA*. C++ Report, 1993. 5(July/August).

19. Wayner, P., *Agents Unleashed: A Public Domain Look at Agent Technology*. 1995: AP Professional.

20. Wooldridge, M.J. and N.R. Jennings. *Agent Theories, Architectures and Languages*. in *ECAI-94 Workshop on Agent Theories, Architectures, and Languages*. 1995. Amsterdam.

Modelling Extendible Mobile Agents

Dickson Lukose

Distributed Artificial Intelligence Centre (DAIC)
Department of Mathematics, Statistics, and Computing Science
The University of New England, Armidale, 2351, N.S.W., AUSTRALIA

Email: lukose@peirce.une.edu.au
Tel.: +61 (0)67 73 2302   Fax.: +61 (0)67 73 3312

Abstract

In this paper, the author describes a graphical conceptual modelling language called MODEL-ECS that is used to model the components of a mobile agent. The use of this language to model the *PROJECTION COMPONENT* of the *Perception Mechanism* of a mobile agent is demonstrated. This modelling language uses conceptual structures (i.e., Conceptual Graphs, Actor Graphs, and Problem Maps) as its primitive modelling constructs. The Knowledge Analysis and Design Support (KADS) conceptual modelling principles are adopted in building the Knowledge Sources and the Problem Solving Methods (PSMs) for constructing the components of a mobile agent. There are three main reasons (resulting in three major advantage) for using MODEL-ECS to construct the components of a mobile agent: (1) the executable components in the form of PSMs are much easier to transport from one *Agent Server* to the next, because you only have to send a flat file consisting of the conceptual structures that make up the PSM; (2) it is much easier to manipulate conceptual structures to construct a PSM, rather then writing a program; (3) the conceptual structures are specifically designed to maintain their current value, thus, enabling the PSMs of a mobile agent to be suspended at any time, so the agent can be transported to the next location, and it can commence execution from where it left off. These three advantages are crucial to the successful implementation of a robust extendable mobile agent architecture.

1. Introduction

In recent years, there has been much effort in building Distributed Artificial Intelligence (DAI) applications. Wooldridge and Jennings [17], and O'Hare and Jennings [13], provide an excellent overview of most of the contemporary developments in this area. Three agent architectures for building DAI systems have evolved to emerge as more prominent. They are: the ARCHON (architecture for cooperative heterogeneous on-line systems) agent architecture which specifically addresses the framework and the methodology necessary for interaction between the components of an integrated community [1]; the CooperA [14] which is a software environment supporting the cooperation of heterogeneous, distributed, semiautonomous KB systems; and finally, the AGenDA agent architecture which is composed of a number of rigorously defined layers which use different types of knowledge representation and different reasoning mechanisms [5]. On the other hand, IMAGINE [16] is a language for implementing DAI systems (i.e., a programming language that can be used to implement agents and their interactions). Further, a framework like TAEMS [3] adopts an agent centred perspective for the analysis and design of coordination mechanisms, and Agent Factory [12] supports systematic development of multi agent systems.

Even though the above-mentioned agent architectures have been successfully used in building DAI systems in industry and commerce, there are still some very fundamental requirements of an agent modelling environment that need to be addressed. In particular, the facilitates that enable mobile agents to efficiently move around in the cyberspace (i.e., from one community of agents to another), cooperate with other agents during problem solving, and collaborate with other agents in carrying out a task. There are three necessary functionalities of an agent architecture of this type. They are: *mobility*; *extendability*; and *current value programming*. MODEL-ECS is a conceptual modelling language specifically designed for implementing agents and their interactions in a multi-agent environment, and which successfully addresses these three necessary functionalities. This paper will describe MODEL-ECS, and provide an example of building a PSM using this language.

The outline of this paper is as follows. Section 2 describes our extendable mobile agent architecture, and the architecture and components of a deliberative agent. In Section 3, the author will describe all the conceptual structures used by MODEL-ECS to realise the primitive executable construct known as the Knowledge Source, and the more complex construct known as the Problem Map, that are used for building the PSMs. Section 4 describes, in detail, the construction of the *PROJECTION COMPONENT* of the *Perception Mechanism* of our mobile agent. Section 5 discusses the advantages of using MODEL-ECS in building our mobile agents, and finally, Section 6 concludes with an outline of the future direction of this research.

2. Mobile Agent Architecture

2.1. Agent Environment

Our mobile agent environment is made up of *Agent Servers*, *Agent Name Servers*, and *Mobile Agents*. An Agent Server is made up of the following components: an *In-Queue*, an *Out-Queue*, several *Service Rooms* and a stationary *Gatekeeper* agent. Each of these is described below:
- **Agent Server:** The *Agent Server* is the point where the agent arrives, performs its tasks and then depart to some other agent server.
- **In-Queue:** The *In-Queue* is where the incoming agents queue up for authentication before being allowed into their room, or before being allocated a new room for first time visitors.
- **Out-Queue:** The *Out-Queue* is where the agent queues up to be transported to its next destination.
- **Service Room:** A Service Room is a work space allocated to a mobile agent. Every agent is allocated a different room. This room is used by the agents to deposit many of its bulky components (ie., in particular site specific components/data). These components will therefore be available on subsequent visits.
- **Gatekeeper:** The *Gatekeeper* is responsible for managing the arrival and departure of the mobile agents. This includes the authentication of incoming agents, registration and allocation of a service room, and the bundling and dispatch of agents leaving the server.

- **Agent Name Server:** The *Agent Name Server* (ANS) functions in a similar way to the *Domain Name Servers* used in the Internet. The ANS can also provide a messaging service and audit trail of an agent's movements.

Figure 1 depicts our mobile agent environment. For a detailed description of the components outlined above, refer to Munday et al. [11].

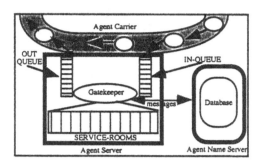

Figure 1: Mobile Agent Environment (adapted from [11])

2.2. Mobile Agent

An extendable architecture for building our autonomous agents has been adopted. This approach enables us to build agents that range from being purely reactive, highly deliberative, or hybrid architecture [11]. Figure 2 depicts the components of a deliberate mobile agent. Some of the components are *Short-Term Memory* (STM), *Long-Term Memory* (LTM), and mechanisms such as *Perception*; *Motivation*; *Prediction*; *Self-Reflexion*; *Goal Creation, Identification* and *Evaluation*; *Planning, Plan Identification* and *Plan Execution*. Each of the components of an agent is modelled as an executable Problem Solving Methods (PSMs). Executability of a PSM is achieved by using a graphical conceptual modelling language called MODEL-ECS [8] [9] [10]. To enable *information passing* between components in an agent, each component also has a set of *plugs* and *sockets* that connects these components together [11].

In the following section, the author will describe the graphical conceptual modelling language called MODEL-ECS, which is used in building the components of an agent (i.e., as PSMs). MODEL-ECS uses Conceptual Graphs, Actors, Executable Conceptual Structures and Complex Modelling Constructs to facilitate graphical conceptual modelling. All of these are briefly described in the following section. For a detailed description, refer to [9].

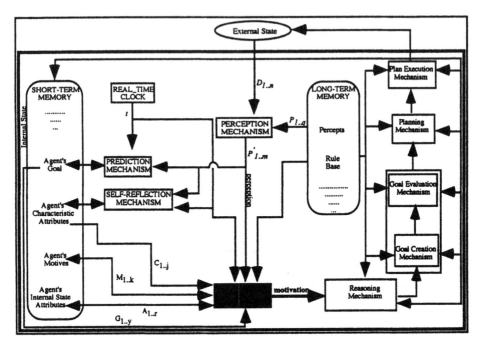

Figure 2: Architecture of a Deliberate Mobile Agent (adapted from[11])

3. MODEL-ECS: Executable Conceptual Modelling Language

3.1. Conceptual Graphs

Conceptual graphs are finite, connected, bipartite graphs. For example, in graphical form, a conceptual graph representation of a natural language sentence "*Dickson went to Calgary by plane*" is shown in Figure 3.

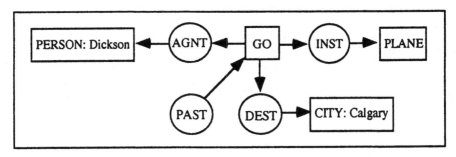

Figure 3: Diagram representation of a simple conceptual graph

A definition can equate an entire graph with a name or type label. Type definitions provide a way of expanding a concept in primitives, or contracting a concept from a graph of primitives. Definitions can specify a type in two different ways: by stating necessary and sufficient conditions for the type, or by giving a few examples and saying that everything similar to these belongs to the type. Conceptual Graphs support type definition by *genus* and *differentiae*, as well as *schemata* and *prototypes*. Both methods are based on abstractions, which are canonical graphs with one or more concepts designated as formal parameters. An *n-adic abstraction*, $\lambda a_1,.....,a_n u$, consists of a canonical graph u, called the body, together with a list of generic concepts $a_1,.....,a_n$ in u, called the formal parameters. A generalisation hierarchy is defined over abstractions.

Definition 1:
A *type definition* declares that a type label t is defined by a monadic abstraction $\lambda a\ u$. It is written, **type** $t(a)$ **is** u. The body u is called the *differentia* of t, and $type(a)$ is called the *genus* of t.

An example of a type definition for OBTAIN is shown in Figure 4.

```
type OBTAIN(x) is:
            [ACT:*x] -
                    --> (OBJ) --> [ENTITY:*m]
                    --> (SRCE) --> [PLACE:*n]
                    --> (AGNT) --> [ENTITY:*o]
                    --> (RCPT) --> [ENTITY:*o].
```

Figure 4: Type Definition for concept type *"OBTAIN"*

Definition 2:
A *relation definition*, written **relation** $t(a_1,....,a_n)$ **is** u, declares that the label t for a conceptual relation is defined by an *n-adic abstraction*, $\lambda a_1,....,a_n u$. The body u is called the *relator* of t.

Figure 5 and 6 shows the relation definition for two temporal relations (i.e., *FINISH_BEFORE_START (FBS)* that indicates sequence, and *START_WHEN_START (SWS)* to indicate concurrency).

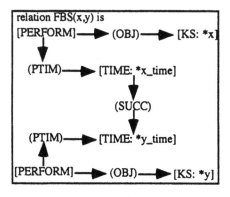

Figure 5: Relation Definition for
FINISH_BEFORE_START

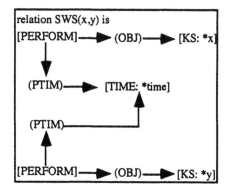

Figure 6: Relation Definition for
START_WHEN_START

3.2. Actor

There two types of actors (objects). They are the *class (type) actor* and the *instance actor*. Class actors are defined as abstractions. An *actor hierarchy* is defined over all the class actors. It responds to an incoming message by executing a method corresponding to the message. A detailed description of each of the components of the Actor (i.e., Class Actor or Instance Actor) is beyond the scope of this paper. Interested readers may refer to [7] for a detailed discussion.

Definition 3:
An *actor type* (or class) t is defined as an *n-adic* abstraction $\lambda\, m_1, m_2, ..., m_n\, u$, written as the **actor** $t\,(\, m_1, m_2, ..., m_n\,)$ is u. The body u is called the "actor", while $m_1, m_2, ...,$ m_n represents the messages that the "actor" can respond to. If r is an actor of class t, then the message handler in r can handle n different messages (i.e., $m_1, m_2, ..., m_n$), represented by n different methods in "actor" u.

An example for actor class (type) for OBTAIN is shown in Figure 7.

```
/* ICS Object for : obtain  */
icsobject(obtain,                                               /* actor name            */
      basicframe(localreg( [post(p1), pre(p2), del(p1)],263  ),   /* long-term memory     */
              defaultrtn( [recallinformation(A,B,Z)]  )  ),
         extentionframe( iopara([iomethodptr(description(A), description(A)), /* message handler*/
                  iomethodptr(graph(G1), process(G1,A,B,Z))
                          ]),
              currentvalue( [0,24], 264),                        /* short-term memory  */
icsfunction([description('Actor Graph OBTAIN'),                  /* methods            */
              ])), 265).                                         /* actor identifier   */
```

Figure 7: Class Actor for *"OBTAIN"*

3.3. Executable Conceptual Structures

3.3.1. Actor Graphs

Actor Graphs are the most primitive Executable Conceptual Structures. Actor Graphs use *conceptual graphs* to represent the declarative knowledge associated with an inference step, and an *actor script* to represent the procedural knowledge [7].

Definition 4:
An *Actor Graph* labelled t is defined as a *dyadic* abstraction $\lambda\, a\, u_1\, m\, u_2$, where **type(a)** is the genus of t, the body u_1 is the differentia of t, and m is the message that will invoke the main method described in the "actor" u_2.

Figure 8 depicts a graphical representation of the Actor Graph. Actor Graphs adopt the semantics of the STRIPS architecture [4]. Each Actor Graph has, associated with it, sets of conceptual graphs representing the "precondition", "postcondition" and "delete" lists. The actor associated with an Actor Graph is made up of three parts: short term memory; long term memory; and main methods. The short term memory is used to record current values associated with the problem domain. The long term memory is used to store the precondition, postcondition and delete lists. The main method section represents the set of methods that the actor is able to call upon. The precondition graphs represent the knowledge which must exist for the inference step represented by the Actor Graph to be executed. The postcondition graphs represent the new knowledge which is created by the inference. Any graphs in the delete list represent knowledge which no longer holds as a result of the inference step.

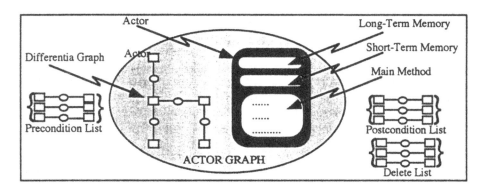

Figure 8: Graphical Representation of an Actor Graph

By combining the differentia of the *type definition* for *OBTAIN* (i.e., Figure 4), with the *actor* for *OBTAIN* (i.e., Figure 7), actor graph for OBTAIN is formed as shown in Figure 9. The execution of OBTAIN takes place only when the graphs in the precondition list is found in the working memory (i.e., state space). If they are found in the working memory, the graphs in the delete list is removed from the working memory, and the graphs in the postconditions list is inserted into the working memory.

```
                              [ACT:*x] -
                                    --> (OBJ) --> [ENTITY:*m]
                                    --> (SRCE) --> [PLACE:*n]
                                    --> (AGNT) --> [ENTITY:*o]
                                    --> (RCPT) --> [ENTITY:*o].
/* ICS Object for : obtain  */
icsobject(obtain,                                    /* actor name          */
        basicframe(localreg( [post(p1), pre(p2), del(p1)],263  ),   /* long-term memory   */
                defaultrtn( [recallinformation(A,B,Z)]  ) ),
            extentionframe( iopara([iomethodptr(description(A), description(A)), /* message handler*/
                    iomethodptr(graph(G1), process(G1,A,B,Z))
                        ]),
                currentvalue( [0,24], 264),                 /* short-term memory  */
icsfunction([description('Actor Graph OBTAIN'),          /* methods            */
        ])), 265).                                           /* actor identifier   */
```

Pre-Condition List:	{[ENTITY:*o] <- (AGNT) <- [ACCESS] -> (OBJ) -> [ENTITY:*m] }	p_1
Post-Condition List:	{[ENTITY:*o] -> (POSS) -> [ENTITY:*m] }	p_2
Delete List	: {[ENTITY:*o] <- (AGNT) <- [ACCESS] -> (OBJ) -> [ENTITY:*m]}	p_1

Figure 9: Actor graph for *OBTAIN*

3.3.2. Problem Maps

The Problem Map is an executable conceptual structure which can be used to represent task knowledge in a KADS model. A Problem Map is formed by specifying a partial temporal ordering of the Actor Graphs [2] which represent the primitive inference steps.

Definition 5:

A *Problem Map* labelled t is defined as a *n-adic* abstraction $\lambda v_1,..,v_n \ w_1,...,w_m \ u$, where u is the conceptual graph (i.e., body) representing the Problem Map, $v_1,..,v_n$ which is in turn the set of conceptual graphs representing the initial state, while $w_1,...,w_m$ is the set of graphs representing the final state.

Two relations are used to specify the partial temporal ordering of the Actor Graphs: FINISH_BEFORE_START (FBS) and START_WHEN_START (SWS). The (FBS) relation is used to represent a temporal constraint between two Actor Graphs. The (SWS) relation is used to link two Actor Graphs when there is no temporal constraint between them [2]. An example of a simple Problem Map is shown below:

$$[KS:ag_1] \to (FBS) \to [KS:ag_2] \to (FBS) \to [KS:ag_3]$$
$$\to (FBS) \to [KS:ag_4] \to (SWS) \to [KS:ag_5]$$
$$\to (SWS) \to [KS:ag_6]$$

The above Problem Map consists of six Actor Graphs (i.e., $ag_1,....,ag_6$). These Actor Graphs are referent to a meta level concept [KS], which stands for "knowledge source".

3.4. Modelling Constructs

3.4.1. Information Hiding

One of the main advantages of using Problem Maps to represent PSMs is its ability for information hiding. That is, the ability to represent a Problem Map within another Problem Map. To enable nesting, the conceptual relations FBS and SWS are extended to point from or into not only Knowledge Sources (i.e., [KS]), but, also to Problem Maps (i.e., [PM]). The following conventions are then available to MODEL-ECS:

(1) [KS: *a] -> (FBS) -> [KS: *b]　　　　　　(2) [KS: *a] -> (FBS) -> [PM:*b]

(3) [PM: *a) -> (FBS) -> [KS: *b]　　　　　　(4) [PM: *a] -> (FBS) -> [PM: *b]

(5) [KS: *a] -> (SWS) -> [KS: *b]　　　　　　(6) [KS:*a] -> (SWS) -> [PM: *b]

(7) [PM: *a] -> (SWS) -> [KS: *b]　　　　　　(8) [PM: *a] -> (SWS) -> [PM: *b]

The level of nesting is not necessarily limited to one, as shown is the above constructs. It is possible to have *n-levels* of nesting, as shown below:

```
[PM: [KS:*w] -
                -> (FBS) -> [PM: [KS: *x] -> (SWS) -> [KS: *y]
              ]
] -> (FBS) -> [KS: *z]
```

We could re-represent the above Problem Map as shown below:

[PM: *b] -> (FBS) -> [KS: *z]　　　　　　　　- nesting at *Depth 0*

where *z* is a Knowledge Source, while *b* is another Problem Map as shown below:

[KS: *x] -> (SWS) -> [KS: *y]   - nesting at *Depth 1*

3.4.2. Knowledge Passing

There is one major issue to be addressed with nested Problem Maps. That is, the flow of information from a sub-component (i.e., concepts) of a knowledge source nested within a Problem Map to concepts in another Problem Map or Knowledge Sources in different context or at different levels of nesting. Knowledge passing of this form is achieved by the use of context, coreference links and line of identity [15]. Definition 6, 7 and 8 briefly describes coreference link, context and line of identity, respectively.

Definition 6:
Coreference links@ show which concepts refer to the same entities. In linear form representation of conceptual graphs, coreference links are represented using variables. For example, consider the following conceptual graph:

[OBTAIN]-
        --> (AGNT) --> [PERSON: *a] -
                                <-- (AGNT) <-- [LIVE] -
                                        --> (LOC) --> [PLACE: Loughborough]
        --> (OBJ) --> [CAR:@2342] --> (ATTR) --> [RED]
        --> (SRCE) --> [PLACE:London]
        --> (RCPT) --> [PERSON: *a].

Here, the agent of *OBTAIN* is the same as the recipient of *OBTAIN*. The variable *a* is used to represent the coreference link between the two concept *PERSON* in the above conceptual graph.

Definition 7:
The *outermost context* is the collection of all conceptual graphs that do not occur in the referent of any concept. If a concept or conceptual graph occurs in the outermost context, it is said to be *enclosed* at *depth 0*. If a context *y* occurs in a context *x*, then *x* is said to *dominate y*. If *y* dominates another context *z*, then *x* also dominates *z*. The outermost context dominates all other contexts& .

Definition 8:
A *line of identity* is a connected, undirected graph *g* whose nodes are concepts and whose arcs are pairs of concepts, called *coreference links**.

3.4.3. Complex Modelling Constructs

The main ingredients for building complex modelling constructs are: Actor Graph, Problem Map, conceptual relations to enable expression of sequence, and special purpose Actor Graphs for expressing condition and iteration. Conceptual Relations, and special purpose Actor Graphs necessary for building complex Problem Maps, are listed in Table 1.

@ In a sentence, these links are expressed as *pronouns* and other *anaphoric references*. Refer to Sowa (1984, pp. 10).
& Refer to Sowa (1984, pp. 141) for more details on *context*.
* Refer to Sowa (1984, pp. 142) for details on *line of identity*.

Conceptual Constructs	Descriptions
(FBS)	Conceptual Relation to indicate sequence
(SWS)	Conceptual Relation to indicate concurrence
[PM: { }]	Problem Map for implementing disjunction
[TRUE_TEST]	Actor Graph to indicate positive test
[FALSE_TEST]	Actor Graph to indicate negative test

Table 1: Conceptual Constructs

Assuming that ϕ and φ denote predicates (i.e., conceptual graphs) and α and β denote Problem Maps, the above conceptual constructs can be used to construct simple Problem Maps shown in Table 2.

Syntactic Representation	Semantics
[PM: α] -> (FBS) -> [PM: β]	do α followed by β
[PM: { [PM: α], [PM: β] }]	do either α or β, non deterministically
[TRUE_TEST: ϕ]	proceed if ϕ is true
[FALSE_TEST: ϕ]	proceed if ϕ is false

Table 2: Syntax and Semantics of Modelling Constructs

Using the simple modelling constructs outlined in Table 2, we are able to build more complex modelling constructs as shown in Table 3. Again, assume that ϕ and φ are predicates (i.e., conceptual graphs), while α and β are Problem Maps.

Modelling Construct	Executable Conceptual Structure Representation
$\alpha;\beta$	[PM: α] -> (FBS) -> [PM: β]
if ϕ then α else β	[PM:{ [KS: [TRUE_TEST: ϕ]]-> (FBS) -> [PM: α], [KS: [FALSE_TEST: ϕ]]-> (FBS) -> [PM: β] }]
while ϕ do α	[PM:{[KS: [TRUE_TEST: ϕ]]->(FBS)->[PM: α] - -> (FBS) -> [KS: *], [KS: [FALSE_TEST: ϕ]] }]
repeat α until ϕ	[PM:α]->(FBS)->[PM:{[KS:[FALSE_TEST:ϕ]]- ->(FBS)->[PM:α], [KS: [TRUE_TEST: ϕ]] }]
case ϕ : α, φ : β	[PM:{[KS: [TRUE_TEST: ϕ]] -> (FBS) -> [PM: α], [KS: [TRUE_TEST: φ]] -> (FBS) -> [PM: β] }]

Table 3: Modelling Constructs representation using Executable Conceptual Structures

4. Problem Solving Methods for Perception

Perception is a process by which the agent is able to understand the external world in terms of its own percepts (i.e. knowledge). The percepts can be thought of as skeleton structures that can be used by the Perception Mechanism of the agent to impose structure on incoming messages, and thereby assist the agent in interpreting the information. These percepts are represented as conceptual graphs in the agents LTM. Figure 10 depicts the architecture of the Perception Mechanism built into our agents.

The Perception Mechanism in the Mobile Agent has two main component: *KQML_PROCESSOR Component*, and *PROJECTION Component*. Figure 11 depicts the Problem Map (i.e., the PSM representation) of the Perception Mechanism using two nested Problem Maps (i.e., *pm_kqml_processor*, and *pm_project*). These two Problem Maps are separated by an *(FBS)* conceptual relation.

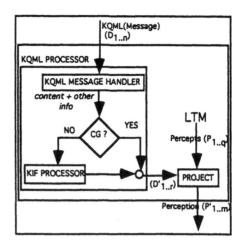

Figure 10: Perception Mechanism
(adapted from [11])

This conceptual relation indicates that the Problem Map *pm_kqml_processor* has to be completed before the commencement of the execution of the Problem Map *pm_project*.

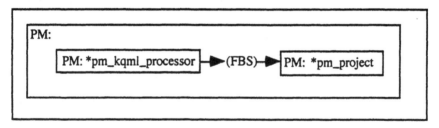

Figure 11: PSM representing the Perception Mechanism

A detailed description of the whole Projection Mechanism is beyond the scope of this paper. We will instead concentrate on the *PROJECTION Component*. A typical pseudo code for the *PROJECTION Component* of the Perception Mechanism is as shown in Figure 12. In this algorithm, *more_message_graphs* and *not_done* are *BOOLEAN*, while the variable b and d represent the pointer to *message graph* and *percept graph*, respectively. The function *select_next_message_graph*$(D'_{1..r})$ selects the next message graph that resulted from the KQML_PROCESSOR. The *function select_next_percept_graph*$(P_{1..q})$ selects a percept graph from the agent LTM. The function *project*(d,b) performs a projection of the percept graph d onto the message graph b to produce interpretations of b (i.e., denoted by $P'_{1..m}$ in Figure 10).

The pseudo code listed in Figure 12 can be modelled into a PSM (i.e., depicted in Figure 13) with MODEL-ECS using four Actor Graphs, together with the complex modelling constructs: "*if* ϕ *then* α *else* β" and "*while* ϕ *do* α". The four Actor Graphs are: *ASSERT*, *RETRACT*, *SELECT*, and *PROJECT*.

```
more_message_graph := true;
WHILE more_message_graph DO
BEGIN
        b := select_next_message_graph(D'1..r);
        IF not(null(b)) THEN
                BEGIN
                        not_done := true;
                        more_percept_graph := true;
                        WHILE (not_done AND more_percept_graph)DO
                        BEGIN
                                d := select_next_percept_graph(P1..q);
                                IF not(null(d)) THEN
                                        BEGIN
                                                e := project(d,b);
                                                IF not(null(e)) THEN
                                                        not_done := false;
                                        END;
                                ELSE
                                        more_percept_graph := false;
                        END;
                END;
        ELSE
                more_message_graph := false;
END;
```

Figure 12: Pseudo Code Representing the *PROJECTION Component*

These Actor Graphs form the Knowledge Source of the PSM. A Knowledge Source is the smallest executable component of the PSM. Each of these Knowledge Sources is described below:

- The *ASSERT* Knowledge Source shown below simply asserts the proposition j into the state space:

    [ASSERT] -
    $\quad$ -> (OBJ) -> [PROPOSITION: *j]

- The *RETRACT* Knowledge Source shown below will retract the proposition k from the state space:

    [RETRACT] -
    $\quad$ -> (OBJ) -> [PROPOSITION: *k]

- The SELECT Knowledge Source shown below selects a proposition n from a set of propositions m of a particular type:

    [SELECT] -
    $\quad$ -> (ARG) -> [T: {*m}]
    $\quad$ -> (OBJ) -> [PROPOSITION: *n]

- The PROJECT Knowledge Source shown below performs the conceptual graph operations projection of conceptual graphs represented by proposition o onto aa conceptual graph represented by proposition p, resulting in a set of graphs represented by propositions q.

    [PROJECT] -
    $\quad$ -> (ARG) -> [PROPOSITION: *o]
    $\quad$ -> (ARG) -> [PROPOSITION: *p]
    $\quad$ -> (RSLT) -> [PROPOSITIONS: {*q}]

5. Discussion

An agent in our Extendable Agent Architecture is made up of many components (c.f. Figure 2). Each of these components is connected by *plugs* and *sockets*. A component can be represented by a PSM (c.f. Figure 12). A PSM is modelled using MODEL-ECS, where the Knowledge Sources are made up of Actor Graphs, and PSM are made up of nested Problem Maps. There are several reasons for modelling agents in this way, which results in major advantage. Each of these reasons (with its advantage) is described below:

The first reason for modelling executable components in the form of PSMs is that it is much easier to transport these types of agent from one *Agent Server* to another, because one only has to send a file of conceptual structures (i.e., the Actor Graphs that represent the Knowledge Sources that form the PSM and its *plugs* and *sockets*). The main advantage of this approach compared to other approaches (like mobile TCL or JAVA) is that the conceptual structures maintain the current value of the agent. The current values of an agent is embedded implicitly in each of the conceptual structure that make up the agent. When an agent with components made up of conceptual structures arrives at an *Agent Server*, the *Gatekeeper* of this *Agent Server* simply places this agent into its allocated *Service Room*. This agent will then proceed to carry out its tasks from this *Service Room*.

The second reason for building a mobile agent using MODEL-ECS is that it is much easier to manipulate conceptual structures to configure a component, rather then writing a computer program. We need our deliberative agent to have the capability to configure less complex (i.e., simple) agents to carry out specific tasks on behalf of the deliberative agent. It is not simple to equip the deliberative agent with the knowledge to construct a program to assemble a simple agent. It is much easier to provide a deliberative agent with sufficient knowledge to enable it to manipulate conceptual structures to put together necessary components to make up the simple agent.

The third reason is that PSMs maintain current values very efficiently. That is, the *differentia graph* and the *actor* that make up an Actor Graph has been designed to maintain its current value (i.e., specifically designed for current value programming) during execution. An Actor Graph can be stopped in the middle of its execution, and then, at a later time, it can be triggered to continue executing from where if left off previously. This capability is a fundamental requirement for mobile agents. That is, when an agent decides to move from one Agent Server to the next, it must be able to suspend all its components (i.e., PSMs), and then, when it arrives at the other Agent Server, it must be able to continue from where it left off just before it departed from the last *Agent Server*. Since PSMs can maintain current values, there is no need to make special provision in our agent architecture to save and restore agent states. This is very important, and is indeed one of the most valuable advantages gained from using MODEL-ECS to build our agents.

This PSM shown in Figure 13 can be built using the Deakin ToolSet [6]. Thus, the *PROJECTION COMPONENT* of the *Perception Mechanism* is made up of the *31* conceptual structures. Thus, for example, when an agent (with this *PROJECTION COMPONENT*) is transported to another *Agent Server* for the very first time, we will be sending these *31* conceptual structures. Certainly, bulky components like the *Perception Component*, *Motivation Component*, etc., will be left in the *Service Room* allocated to it by the *Gatekeeper* of the *Agent Server* [11].

45

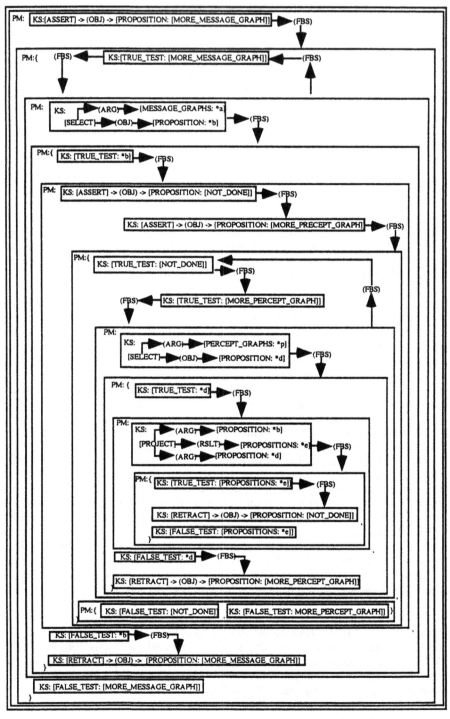

Figure 13: Problem Map Representing "pm_project"

6. Conclusion

In this paper, the author demonstrated the use of a executable conceptual modelling language called MODEL-ECS to build PSMs that represent the components of mobile agents. MODEL-ECS use conceptual structures (i.e., Conceptual Graphs, Actors, Actor Graphs, and Problem Maps) to build complex executable PSMs (c.f. Section 3). The use of MODEL-ECS is successfully demonstrated by building the *PROJECTION COMPONENT* of the *Perception Mechanism* of our mobile agents. MODEL-ECS address all three necessary functionalities of an agent architecture for building mobile agents and their interactions. These functionalities are: *mobility*; *extendability*; and *current value programming* (c.f. Section 5).

The prototype components of our mobile agent are implemented using the Deakin ToolSet [6]. Currently, testing and evaluations of the *PERCEPTION Components* are being conducted, as they are the most fundamental components of an agent. An agent must be able to perceive its environment and the messages it receives from other agents in the environment. Meanwhile, other members of the team are building the necessary techniques to realise light-weight mobile agents, and efficient reasoning mechanisms to implement the agent's Planning Mechanism.

Acknowledgments

We would like to take this opportunity to thank all the members of the Distributed Artificial Intelligence Centre (DAIC) at The University of New England for all their contributions in developing the modelling constructs described in this paper. Also, a very special thanks to all the paper reviewers who have made valuable suggestions.

References

1. Cockburn, D., and Jennings, N. R., (1996). ARCHON: A Distributed Artificial Intelligence System for Industrial Applications, *Foundations of Distributed Artificial Intelligence*, G. H. P. O'Hare and N. R. Jennings (Eds.), John Wiley & Sons, Inc., New York, 1996.

2. Cross, T. and Lukose, D., (1994). The representation of non-linear hierarchical executable plans, in *Proceedings of the 1st Australian Workshop on Conceptual Structures*, Armidale, N.S.W., Australia, pages 58 - 69.

3. Decker, K. S., (1996). TAEMS: A Framework for Environment Centered Analysis and Design of Coordination Mechanisms, *Foundations of Distributed Artificial Intelligence*, G. H. P. O'Hare and N. R. Jennings (Eds.), John Wiley & Sons, Inc., New York, 1996.

4. Fikes, R. E., and Nilsson, N. J., (1971). STRIPS: A new approach to the application of theorem proving to problem solving, *Artificial Intelligence* 2(3-4):189-208.

5. Fischer, K., Muller, J. P., and Pischel, M., (1996). AGenDA - A General Testbed for Distributed Artificial Intelligence Applications, *Foundations of Distributed Artificial*

Intelligence, G. H. P. O'Hare and N. R. Jennings (Eds.), John Wiley & Sons, Inc., New York, 1996.

6. Lukose, D. (1991). *Conceptual Graph Tutorial*, Department of Computing and Mathematics, School of Sciences, Deakin University, Geelong, Australia, 3217.

7. Lukose, D., (1993). Executable Conceptual Structures, in G.W. Mineau, B. Moulin and J.F. Sowa (eds.), *Conceptual Graphs for Knowledge Representation*, Lecture Notes in Artificial Intelligence (699), Springer-Verlag, Berlin.

8. Lukose, D., (1995). Using Executable Conceptual Structures for Modelling Expertise, in *Proceedings of the 9th Banff Knowledge Acquisition For Knowledge-Based Systems Workshop*, Banff Conference Centre, Banff, Alberta, Canada, February 26 - March 3, 1995, Paper No: 8.

9. Lukose, D., (1996). MODEL-ECS: Executable Conceptual Modelling Language, in Proceedings of the 10 Banff Knowledge Acquisition For Knowledge-Based Systems Workshop, Banff, Alberta, Canada, November 1996.

10. Lukose, D., Cross, T., Munday, C., and Sobora, F., (1995a). Operational KADS Conceptual Model using Conceptual Graphs and Executable Conceptual Structures, in *Proceedings of the International Conference on Conceptual Structures* (ICCS'95), USA.

11. Munday, C., Daengdej, J., Cross, T., and Lukose, D., (1996). Motivation and Perception Mechanisms in Mobile Agents for Electronic Commerce, in Lecture Notes in Artificial Intelligence, *Distributed Artificial Intelligence - Architecture and Modelling*, edited by Chengqi Zhang and Dickson Lukose, Springer Verlag Publishers, 1996.

12. O'Hare, G. M., (1996). Agent Factory: An Environment for the Fabrication of Multiagent Systems, *Foundations of Distributed Artificial Intelligence*, G. H. P. O'Hare and N. R. Jennings (Eds.), John Wiley & Sons, Inc., New York, 1996.

13. O'Hare, G. M., and Jennings, N. R., (1996). *Foundations of Distributed Artificial Intelligence*, G. H. P. O'Hare and N. R. Jennings (Eds.), John Wiley & Sons, Inc., New York, 1996.

14. Sommaruga, L., Avouris, N. M., and van Liedekerke, M. H., (1996). The Evolution of the CooperA Platform, *Foundations of Distributed Artificial Intelligence*, G. H. P. O'Hare and N. R. Jennings (Eds.), John Wiley & Sons, Inc., New York, 1996.

15. Sowa, J.F., (1984). *Conceptual Structures: Information Processing in Mind and Machine*, Addison Wesley, Reading, Mass., USA.

16. Steiner, D. D., (1996). IMAGINE: An Integrated Environment for Constructing Distributed Artificial Intelligence Systems, *Foundations of Distributed Artificial Intelligence*, G. H. P. O'Hare and N. R. Jennings (Eds.), John Wiley & Sons, Inc., New York, 1996.

17. Wooldridge, M. J., and Jennings, N. R., (1994). Intelligent Agents, Lecture Notes in Artificial Intelligence (890), Springer Verlag, Berlin, 1994.

Making and Breaking Engagements: An Operational Analysis of Agent Relationships

Mark d'Inverno[1] and Michael Luck[2]

[1] School of Computer Science, University of Westminster, London, W1M 8JS, UK.
Email: dinverm@westminster.ac.uk
[2] Department of Computer Science, University of Warwick, Coventry, CV4 7AL, UK.
Email: mikeluck@dcs.warwick.ac.uk

Abstract. Fundamental to the operation of multi-agent systems is the concept of cooperation between individual agents by which the overall system exhibits significantly greater functionality than the individual components. Not only is it important to understand the structure of such relationships in multi-agent systems, it is also important to understand the ways in which cooperative relationships come about. This is particularly true if such an analysis is to be relevant to, and useful for, the construction of real systems for which the invocation and destruction of such relationships is critical. This paper extends previous work concerned with formalising the structure of inter-agent relationships to provide an operational analysis of the invocation and destruction of engagement and cooperation within our formal agent framework.

1 Introduction

Fundamental to the operation of multi-agent systems is the concept of cooperation between individual agents. If single agent systems can cooperate, they can exploit the capabilities and functionality of others to achieve their own individual goals. This moves beyond the advantages of robustness in traditional distributed systems in the face of individual component failure since components can be replaced and cooperation configurations realigned. It allows the specific expertise and competence of different agents to complement each other so that in addition to general resilience, the overall system exhibits significantly greater functionality than individual components.

Durfee, for example, defines a multi-agent system as a collection of problem solvers that "work together" to achieve goals that are beyond the scope of their individual abilities [2]. This notion of agents helping each other, working together or cooperating in some way is common. Huberman and Clearwater similarly characterise multi-agent systems by the interaction of many agents trying to solve problems in a cooperative fashion [3], and Lesser describes a multi-agent system as a computational system in which several semi-autonomous agents interact or work together to perform some tasks or satisfy some goals [4].

Since cooperation underlies the structure of multi-agent systems, it is important to be able to model and anlayse it in detail in the context of a well-founded framework. Moreover, the ways in which cooperative relationships come about are also important for a complete understanding of the nature of cooperation. This is especially true if such an analysis is to be relevant to real systems for which the invocation and destruction of such relationships is critical.

Previous work has focussed on taxonomising the types of interactions that occur between agents in a multi-agent system, distinguishing in particular between *engagements* of non-autonomous agents and *cooperation* between autonomous agents [7]. This work was based on our agent hierarchy which defined *agency* and *autonomy*, and specified how autonomy is distinct but is achieved by *motivating* agency and generating goals [5]. In this paper we aim to extend this work on cooperation and engagement by describing the operations necessary for their invocation and destruction, and providing a formal specification in the context of the existing framework. First, we briefly review the agent framework and the nature of engagement and cooperation within it. We then address the invocation and destruction of such structures, enumerating the variety of situations in which they arise. Finally, we discuss what benefits such an analysis provides.

2 Background

To present a mathematical description of our definitions, we use the specification language, Z [8]. Space constraints prohibit a detailed explanation of the notation here, but our use should be clear from the combination of text and formalism. (A brief introduction to Z can be found in the appendix of [1].) In this section, we sketch previous work on the agent framework. Details may be found in [5, 7].

An *object* comprises a set of *motivations*, a set of *goals*, a set of *actions*, and a set of *attributes* such that the attributes and actions are non-empty.

```
┌─ Object ─────────────────────────────────────────────────────
│  attributes : P Attribute
│  capableof : P Action
│  goals : P Goal
│  motivations : P Motivation
├──────────────────────────────────────────────────────────────
│  attributes ≠ { } ∧ capableof ≠ { }
└──────────────────────────────────────────────────────────────
```

An object, described by its features and capabilities, is just an automaton and cannot engage other entities to perform tasks, nor is it itself used in this way. However, it serves as a useful abstraction mechanism by which it is regarded as distinct from the remainder of the environment, and can subsequently be transformed into an agent, an augmented object, engaged to perform some task or satisfy some goal. Viewing something as an agent means that we regard it as satisfying or pursuing some goal. Furthermore, it means that it must be doing so either for another agent, or for itself, in which case it is autonomous. If it is for itself, it must have generated the goal through its motivations. Autonomous agents are thus just agents that can generate their own goals from motivations.

```
┌─ Agent ─────────────────────────────────────────────────────────────────
│ Object
├──────────────────────────────────
│ goals ≠ { }
└─────────────────────────────────────────────────────────────────────────
```

```
┌─ AutonomousAgent ───────────────────────────────────────────────────────
│ Agent
├──────────────────────────────────
│ motivations ≠ { }
└─────────────────────────────────────────────────────────────────────────
```

For ease of exposition, we further refine the agent hierarchy with two new definitions. A *neutral-object* is an object that is *not* an agent, and a *server-agent* is an agent that is *not* an autonomous agent.

```
┌─ NeutralObject ─────────────────────────────────────────────────────────
│ Object
├──────────────────────────────────
│ goals = { } ∧ motivations = {}
└─────────────────────────────────────────────────────────────────────────
```

```
┌─ ServerAgent ───────────────────────────────────────────────────────────
│ Agent
├──────────────────────────────────
│ motivations = { }
└─────────────────────────────────────────────────────────────────────────
```

Now, we consider a multi-agent system as a collection of objects, agents and autonomous as defined below. In this view, a multi-agent system contains autonomous agents which are all agents, and in turn, all agents are objects. An agent is either a server-agent or an autonomous agent, and an object is either a neutral-object or an agent.

```
┌─ MultiAgentSystemComponents ────────────────────────────────────────────
│ objects : P Object
│ agents : P Agent
│ autonomousagents : P AutonomousAgent
│ neutralobjects : P NeutralObject
│ serveragents : P ServerAgent
├──────────────────────────────────
│ autonomousagents ⊆ agents ⊆ objects
│ agents = autonomousagents ∪ serveragents
│ objects = neutralobjects ∪ agents
└─────────────────────────────────────────────────────────────────────────
```

3 Engagement and Cooperation

In this section, we briefly review previous work that categorised inter-agent relationships into two distinct classes, engagements and cooperations. We provide formal descriptions and brief explanations. For a full exposition on the nature of these relationships, see [7]. Note, however, that there have been several minor modifications to the earlier formal specification.

3.1 Engagement

A direct engagement occurs when a neutral-object or a server-agent adopts some goals. In a direct engagement, a *client*-agent with some goals uses another *server*-agent to assist them in the achievement of those goals. A server-agent either exists already as a result of another engagement, or is instantiated from a neutral-object for the current engagement. No restriction is placed on a client-agent.

We define a *direct engagement* below to consist of a client agent, *client*, a server agent, *server*, and the goal that *server* is satisfying for *client*. An agent cannot engage itself, and both agents must have the goal of the engagement.

$$
\begin{array}{|l}
\underline{\ DirectEngagement\ } \\
client : Agent \\
server : ServerAgent \\
goal : Goal \\
\hline
client \neq server \\
goal \in (client.goals \cap server.goals) \\
\end{array}
$$

The set of all *direct* engagements in a system is given by *direngagements* in the following schema. For any direct engagement in *direngagements*, there can be no intermediate *direct* engagements of the goal, so there is no other agent, y, where *client* engages y for *goal*, and y engages *server* for *goal*.

$$
\begin{array}{|l}
\underline{\ SystemEngagements\ } \\
MultiAgentSystemComponents \\
direngagements : \mathbf{P}\ DirectEngagement \\
\hline
\forall eng : direngagements \bullet \neg\ (\exists y : Agent;\ e_1, e_2 : direngagements\ | \\
\quad e_1.goal = e_2.goal = eng.goal \bullet e_1.server = eng.server \wedge \\
\quad\quad e_2.client = eng.client \wedge e_1.client = e_2.server = y) \\
\end{array}
$$

An *engagement chain* represents a sequence of *direct engagements*. Specifically, an *engagement chain* comprises a goal, *goal*, the autonomous client that generated the goal, *autoagent*, and a sequence of server-agents, *agentchain*, where each agent in the sequence directly engages the next. For any engagement chain, there must be at least one server-agent, all agents must share *goal*, and each agent can only be involved once. seq_1 represents a non-empty sequence.

$$
\begin{array}{|l}
\underline{\ EngagementChain\ } \\
goal : Goal \\
autoagent : AutonomousAgent \\
agentchain : \mathsf{seq}_1\ Agent \\
\hline
goal \in autoagent.goals \\
goal \in \bigcup\{s : Agent\ |\ s \in \mathsf{ran}\ agentchain \bullet s.goals\} \\
\#(\mathsf{ran}\ agentchain) = \#agentchain \\
\end{array}
$$

The set of all engagement chains in a system is given in the schema below by *engchains*. For every engagement chain, *ec*, there must be a direct engagement between the autonomous agent, *ec.autoagent*, and the first client of *ec*, *head ec.agentchain*, with respect to the goal of *ec*, *ec.goal*. There must also be a direct engagement between any two agents which follow each other in *ec.agentchain* with respect to *ec.goal*. In general, an agent *engages* another agent if there is some engagement chain in which it precedes the server agent.

```
┌─ SystemEngagementChains ──────────────────────────────────────
│ SystemEngagements
│ engchains : P EngagementChain
├───────────────────────────────────────────────────────────────
│ ∀ ec : engchains; s₁, s₂ : Agent •
│     (∃ d : direngagements • d.goal = ec.goal ∧ d.client = ec.autoagent
│                          ∧ d.server = head ec.agentchain) ∧
│     ⟨s₁, s₂⟩ in ec.agentchain ⇒ (∃ d : direngagements •
│                          d.client = s₁ ∧ d.server = s₂ ∧ d.goal = ec.goal)
└───────────────────────────────────────────────────────────────
```

3.2 Cooperation

Two autonomous agents are said to be *cooperating* with respect to some goal if one of the agents has adopted goals of the other. This notion of autonomous goal acquisition applies both to the *origination* of goals by an autonomous agent for its own purposes, and the *adoption* of goals from others, since in each case the goal must have a positive motivational effect [6]. For autonomous agents, the goal of another can only be adopted if it has such an effect, and this is also exactly why and how goals are originated. Thus goal adoption and origination are related forms of goal generation. The term *cooperation* can be used only when those involved are autonomous and, potentially, capable of resisting. If they are not autonomous, nor capable of resisting, then one simply *engages* the other.

A *cooperation* describes a goal, the autonomous agent that generated the goal, and those autonomous agents who have adopted that goal from the generating agent. In addition, all the agents involved have the goal of the cooperation, an agent cannot cooperate with itself, and the set of cooperating agents must be non-empty. Cooperation cannot, therefore, occur unwittingly between agents, but must arise as a result of the motivations of an agent and that agent recognising the goal in another.

```
┌─ Cooperation ─────────────────────────────────────────────────
│ goal : Goal
│ generatingagent : AutonomousAgent
│ cooperatingagents : P AutonomousAgent
├───────────────────────────────────────────────────────────────
│ goal ∈ generatingagent.goals
│ ∀ aa : cooperatingagents • goal ∈ aa.goals
│ generatingagent ∉ cooperatingagents
│ cooperatingagents ≠ { }
└───────────────────────────────────────────────────────────────
```

The set of cooperations in a multi-agent system is given by the *cooperations* variable in the schema, *SystemCooperations*. The predicate part of the schema states that for any cooperation, the union of the cooperating agents and the generating agent is a *subset* of the set of all autonomous agents which have that goal. As a consequence, two agents sharing a goal are not necessarily cooperating. In addition, the set of all cooperating agents is a subset of all autonomous agents of the system since not all are necessarily participating in cooperations.

$SystemCooperations$
$MultiAgentSystemComponents$
$cooperations : \mathbf{P}\ Cooperation$

$\forall c : cooperations \bullet (c.cooperatingagents \cup \{c.generatingagent\}) \subseteq$
$\qquad\qquad\qquad\qquad \{a : autonomousagents \mid c.goal \in a.goals \bullet a\}$
$\bigcup\{c : cooperations \bullet c.cooperatingagents\} \subseteq autonomousagents$

---

4 Operational Aspects of Engagement and Cooperation

So far we have provided an analysis of the *structure* of multi-agent systems based on inter-agent relationships. In this section, we provide an operational analysis of how these cooperations and direct engagements are created and destroyed, and how this affects the configuration of inter-agent relationships.

There are four principal operations to be considered, as follows:

- a server-agent adopting the goals of an agent giving rise to a new engagement;
- a server-agent being released from some or all of its agency obligations by an engaging agent, thus destroying a direct engagement;
- an autonomous agent adopting the goal of another, so that either a new cooperation is formed, or the agent joins an existing cooperation;
- an autonomous agent destroying the goals of an existing cooperation, resulting in either the destruction of the cooperation, or the removal of the autonomous agent from the cooperation.

To provide an operational account of these relationships we must specify how they are affected when new cooperations and engagements are invoked and destroyed. Before considering the operations in detail we first specify some general functions to create relationships from individual components. Thus, *MakeEng*, *MakeEngChain* and *MakeCoop* below simply construct the schema types, *Engagment*, *EngagementChain* and *Cooperation* respectively. The functions, *MakeEng* and *MakeCoop*, are partial; *MakeEng* is not defined if the two agents involved in the cooperation are the same, and *MakeCoop* is not defined if the single autonomous agent initiating the cooperation is in the set of other autonomous agents. Note that $\mathbf{P}_1\ AutonomousAgent$, represents non-empty sets of elements of type *AutonomousAgents*. The schema also makes use of the *mu-expression*. In general, the value of a in the mu-expression, $\mu\, a : A \mid p$, is the unique value of type A which satisfies predicate p. [3]

$MakeEng : (Goal \times Agent \times ServerAgent) \twoheadrightarrow DirectEngagement$
$MakeEngChain : (Goal \times AutonomousAgent \times \text{seq}_1\, ServerAgent)$
$ \twoheadrightarrow EngagementChain$
$MakeCoop : (Goal \times AutonomousAgent \times \mathbf{P}_1\, AutonomousAgent)$
$ \longrightarrow Cooperation$

$\forall\, g : Goal;\ a : Agent;\ aa : AutonomousAgent;\ s : ServerAgent;$
$ ch : \text{seq}_1\, ServerAgent;\ aas : \mathbf{P}_1\, AutonomousAgent \bullet$
$ MakeEng(g, a, s) = (\mu\, d : DirectEngagement \mid$
$ d.goal = g \wedge d.client = a \wedge d.server = s) \wedge$
$ MakeEngChain(g, a, ch) = (\mu\, ec : EngagementChain \mid$
$ ec.goal = g \wedge ec.autoagent = a \wedge ec.agentchain = ch) \wedge$
$ MakeCoop(g, aa, aas) = (\mu\, c : Cooperation \mid$
$ c.goal = g \wedge c.generatingagent = aa \wedge c.cooperatingagents = aas)$

Next, we define the generic function, *cut*, which takes an injective sequence (where no element appears more than once) and an element, and removes all the elements of the sequence which appear after this element. If the element does not exist in the sequence, the sequence is left unaltered.

$[X]$

$cut : (\text{iseq}\, X \times X) \twoheadrightarrow \text{iseq}\, X$

$\forall\, x : X;\ s, t : \text{seq}\, X \bullet cut(s, x) = t \Leftrightarrow$
$ last\, t = x \wedge (\exists\, u : \text{seq}\, X \bullet s = t \frown u)$

We also define a total function that creates a new object by ascribing a set of goals to an existing object. It is valid for any object and any set of goals. This is detailed elsewhere with a complete formalisation of goal generation [6].

$ObjectAdoptGoals : (Object \times \mathbf{P}\, Goal) \longrightarrow Object$

$\forall\, gs : \mathbf{P}\, Goal;\ old, new : Object \bullet$
$ ObjectAdoptGoals(old, gs) = new \Leftrightarrow new.goals = old.goals \cup gs$
$ \wedge\, new.capableof = old.capableof \wedge new.attributes = old.attributes$

This allows us to define two further functions, *ExtendChain* and *CutChain*. The first takes an engagement chain and an object, and extends the engagement chain to include the object. The second function cuts an engagement chain after the occurrence of an object.

---

[3] For example, the expression $\mu\, n : \mathbb{N} \mid (n * n) \bmod 2 = 0 \wedge 0 < (n * n) \le 10l$ binds the variable n to the value 10.

$$ExtendChain : EngagementChain \times Object \longrightarrow EngagementChain$$
$$CutChain : EngagementChain \times Agent \nrightarrow EngagementChain$$

$\forall c : EngagementChain; \; e : Object \; \bullet$
$\quad ExtendChain(c, e) = (\mu \; new : EngagementChain \; |$
$\qquad new.goal = c.goal \wedge new.autoagent = c.autoagent$
$\qquad \wedge \; new.agentchain = c.agentchain\frown$
$\qquad\qquad\qquad \langle ObjectAdoptGoals(e, \{c.goal\}) \rangle) \wedge$
$\quad CutChain(c, e) = (\mu \; new : EngagementChain \; |$
$\qquad new.goal = c.goal \wedge new.autoagent = c.autoagent$
$\qquad \wedge \; new.agentchain = cut(c.agentchain, e)))$

Formally, the structure of multi-agent systems is defined below. It states that a multi-agent system must contain at least one relationship between two agents.

_MultiAgentSystemStructure_____
$MultiAgentSystemComponents$
$SystemEngagements$
$SystemEngagementChains$
$SystemCooperations$
_____
$\#cooperations + \#direngagements \geq 1$

4.1 Making Engagements

When a new direct engagement is formed between an agent and a server agent, the associated engagement chain may be altered in several ways. The different possibilities depend on whether the engaging agent is at the tail, the head, or in the middle of the chain. Consider an engagement chain where A is an autonomous agent at the head of the chain directly engaging the server-agent, $S1$, which is directly engaging server-agent, $S2$, in turn directly engaging $S3$, as in Figure 1(a).

- If the last agent in the chain, $S3$, engages a neutral-object, O, the chain is extended to include the engagement between $S3$ and O, as in Figure 1(b).
- If the autonomous agent, A, directly engages O, a new engagement chain is created solely comprising A and O, as in Figure 1(c).
- If any _server_-agent, other than that at the tail of the engagement chain, engages O, then a new engagement chain is formed between them. Thus if $S1$ engages O, the existing chain is unchanged, but a new chain is formed from the engagements up to and including $S1$ in the original chain, with the addition of the new engagment of O by $S1$, as in Figure 1(d).

The aspects of forming a new engagement common to all three scenarios are described in the next schema. Here, the engaging agent, _agent?_, the engaged object, _e?_, the goal of the engagement, _goal?_, and an optional engagement chain, _chain?_, are given as input to the operation, and the structure of the multi-agent system changes. The predicate part states that the object is a system object, and the agent is a known agent with the goal, _goal?_. If no engagement

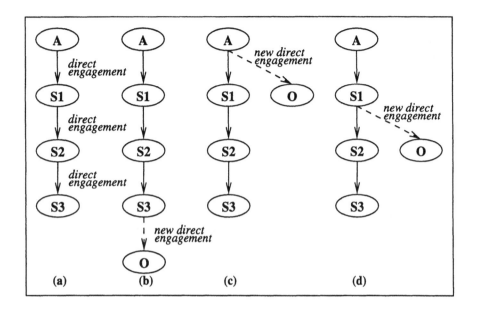

Fig. 1. Alternative ways to make engagements

chain already exists, so that *chain?* is not defined, then *agent?* must be autonomous. Conversely, if *chain?* is defined, *agent?* must be a server-agent, the goal of *chain?* must be *goal?*, and *agent?* must be part of *chain?*. (Formal definitions for optional, defined, undefined and the are given in the appendix.) There is no change to the set of cooperations, but the set of direct engagements is updated to include the new engagement between the agent and the object.

```
┌─ GeneralEngage ──────────────────────────────────────
│ agent? : Agent
│ e? : Object
│ goal? : Goal
│ chain? : optional [EngagementChain]
│ ∆ MultiAgentSystemStructure
├──────────────────────────────────────────────────────
│ e? ∈ objects
│ agent? ∈ agents
│ goal? ∈ agent?.goals
│ undefined chain? ⇔ agent? ∈ autonomousagents
│ defined chain? ⇒
│         (agent? ∈ serveragents ∧
│         ( the chain?).goal = goal? ∧
│         agent? ∈ ran ( the chain?).agentchain)
│ cooperations' = cooperations
│ direngagements' = direngagements∪
│    {MakeEng(goal?, agent?, (ObjectAdoptGoals (e?, {goal?})))}
└──────────────────────────────────────────────────────
```

The distinct aspects of the ways in which the set of engagement chains are affected in each scenario are detailed below. First, the engaging agent is a server-agent at the end of the chain so that the chain is extended to include this new direct engagement.

```
__ EngageExtendChain _____
GeneralEngage
_____
defined chain? ∧ e? = last(the chain?).agentchain ⇒
    engchains' = engchains \ chain?∪
        {ExtendChain((the chain?), e?)}
```

Second, the engaging agent is autonomous, and a new engagement chain is formed from *goal?*, *agent?*, and the sequence consisting of *agent?* and the newly instantiated agent.

```
__ StartNewChain _____
GeneralEngage
_____
agent? ∈ autonomousagents ⇒
    engchains' = engchains∪
        {MakeEngChain(goal?, agent?, ⟨agent?, ObjectAdoptGoals(e?, {goal?})⟩)}
```

Third, if *agent?* is not at head or tail of the chain, then the original chain is unchanged, and a new chain is formed from the direct engagements in the original chain up to the agent, plus the new direct engagement between *agent?* and the newly instantiated object.

```
__ CutandAddChain _____
GeneralEngage
_____
(defined chain?) ∧ (e? ≠ last(the chain?).agentchain)
        ∧ e? ≠ (head(the chain?).agentchain) ⇒
    engchains' = engchains∪
        {ExtendChain((CutChain((the chain?), agent?)), e?)}
```

The operation of making an engagement can then be defined using schema disjunction. Thus, the *Engage* operation is applied when any of the following three occur: *CutandAddChain*, *EngageExtendChain* or *StartNewChain*.

$$Engage \mathrel{\widehat{=}} EngageExtendChain \lor StartNewChain \lor CutandAddChain$$

4.2 Breaking Engagements

If an autonomous agent or a server-agent in an engagement chain *disengages* another server-agent, either through destroying the goal itself or because the agent is no longer required to achieve it, all subsequent engagements in the chain are destroyed. This is because the subsequent agents no longer satisfy a goal that can be attributed to an autonomous agent. Thus, whenever an engagement is broken, all subsequent engagements of that engagement chain are also broken.

The schema, *Disengage*, formally defines the breaking of a direct engagement between engaging and engaged agents, *engaging?* and *engaged?* respectively, and specifies the propagation of broken direct engagements for the goal, *goal?*, down through the associated engagement chain, *chain?*. All of these components are inputs. The predicates ensure that there is a direct engagement between *engaging?* and *engaged?* with respect to *goal?*, that *chain?* is an engagement chain, and that the goal of the chain is equal to the input *goal?*. The set of cooperations remains unchanged, but the engagement chain, *chain?*, is removed from the system and replaced with the chain resulting from cutting the original chain at the engaging agent. Finally, the direct engagements are updated accordingly.

Disengage

engaging? : *Agent*
engaged? : *ServerAgent*
goal? : *Goal*
chain? : *EngagementChain*
$\Delta MultiAgentSystemStructure$

$MakeEng(goal?, engaging?, engaged?) \in direngagements$
$chain? \in engchains$
$chain?.goal = goal?$
$cooperations' = cooperations$
$engchains' = engchains \setminus \{chain?\} \cup \{CutChain(chain?, engaging?)\}$
$direngagements' = direngagements \setminus$
$\quad \{d : DirectEngagement \mid$
$\quad \quad (\langle d.client, d.server \rangle \text{ in } chain?.agentchain)$
$\quad \quad \quad \quad \quad \quad \quad \quad \wedge d.goal = chain?.goal \bullet d\} \cup$
$\quad \{d : DirectEngagement \mid$
$\quad \quad (\langle d.client, d.server \rangle \text{ in } (CutChain(chain?, engaging?)).agentchain$
$\quad \quad \quad \quad \quad \quad \quad \quad \wedge d.goal = chain?.goal) \bullet d\}$

4.3 Joining a Cooperation

A cooperation occurs when an autonomous agent generates a goal by recognising that goal in another autonomous agent. There are two cases when one autonomous agent, C, adopts the goal, g, of another, G. If no cooperation exists between any other autonomous agents and G with respect to g, then a new cooperation structure is created. Alternatively, if a cooperation already exists between another agent and G with respect to g, then C joins this cooperation.

Formally, the following schema, *GeneralCooperate* describes the general system change when a cooperating agent, *coopagent?*, adopts the goal, *goal?*, of the generating agent, *genagent?*, where all are inputs. The predicate part of the schema states that *genagent?* has *goal?*, that *coopagent?* does not, and that both agents are autonomous. The sets of direct engagements and engagement chains remain unchanged.

$$
\begin{array}{|l}
\hline
\text{\_\_}\ GeneralCooperate\ \text{_____} \\
goal?: Goal \\
genagent?, coopagent?: AutonomousAgent \\
\Delta MultiAgentSystemStructure \\
\hline
goal? \in genagent?.goals \\
goal? \notin coopagent?.goals \\
\{genagent?, coopagent?\} \subseteq autonomousagents \\
direngagements' = direngagements \\
engchains' = engchains \\
\hline
\end{array}
$$

Then a new cooperation is formed when there is no existing cooperation for $goal?$ with $genagent?$ as the generating agent. This is described formally below.

$$
\begin{array}{|l}
\hline
\text{\_\_}\ NewCooperation\ \text{_____} \\
GeneralCooperate \\
\hline
\neg\,(\exists\,c: cooperations \bullet c.goal = goal? \wedge c.generatingagent = genagent?) \wedge \\
\quad cooperations' = cooperations \cup \\
\qquad \{MakeCoop(goal?, genagent?, \{coopagent?\})\} \\
\hline
\end{array}
$$

If such a cooperation does exist, then $coopagent?$ is added to it. Specifically, it adopts the goal, $goal?$, and joins the cooperation, as specified in the $JoinCooperation$ schema.

$$
\begin{array}{|l}
\hline
\text{\_\_}\ JoinCooperation\ \text{_____} \\
GeneralCooperate \\
\hline
\exists\,c: cooperations \bullet c.goal = goal? \wedge c.generatingagent = genagent? \wedge \\
\quad c.goal = goal? \wedge c.generatingagent = genagent? \wedge \\
\quad cooperations' = cooperations \setminus \{c\} \cup \\
\qquad \{MakeCoop(goal?, genagent?, c.cooperatingagents \cup \\
\qquad\quad \{ObjectAdoptGoals(coopagent?, \{goal?\})\})\} \\
\hline
\end{array}
$$

4.4 Breaking or Leaving a Cooperation

There are three cases for autonomous agents destroying the goal of a cooperation in which they are involved, illustrated in Figure 2. First, the generating agent, G, destroys the goal of a cooperation with the result that the cooperation is itself destroyed. This does not imply that $C1$ and $C2$ have destroyed the goal. Second, the cooperation is also destroyed when the only cooperating agent destroys the cooperation goal. Finally, when there are many cooperating agents, one of which destroys the cooperation goal, the cooperation is not destroyed but modified so that only one agent *leaves* the cooperation.

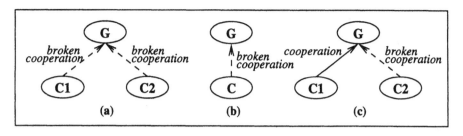

Fig. 2. Breaking a cooperation

In all three cases, however, the state is changed and the set of engagements is unaltered as defined by *CommonBreakCooperation*. A goal, *goal?*, a cooperation, *coop?*, and, optionally, two autonomous agents, *genagent?*, and *coopagent?* are inputs. The preconditions state that either *genagent?* or *coopagent?* is input. In addition, the schema checks that *genagent?* is the generating agent and that *coopagent* is a cooperating agent of *coop?*. The sets of direct engagements and engagement chains are unchanged.

$$
\begin{array}{|l}
\_\,CommonBreakCooperation\,\_\!\!\_\!\!\_\!\!\_\!\!\_\!\!\_\!\!\_\!\!\_ \\
goal? : Goal \\
coop? : Cooperation \\
genagent?, coopagent? : \text{optional}\,[AutonomousAgent] \\
\Delta MultiAgentSystemStructure \\
\hline
\#(genagent? \cup coopagent?) = 1 \\
genagent? \subseteq \{coop?.generatingagent\} \\
coopagent? \subseteq coop?.cooperatingagents \\
direngagements' = direngagements \\
engchains' = engchains
\end{array}
$$

Each of the three different scenarios can now be specified formally as refinements to this general operation schema. First, the generating agent of the cooperation destroys the goal of the cooperation. The cooperation, *coop?*, is destroyed and removed from *cooperations*.

$$
\begin{array}{|l}
\_\,GeneratingAgentDestroysCooperation\,\_\!\!\_\!\!\_\!\!\_\!\!\_\!\!\_ \\
CommonBreakCooperation \\
\hline
\text{defined } genagent? \Rightarrow \\
\quad cooperations' = cooperations \setminus \{coop?\}
\end{array}
$$

Second, the only cooperating agent destroys the goal of the cooperation. In this case, the cooperation is similarly destroyed and removed from *cooperations*.

```
┌─ CooperatingAgentDestroysCooperation ──────────────────────
│ CommonBreakCooperation
├──────────────────────────────────────────────────
│ (defined coopagent? ∧ coopagent? = coop?.cooperatingagents)
│    ⇒ cooperations' = cooperations \ {coop?}
└──────────────────────────────────────────────────
```

Finally, a cooperating agent which is not the only cooperating agent destroys the goal of the cooperation. It is removed from the cooperation and the remaining cooperation is added to *cooperations*.

```
┌─ CooperatingAgentLeavesCooperation ──────────────────────
│ CommonBreakCooperation
├──────────────────────────────────────────────────
│ (defined coopagent? ∧ coopagent? ⊂ coop?.cooperatingagents)
│    ⇒ cooperations' = cooperations \ {coop?}∪
│         {MakeCoop(goal?, coop?.generatingagent,
│                    (coop?.cooperatingagents \ coopagent?))}
└──────────────────────────────────────────────────
```

Schema disjunction is then used to define *BreakCooperation*.

$$BreakCooperation \mathrel{\widehat{=}} GeneratingAgentDestroysCooperation \lor$$
$$CooperatingAgentDestroysCooperation \lor CooperatingAgentLeavesCooperation$$

5   Discussion

Identifying the structures and relationships between agents in multi-agent systems provides a way of understanding the nature of the system, its purpose and functionality. This is typical of existing analyses. However, if we are to build systems based on a recognition of these relationships, so that prior relationships are not destroyed when new ones are created, we must extend such analyses into *operational* areas. This paper has provided just such an analysis, explicating the different kinds of structures that can arise, and showing how different configurations of agents and relationships can evolve by invoking and and destroying them. As part of the analysis, we have had to consider a range of scenarios and the effects of changing relationships upon them.

This is particularly important for system developers aiming to build programs that are capable of exploiting a dynamic multi-agent environment. An operational analysis is vital in providing a link from the structural account to methods for accessing and manipulating these structures. If such operational analyses are avoided, then the merit of research that aims to lay a foundation for the practical aspects of multi-agent systems is limited. Indeed, most existing research has concentrated on addressing either theoretical or practical problems, and has not managed to cross the boundary between the two. Our work strives to place a foot firmly in both camps. We have constructed a formal specification of the structures necessary for an understanding of multi-agent systems and the relationships therein, and we have also shown how it is possible to set about using this understanding in the development of practical systems. Certainly, more work is required for a complete move from theory to practice, but the current work takes us a large part of the way down that road.

References

1. M. d'Inverno and M. Luck. A formal view of social dependence networks. In *Proceedings of the First Australian DAI Workshop, Lecture Notes in Artificial Intelligence, 1087*, pages 115–129. Springer Verlag, 1996.
2. E. H. Durfee and T. Montgomery. MICE: A flexible testbed for intelligent coordination experiments. In *Proceedings of the 1989 International Workshop on Distributed Artificial Intelligence (IWDAI-89)*, 1989.
3. B. A. Huberman and S. H. Clearwater. A multiagent system for controlling building environments. In *Proceedings of the First International Conference on Multi-Agent Systems (ICMAS-95)*, pages 171–176, San Francisco, CA, June 1995.
4. V. Lesser. Preface. In *Proceedings of the First International Conference on Multi-Agent Systems*, page xvii, 1995.
5. M. Luck and M. d'Inverno. A formal framework for agency and autonomy. In *Proceedings of the First International Conference on Multi-Agent Systems*, pages 254–260. AAAI Press / MIT Press, 1995.
6. M. Luck and M. d'Inverno. Goal generation and adoption in hierarchical agent models. In *AI95: Proceedings of the Eighth Australian Joint Conference on Artificial Intelligence*. World Scientific, 1995.
7. M. Luck and M. d'Inverno. Engagement and cooperation in motivated agent modelling. In *Proceedings of the First Australian DAI Workshop, Lecture Notes in Artificial Intelligence, 1087*, pages 70–84. Springer Verlag, 1996.
8. J. M. Spivey. *The Z Notation*. Prentice Hall, Hemel Hempstead, 2nd edition, 1992.

Appendix: Z Extensions

We have found it useful in this specification to be able to assert that an element is optional. The following definitions provide for a new type, optional T, for any existing type, T, along with the predicates defined and undefined which test whether an element of optional T is defined or not. The function, the, extracts the element from a defined member of optional T.

$$\text{optional}\,[X] == \{xs : \mathbf{P}\,X \mid \# xs \leq 1\}$$

$$
\begin{array}{l}
\rule{4cm}{0.4pt}\,[X]\,\rule{4cm}{0.4pt} \\
\quad \text{defined}\,\_,\ \text{undefined}\,\_ : \mathbf{P}(\,\text{optional}\,[X]) \\
\quad \text{the:}\ \text{optional}\,[X] \rightarrowtail X \\
\rule{9cm}{0.4pt} \\
\quad \forall\,xs : \text{optional}\,[X] \bullet \text{defined}\,xs \Leftrightarrow \# xs = 1 \wedge \\
\qquad\qquad\qquad\qquad \text{undefined}\,xs \Leftrightarrow \# xs = 0 \\
\quad \forall\,xs : \text{optional}\,[X] \mid \text{defined}\,xs \bullet \\
\qquad\qquad\qquad \text{the}\,xs = (\mu\,x : X \mid x \in xs)
\end{array}
$$

Cloning for Intelligent Adaptive Information Agents

Keith Decker[1], Katia Sycara[2], and Mike Williamson[2]

[1] Dept. of Computer and Information Sciences
University of Delaware, Newark, DE 19716
decker@cis.udel.edu
[2] The Robotics Institute
Carnegie Mellon University, Pittsburgh, PA 15213
(sycara,mikew)@cs.cmu.edu

Abstract. Adaptation in open, multi-agent information gathering systems is important for several reasons. These reasons include the inability to accurately predict future problem-solving workloads, future changes in existing information requests, future failures and additions of agents and data supply resources, and other future task environment characteristic changes that require system reorganization. We are developing a multi-agent financial portfolio management system that must deal with all of these problems. This paper will briefly describe our approaches and solutions at several different levels within the agents: adaptation at the organizational, planning, scheduling, and execution levels. We discuss our solution for execution-level adaptation ("cloning") in detail, and present empirical evidence backing up the theory behind this execution-level solution.

1 Introduction

Adaptation is behavior of an agent in response to unexpected (i.e., low probability) events or dynamic environments. Examples of unexpected events include the unscheduled failure of an agent, an agent's computational platform, or underlying information sources. Examples of dynamic environments include the occurrence of events that are expected but it is not known *when* (e.g., an agent may reasonably expect to become overloaded), events whose importance fluctuates widely (e.g., price information on a stock is much more important while a transaction is in progress), the appearance of new information sources and agents, and finally underlying environmental uncertainty (e.g., not knowing the duration of a query).

We have been involved in designing, building, and analyzing multi-agent systems that exist in these types of dynamic and partially unpredictable environments [18]. These agents handle adaptation at several different levels, from the high-level multi-agent organization down to the monitoring of individual method executions. In the next section we will discuss an agent's internal architecture. Then we will discuss agent adaptation at the organizational, planning, scheduling, and execution monitoring levels. In particular, we will discuss how our architecture supports organizational and planning-level adaptation currently and what areas are still under active investigation. We will discuss schedule adaptation only in passing and refer the interested reader to work elsewhere. Finally, we will present a detailed model and some experiments with one particular execution-level behavior, agent self-cloning.

2 Agent Architecture

Most of our work in the information gathering domain to date has been centered on the most basic type of intelligent agent: the *information* agent, which is tied closely to a single data source [2]. The dominant domain level behaviors of an information agent are: retrieving information from external information sources in response to one shot queries (e.g. "retrieve the current price of IBM stock"); requests for periodic information (e.g. "give me the price of IBM every 30 minutes"); monitoring external information sources for the occurrence of given information patterns, called change-monitoring requests, (e.g. "notify me when IBM's price increases by 10% over $80"). Information originates from external sources. Because an information agent does not have control over these external information sources, it must extract, possibly integrate, and store relevant pieces of information in a database local to the agent. The agent's information processing mechanisms then process the information in the local database to service information requests received from other agents or human users. Other simple behaviors that are used by all information agents include advertising their capabilities, managing and rebuilding the local database when necessary, and polling for KQML messages from other agents.

An information agent's reusable behaviors are facilitated by its reusable agent architecture, i.e. the domain-independent abstraction of the local database schema, and a set of generic software components for knowledge representation, agent control, and interaction with other agents. The generic software components are common to all agents, from the simple information agents to more complex multi-source information agents, task agents, and interface agents. The design of useful basic agent behaviors for all types of agents rests on a deeper specification of agents themselves, and is embodied in an agent architecture. Our current internal agent architecture is an instantiation of the DECAF (Distributed, Environment-Centered Agent Framework) architecture [8].

2.1 Control: Planning, Scheduling, and Action Execution

The control process for information agents includes steps for planning to achieve local or non-local objectives, scheduling the actions within these plans, and actually carrying out these actions. In addition, the agent has a shutdown and an initialization process. The agent executes the initialization process upon startup; it bootstraps the agent by giving it initial objectives to poll for messages from other agents and to advertise its capabilities. The shutdown process is executed when the agent either chooses to terminate or receives an uncontinueable error signal. The shutdown process assures that messages are sent from the terminating agent asserting goal dissolution to client agents and requesting goal dissolution to server agents (see the section on planning adaptation).

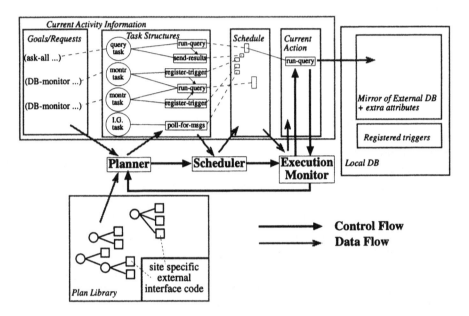

Fig. 1. Overall view of data and control flow in an information agent.

The agent planning process (see Figure 1) takes as input the agent's current set of goals $\mathcal{G}$ (including any new, unplanned-for goals $\mathcal{G}_n$), and the set of current task structures (plan instances) $\mathcal{T}$. It produces a new set of current task structures [21].

- Each individual task T represents an instantiated approach to achieving one or more of the agent's goals $\mathcal{G}$—it is a unit of goal-directed behavior. Every task has an (optional) deadline.
- Each task consists of a partially ordered set of subtasks and/or basic actions **A**. Currently, tasks and actions are related by how information flows from the *outcomes* of one task or action to the *provisions* of anther task or action. Subtasks may inherit provisions from their parents and provide outcomes to their parents. Actions may be periodic or have a deadline.

The most important constraint that the planning/plan retrieval algorithm needs to meet (as part of the agent's overall properties) is to guarantee at least one task for every goal until the goal is accomplished, removed, or believed to be unachievable [1]. For information agents, a common reason that a goal in unachievable is that its specification is malformed, in which case a task to respond with the appropriate KQML error message is instantiated. An information agent receives in messages from other agents three important types of goals: one shot queries, periodic queries, and requests to monitor the database for some condition.

The agent scheduling process in general takes as input the agent's current set of task structures $\mathcal{T}$, in particular, the set of all basic actions, and decides which basic action, if any, is to be executed next. This action is then identified as a fixed intention until it is actually carried out (by the execution component). Constraints on the scheduler include: no action can be intended unless it is enabled; periodic actions must be executed at least once during their period (as measured from the previous execution instance); actions must begin execution before their deadline; actions that miss either their period or deadline are considered to have failed[1]; the scheduler attempts to maximize some predefined utility function defined on the set of task structures. For the information agents, we use a very simple notion of utility—every action needs to be executed in order to achieve a task, and every task has an equal utility value.

In our initial implementation, we use a simple earliest-deadline-first scheduling heuristic. A list of all actions is constructed (the schedule), and the earliest deadline action that is enabled is chosen. Enabled actions that have missed their deadlines are still executed but the missed deadline is recorded and the start of the next period for the task is adjusted to help it meet the next period deadline. When a periodic task is chosen for execution, it is reinserted into the schedule with a deadline equal to the current time plus the action's period.

The execution monitoring process takes the agent's next intended action and prepares, monitors, and completes its execution. The execution monitor prepares an action for execution by setting up a context (including the results of previous actions, etc.) for the action. It monitors the action by optionally providing the associated computation-limited resources—for example, the action may be allowed only a certain amount of time and if the action does not complete before that time is up, the computation is interrupted and the action is marked as having failed. Upon completion of an action, results are recorded, downstream actions are passed provisions if so indicated, and runtime statistics are collected.

3 Agent Adaptation

In this section we briefly consider several types of adaptation supported by this individual agent architecture in our current and previous work. These types include organizational, planning, scheduling, and execution-time adaptation. We are currently actively involved in expanding an agent's adaptation choices at the organizational and planning levels—in this short paper we will only describe how our architecture supports organizational and planning-level adaptation, what we have currently implemented, and what directions we are currently pursuing. We have not, in our current work, done much with schedule adaptation; instead we

---

[1] The scheduler must report all failed actions. Sophisticated schedulers will report such failures (or probable failures) before they occur by reasoning about action durations (and possibly commitments from other agents) [10].

indicate future potential by pointing to earlier work within this general architecture that addresses precisely schedule adaptation. Finally, we present a fairly comprehensive account of one type of execution-time adaptation ("self-cloning").

3.1 Organizational Adaptation

It has been clear to organizational theorists since at least the 60's that there is no one good organizational structure for human organizations [13]. Organizations must instead be chosen and adapted to the task environment at hand. Most important are the different types and qualities of uncertainty present in the environment. These types include uncertainty associated with inputs and output measurements, uncertainty associated with causal relationships in the environment, the time span of definitive feedback after making a decision [15]. Recently, researchers have proposed that organizations grow toward, and structure themselves around, sources of information that are important to them because they are sources of news about how the future is (evidently) turning out [17].

In multi-agent information systems, one of the most important sources of uncertainty revolves around what information is available from whom (and at what cost). We have developed a standard basic advertising behavior that allows agents to encapsulate a model of their capabilities and send it to a "matchmaker" information agent [12]. Such a matchmaker agent can then be used by a multi-agent system to form several different organizational structures[4] as follows:

Uncoordinated Team: Agents first query the matchmaker as to who might answer the query, and then choose an agent randomly for the target query. Very low overhead, but potentially unbalanced loads, reliability limited by individual data sources, and problems linking queries across multiple ontologies. Our initial implementation used this organization exclusively.

Federations: (e.g., [20,11,9]) Agents give up individual autonomy over choosing who they will do business with to a locally centralized "facilitator" (an extension of the matchmaker concept) that "brokers" requests. Centralization of message traffic potentially allows greater load balancing and the provision of automatic translation and mediation services. We have constructed general purpose brokering agents, and are currently conducting an empirical study of matchmaking vs. brokering behavior. Of course, a hybrid organization is both possible and compelling in many situations.

Economic Markets: (e.g., [19]) Agents use price, reliability, and other utility characteristics with which to choose another agent. The matchmaker can supply to each agent the appropriate updated pricing information as new agents enter and exit the system, or alter their advertisements. Agents can dynamically adjust their organization as often as necessary, limited by transaction costs. Potentially such organizations provide efficient load balancing and the ability to provide truly expensive services (expensive in terms of the resources required). Both brokers and matchmakers can be used in market-based systems (corresponding to centralized and decentralized markets, respectively).

Bureaucratic Functional Units: Traditional manager/employee groups of a single multi-source information agent (manager) and several simple information agent (employees). By organizing into functional units, i.e., related information sources, such organizations concentrate on providing higher reliability (by using multiple underlying sources), simple information integration (from partially overlapping information), and load balancing. "Managing" can be viewed as brokering with special constraints on worker behavior brought about by the manager-worker authority relationship.

This is not an exhaustive list. Our architecture has supported other explorations into understanding the effects of organizational structures [5].

3.2 Planning Adaptation

The "planner" portion of our agent architecture consists of a new hierarchical task network based planner using a plan formalism that admits sophisticated control structures such as looping and periodic tasks [21]. It has features derived from earlier classical planning work, as well as task structure representations such as TCA/TCX [16] and TÆMS [6]. The focus of planning in our system is on explicating the basic information flow relationships between tasks, and other relationships that affect control-flow decisions. Most control relationships are *derivative* of these more basic relationships. Final action selection, sequencing, and timing are left up to the agent's local scheduler (see the next subsection). Some types of adaptation expressed by our agents at this level in our current implementation include the following:

Adapting to failures: At any time, any agent in the system might be unavailable or might go off-line (even if you are in the middle of a long term monitoring situation with that agent). Our planner's task reductions handle these situations so that such failures are dealt with smoothly. If alternate agents are available, they will be contacted and the subproblem restarted (note that unless there are some sort of partial solutions, this could still be expensive). If no alternate agent is available, the task will have to wait. In the future, such failures will signal the planner for an opportunity to replan.

Multiple reductions: Each task can potentially be reduced in several different ways, depending on the current situation. Thus even simple tasks such as answering a query may result in very different sequences of actions (e.g., looking up an agent at the matchmaker; using an already known agent, using a cached previous answer).

Interleaved planning and execution: The reduction of some tasks can be delayed until other, "information gathering" tasks, are completed.

Previous work has focussed on coordination mechanisms alone. In particular, the Generalized Partial Global Planning family of coordination mechanisms is a domain-independent approach to multi-agent scheduling-level and planning-level coordination that works in conjunction with an agent's existing local scheduler to adapt a plan by adding certain constraints [7]. These include commitments to do a task with a minimum level of quality, or commitments to do a task by a certain deadline. If the resulting plan can be successfully scheduled, these local commitments can be communicated to other agents where they become non-local commitments to those agent's local schedulers. Not all mechanisms are needed in all environments. Nagendra-Prasad has begun work on learning which mechanisms are needed in an environment automatically [14].

3.3 Scheduling Adaptation

In our current work, we have been using a fairly simple earliest deadline first scheduler that does little adaptation besides adjusting the deadlines of periodic (technically "max invocation separation constrained") actions that miss or are about to miss their initial deadlines. Also, agents can dynamically change their information request periods which affect only the scheduling of the related actions.

Earlier work within this architecture has used a more sophisticated "Design-to-Time" scheduling algorithm, which adapts the local schedule in an attempt to maximize schedule quality while minimizing missed deadlines [10,7]. In doing so, the scheduler may choose from both "multiple methods" (different algorithms that represent difference action duration/result quality tradeoffs) and anytime algorithms (summarized by duration/quality probability distribution tables [22]).

3.4 Execution Adaptation

Within this architecture, previous execution-time adaptation has focussed on monitoring actions [10]. Recently, we have begun looking at load-balancing/rebalancing behaviors such as agent cloning.

Cloning is one of an information agent's possible responses to overloaded conditions. When an information agent recognizes via self-reflection that it is becoming overloaded, it can remove itself from actively pursuing new queries ("unadvertising" its services in KQML) and create a new information agent that is a clone of itself. To do this, it uses a simple model of how its ability to meet new deadlines is related to the characteristics of it's current queries and other tasks. It compares this model to a hypothetical situation that describes the effect of adding a new agent. In this way, the information agent can make a rational meta-control decision about whether or not it should undertake a cloning behavior.

This self-reflection phase is a part of the agent's execution monitoring process. The start and finish time of each action is recorded as well as a running average duration for that action class. A periodic task is created to carry out the calculations required by the model described below.

The key to modeling the agent's load behavior is its current task structures. Since one-shot queries are transient, and simple repeated queries are just a subcase of database monitoring queries, we focus on database monitoring queries only. Each monitoring goal is met by a task that consists of three activities; run-query, check-triggers, and send-results. Run-query's duration is mostly that of the external query interface function. Check-triggers, which is executed whenever the local DB is updated and which thus is an activity shared by all database monitoring tasks, takes time proportional to the number of queries. Send-results takes time proportional to the number of returned results. Predicting performance of an information agent with n database monitoring queries would thus normally involve a quadratic function. We can make a simplification by observing that the external query interface functions, in all of the information agents we have implemented so far using the Internet (e.g., stock tickers, news, airfares), take an order of magnitude more time than any other part of the system (including measured planning and scheduling overhead). If we let E be the average time to process an external query, then with n queries of average period p, we can predict an idle percentage of:

$$I\% = \frac{p - En}{p} \qquad (1)$$

We validate this model in the next section.

When an information agent gets cloned, the clone could be set up to use the resources of another processor (via an 'agent server', or a migratable Java or Telescript program). However, in the case of information agents that already spend the majority of their processing time in network I/O wait states, an overhead proportion $O < 1$ of the En time units each period are available for processing.[2] Thus, as a single agent becomes overloaded as it reaches p/E queries, a new agent can be cloned on the same system to handle another $m = On$ queries. When the second agent runs on a separate processor, $O = 1$. This can continue, with the ith agent on the same processor handling $m_i = O^i m_{i-1}$ queries (note the diminishing returns). We also demonstrate this experimentally in the next section. For two agents, the idle percentage should then follow the model

$$I_{1+2}\% = \frac{(p - En) + (OEn - Em)}{p + OEn} \qquad (2)$$

It is important to note how our architecture supports this type of introspection and on-the-fly agent creation. The execution monitoring component of the architecture computes and stores timing information about each agent action, so that the agent learns a good estimate for the value of E. The scheduler, even the simple earliest-deadline-first scheduler, knows the actions and their periods, and so can compute the idle percentage $I\%$. In the systems we have been building, new queries arrive slowly and periods are fairly long, in comparison to E, so the cloning rule waits until there are $(p/E - 1)$ queries before cloning. In a faster environment, with new queries arriving at a rate r and with cloning taking duration C, the cloning behavior should be begun when the number of queries reaches

$$\frac{p}{E} - \lceil rc \rceil$$

---

[2] Another way to recoup this time is to run the blocking external query in a separate process, breaking run-query into two parts. We are currently comparing the overhead of these two different uni-processor solutions—in any case we stress that both behaviors are reusable and can be used by any existing information agent without reprogramming. Cloning to another processor still has the desired effect.

4 Execution Adaptation: Experimental Results

We undertook an empirical study to measure the baseline performance of our information agents, and to empirically verify the load models presented in the previous section for both a single information agent without the cloning behavior, and an information agent that can clone onto the same processor. We also wanted to verify our work in the context of a real application (monitoring stock prices).

Our first set of experiments were oriented toward the measurement of the baseline performance of an information agent. Figure 2 shows the average idle percentage, and the average percentage of actions that had deadlines and that missed them, for various task loads. The query period was fixed at 60 seconds, and the external query time fixed at 10 seconds (but nothing else within the agent was fixed). Each experiment was run for 10 minutes and repeated 5 times. As expected, the idle time decreases and the number of missed deadlines increases, especially after the predicted saturation point ($n = 6$). The graph also shows the average amount of time by which an action misses its deadline.

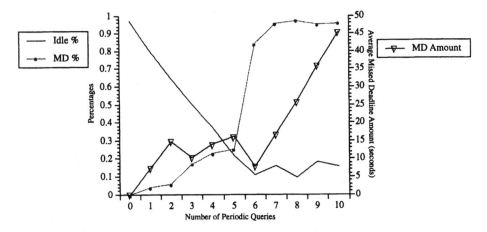

Fig. 2. A graph of the average percentage idle time and average percentage of actions with deadlines that missed them for various loads (left Y axis). Superimposed on the graph, and keyed to the right axis, are the average number of seconds by which a missed deadline [MD] is missed.

The next step was to verify our model of single information agent loading behavior (Equation 1). We first used a partially simulated information agent to minimize variation factors external to the information agent architecture. Later, we used a completely real agent with a real external query interface (the Security APL stock ticker agent).

On the left of Figure 3 is a graph of the actual and predicted idle times for an information agent that monitors a simulated external information source that takes a constant 10 seconds.[3] The information agent being examined was given tasks by a second experiment-driver agent. Each experiment consisted of a sequence of 0 through 10 tasks (n) given to the information agent at the start. Each task had a period of 60 seconds, and each complete experiment was repeated 5 times. Each experiment lasted 10 minutes. The figure clearly shows how the agent reaches saturation after the 6th task as predicted by the model ($p/E = 6$). The idle time never quite drops below 10% because the first minute is spent idling between startup activities (e.g., making the initial connection and sending the batch of tasks). After adding in this extra base idle time, our model predicts the actual utilization quite well ($R^2 = 0.97$; R^2 is a measure of the total variance explained by the model).

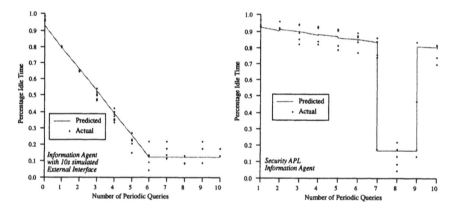

Fig. 3. On the left, graph of predicted and actual utilization for a real information agent with a simulated external query interface. On the right, the same graph for the Security APL stock ticker agent.

We also ran this set of experiments using a real external interface, that of the Security APL stock ticker. The results are shown graphically on the right in Figure 3. 5 experiments were again run with a period of 60 seconds (much faster than normal operation) and 1 through 10 tasks. Our utilization model also correctly predicted the performance of this real system, with $R^2 = 0.96$ and the differences between the model and the experimental results were not significant by either t-tests or non-parametric signed-rank tests. The odd utilization results that occurred while testing $n = 7, 8, 9$ were caused by network delays that significantly changed the average value of E (the duration of the external query). However, since the agent's execution monitor measures this value during problem solving, the agent can still react appropriately (the model still fits fine).

---

[3] All the experiments described here were done on a standard timesharing Unix workstation while connected to the network.

Finally, we extended our model to predict the utilization for a system of agents with the cloning behavior, as indicated in the previous section. Figure 4 shows the predicted and actual results over loads of 1 to 10 tasks with periods of 60 seconds, $E = 10$, and 5 repetitions. Agent 1 clones itself onto the same processor when $n > 5$. In this case, model $R^2 = 0.89$, and the differences between the model and the measured values are not significant by t-test or signed-ranks. The same graph shows the predicted curve for one agent (from the left side of Figure 3) as a comparison.[4]

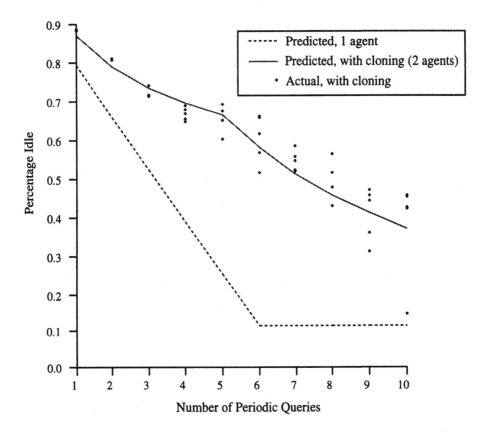

Fig. 4. Predicted idle percentages for a single non cloning agent, and an agent with the cloning behavior across various task loads. Plotted points are the measured idle percentages from experimental data including cloning agents.

---

[4] Since the potential second agent would, if it existed, be totally idle from $1 < n < 6$, the idle curve differs there in the cloning case.

5 Current & Future Work

This paper has discussed adaptation in a system of intelligent agents at four different levels: organizational, planning, scheduling, and execution. Work at the organizational and planning levels is our current pursuit; we will return to schedule adaptation as time and resources permit. Currently, we are conducting an empirical study into matchmakers, brokers, and related hybrid organizations. Our initial results are reported in [3].

This paper also discussed a fairly detailed model of, and experimentation with, a simple cloning behavior we have implemented. Several extensions to this cloning model are being considered. In particular, there are several more intelligent ways with which to divide up the tasks when cloning occurs in order to use resources more efficiently (and to keep queries balanced after a cloning event occurs). These include:

- partitioning existing tasks by time/periodicity, so that the resulting agents have a balanced, schedulable set of tasks;
- partitioning tasks by client so all tasks from agent 1 end up at the same clone;
- partitioning tasks by class/type/content so all tasks about one subject (e.g., the stock price of IBM) end up at the same clone;
- for multi-source information agents, partitioning tasks by data source so all tasks requiring the use of source X end up at the same clone.

Acknowledgements

This work has been supported in part by ARPA contract F33615–93–1–1330, in part by ONR contract N00014–95–1–1092, and in part by NSF contract IRI–9508191.

References

1. Philip R. Cohen and Hector J. Levesque. Intention is choice with commitment. *Artificial Intelligence*, 42(3):213–261, 1990.
2. K. Decker, A. Pannu, K. Sycara, and M. Williamson. Designing behaviors for information agents. In *Proceedings of the 1st Intl. Conf. on Autonomous Agents*, pages 404–413, Marina del Rey, February 1997.
3. K. Decker, M. Williamson, and K. Sycara. Matchmaking and brokering [poster]. In *Proceedings of the 2nd Intl. Conf. on Multi-Agent Systems*, 1996.
4. K. Decker, M. Williamson, and K. Sycara. Modeling information agents: Advertisements, organizational roles, and dynamic behavior. In *Proceedings of the AAAI-96 Workshop on Agent Modeling*, 1996. AAAI Report WS-96-02.
5. Keith S. Decker. Task environment centered simulation. In M. Prietula, K. Carley, and L. Gasser, editors, *Simulating Organizations: Computational Models of Institutions and Groups*. AAAI Press/MIT Press, 1996. Forthcoming.

6. Keith S. Decker and Victor R. Lesser. Quantitative modeling of complex computational task environments. In *Proceedings of the Eleventh National Conference on Artificial Intelligence*, pages 217–224, Washington, July 1993.

7. Keith S. Decker and Victor R. Lesser. Designing a family of coordination algorithms. In *Proceedings of the First International Conference on Multi-Agent Systems*, pages 73–80, San Francisco, June 1995. AAAI Press. Longer version available as UMass CS-TR 94-14.

8. K.S. Decker, V.R. Lesser, M.V. Nagendra Prasad, and T. Wagner. MACRON: an architecture for multi-agent cooperative information gathering. In *Proccedings of the CIKM-95 Workshop on Intelligent Information Agents*, Baltimore, MD, 1995.

9. T. Finin, R. Fritzson, D. McKay, and R. McEntire. KQML as an agent communication language. In *Proceedings of the Third International Conference on Information and Knowledge Management CIKM'94*. ACM Press, November 1994.

10. Alan Garvey and Victor Lesser. Representing and scheduling satisficing tasks. In Swaminathan Natarajan, editor, *Imprecise and Approximate Computation*, pages 23–34. Kluwer Academic Publishers, Norwell, MA, 1995.

11. M.R. Genesereth and S.P. Ketchpel. Software agents. *Communications of the ACM*, 37(7):48–53,147, 1994.

12. D. Kuokka and L. Harada. On using KQML for matchmaking. In *Proceedings of the First International Conference on Multi-Agent Systems*, pages 239–245, San Francisco, June 1995. AAAI Press.

13. Paul Lawrence and Jay Lorsch. *Organization and Environment*. Harvard University Press, Cambridge, MA, 1967.

14. M.V. Nagendra Prasad and V.R. Lesser. Learning situation-specific coordination in generalized partial global planning. In *AAAI Spring Symposium on Adaptation, Co-evolution and Learning in Multiagent Systems*, Stanford, March 1996.

15. W. Richard Scott. *Organizations: Rational, Natural, and Open Systems*. Prentice-Hall, Inc., Englewood Cliffs, NJ, 1987.

16. R. Simmons. Structured control for autonomous robots. *IEEE Trans. on Robotics and Automation*, 10(1), February 1994.

17. Arthur L. Stinchcombe. *Information and Organizations*. University of California Press, Berkeley, CA, 1990.

18. K. Sycara, K. Decker, A. Pannu, M. Williamson, and D. Zeng. Distributed intelligent agents. *IEEE Expert*, 11(6):36–46, December 1996.

19. Michael Wellman. A market-oriented programming environment and its application to distributed multicommodity flow problems. *Journal of Artificial Intelligence Research*, 1:1–23, 1993.

20. G. Wiederhold, P. Wegner, and S. Cefi. Toward megaprogramming. *Communications of the ACM*, 33(11):89–99, 1992.

21. M. Williamson, K. Decker, and K. Sycara. Unified information and control flow in hierarchical task networks. In *Proceedings of the AAAI-96 workshop on Theories of Planning, Action, and Control*, 1996.

22. Shlomo Zilberstein and Stuart J. Russell. Constructing utility-driven real-time systems using anytime algorithms. In *Proceedings of the IEEE Workshop on Imprecise and Approximate Computation*, pages 6–10, Phoenix, AZ, December 1992.

ACACIA: An Agency Based Collaboration Framework for Heterogeneous Multiagent Systems *

Wilfred C. Jamison

Department of Computer and Information Science
Syracuse University
Syracuse, NY, USA 13244
wcjamiso@cat.syr.edu

Abstract. We introduce a collaboration framework called ACACIA for multi-agent systems (MAS). ACACIA is a high level framework that focuses on heterogeneous agents. Our main goal is to create a collaboration framework that precludes the re-engineering of existing software agents. We also apply a case-based coordination scheme in which a database of *collaboration protocols* can be consulted during the collaboration process. This paper gives a macro-level description of our framework which is based mainly on the notion of *agencies*. First, we give our own view of agents and then present *agency* as our metaphor for agent organization. The rest of the paper will discuss ACACIA's problem solving paradigm and runtime system.

KEYWORDS: Heterogenous Agent Architecture, Agent Collaboration, Multiagent Systems

---

* My sincere appreciation for Dr. Gary Craig of Superlative Software Solutions, Inc.;
Joe Ciccarino, Betty Atkinson and Steven Pritko of IBM Endicott, NY, USA .

1 Introduction

Research works in multiagent systems (MAS) have introduced numerous concepts in the past years [2] [8]. For instance, a breed of deceitful agents that negotiate dishonestly are known to exist [13]. Depending on their "personalities", some agents may cooperate only in certain conditions. Agents are diverse in many ways and one fundamental source of this diversity is the framework in which these agents rest upon.

We are interested in a system of *heterogeneous agents*[2] that cooperate and collaborate in solving a problem. Our framework aims at integrating a number of MAS together and form a more powerful agency system. The *Agency Collaboration Architecture for Cooperating Intelligent Agents* (ACACIA) framework treats agency as the baseline for collaboration. This gives us a well-understood metaphor from which we base our framework's organizational structure. In the following sections, we shall present our motivations for the project and outline the framework design by describing its problem solving paradigm, organization and architecture, and the runtime system.

2 Motivation

Interests in agent systems are growing fast these years. More and more research in agents and multi-agent systems or MAS are being heard and written about. In our research, we are motivated by the potential power that a system of collaborating agents can give to us. We address issues on heterogeneity, inter-agent communication, coordination protocols and others. With such a collaborative environment, knowledge sources can be shared and utilized maximally among a wider group of agents. This means that knowledge engineering will be less of a burden since knowledge bases are available. Consequently, a more diverse collection of expertise becomes accessible giving us more possibilities for problem solving. Hopefully, such would mean quicker and better solutions. With collaboration, a quite obvious advantage is the increased degree of task parallelism.

---

[2] Those that were developed on different frameworks and possibly for different platforms.

It also supports the modern user's perception of interoperability and open computing.

An approach to solve interoperability problems is to introduce a common layer underneath the heterogeneous systems. Such approach is used by CORBA [12]. Protocols for low level communication are established and runtime system supports are implemented. On the other hand, we approach the problem by providing an environment *above* the heterogeneous MAS. Adapting the first approach introduces more complexities when building a new MAS. Moreover, existing MAS's cannot benefit from this unless they are re-engineered and recoded. Our contribution is to provide the mechanism for building an interoperable agent environment for both new and existing MAS. Hence, we avoid complexities on the part of the agent builders.

3 The ACACIA Framework

The inherent requirement for agent interaction and the complex nature of cooperation make the design of agents in MAS much more involved. Here, we deal with issues concerning coordination, negotiation, conflict resolution, task allocation and others [1]. In this section, we discuss the following: *Agent Model*, *Organization*, *Problem Solving* and *Communication*. For the purposes of this paper, we abstract most of the fine details.

3.1 An Agent Model

Most frameworks agree more or less on a common notion of agents [8] [2] [16]. A typical agent model has 3 major components as can be seen in Fig. 1.

The *Knowledge System* is the embodiment of the agent's knowledge and intelligence. It consists of a knowledge base and an inference engine. At the very foundation of the agent are a number of knowledge systems. The *Thought System* is the agent's internal control and processing system. It consists of its belief system, intentions, acquaintances, preferences, plans, desires, emotion and other internal information [1]. The *Communication System* is the agent's sensory system. With this, it reveals its state and affects the environment. Also, by

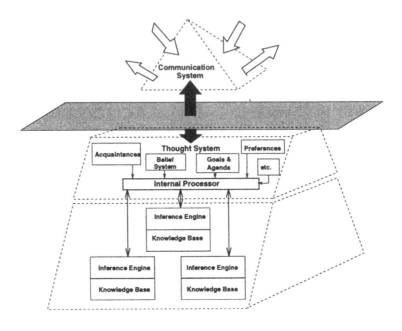

Fig. 1. An Agent Model

receiving information it changes its current state [2]. We broadly define agent *competence* as the quality measurement of these three components.

The agents' suite of capabilities or *expertise* and their competence level are the most vital piece of information. They can be taken out from the agents normally by their explicit and voluntary declaration of themselves, by explicit interrogation, or by direct monitoring [2]. Finally, issues have been raised regarding benevolence versus self-interest as determinants for cooperation [6] [13]. In ACACIA, an agent will be cooperative in any case.

3.2 Agency as a Metaphor for Organizing Agents

We may view an *agency* as a convenient place to secure needed services such as a travel agency. It is a means for achieving our goals through *representation* or *delegation*. It is also a mechanism for an organized agent management procedures. We also regard it as a market for expertise where the client and the agent meet.

We use these notions as metaphors for structuring and organizing software agents. By incorporating management to an existing group of agents (in this case, a MAS), an agency is formed. The whole agency becomes a single entity with collective services. These services are advertised using a system *directory*[3].

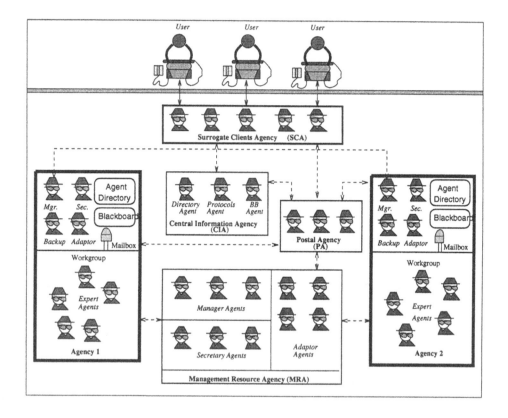

Fig. 2. Logical View of the ACACIA Framework

Fig. 2 is a logical model of the framework. The arrows depict the lines of communications. There are two types of agencies: the *system agencies* defined by ACACIA and the *transient agencies* that join and leave the system[4]. An agency has two subgroups, the *management group* which is comprised of specialized agents that manage the agency's external and internal affairs and the *workgroup* which is comprised of the expert agents that perform the actual problem solving.

---

[3] The directory is updated regularly as agents come and go.

[4] In our context, we shall refer to transient agencies as simply *agencies*.

Below is a summary of important notes.

1. An ACACIA system is composed of at least one transient agency apart from the system agencies. Each has one or more services registered in the *Agency Directory*.

2. The management group is composed of an *agency manager* that represents the agency in all planning activities, a *backup manager* that supports the agency manager and takes over in case the former faults or terminates, a *secretary* that is responsible for maintaining information for the agency, and an *adaptor* that handles all communications between the management and the workgroup.

3. A workgroup is a collection of expert agents.

4. An agency can join an existing ACACIA system anytime but can only leave if it is no longer committed to any project. A project is a joint effort problem solving activity by one or more workgroups. An agent may be involved in only one project at a time.

5. The system agencies consist of the *Surrogate Client Agency* (SCA), *Central Information Agency* (CIA), *Postal Agency* (PA), and *Management Resource Agency* (MRA). The SCA is composed of agents called surrogate clients who serve as the interface to the user clients and deal on their behalf with the ACACIA system. The CIA is the agency that keeps all central information. Agents are also assigned to manage and maintain the *global directory*, the *collaboration protocol repository*, and the *global blackboard*. The PA provides communication services across all agencies. Finally, the MRA is where management services can be sought. Whenever a new agency joins, a management group for it is formed from the MRA.

We should mention that the management group and workgroup are mapped separately. A workgroup is any existing MAS that is based on any framework. Hence, the entire system is a collection of heterogeneous MAS frameworks. On the other hand, all of the management groups are defined uniquely by ACACIA. This homogeneity facilitates the communication and cooperation among the agent managers. The management group is implemented in Java to achieve a platform-independent runtime environment.

The management and the workgroup interface with each other through the adaptor agent who sits in between and performs a two-way message translation service.

3.3 System Configuration

We look at the configuration of the system in two levels. At the workgroup level, the configuration is that of the underlying framework. This means that both distributed and non-distributed set up are possible. At the ACACIA level, we collect the individual workgroup configurations. The situation becomes a network of workstations where each one hosts one or more workgroups. The simplest form is for all workgroups to be in the same host[5]. For instance in Fig 2, the workgroups for agency 1 and agency 2 can be placed in two separate hosts. Meanwhile, the management group of an agency can be placed in any host for as long as its members are together and the adaptor is able to locate its associated workgroup. The best design of course is to place the pair in the same host.

3.4 Paradigm for Problem Solving

The whole idea of our paradigm is to form a coalition of agencies that will plan and collaborate together when no single agency is capable of solving a problem alone. Fig. 3 summarizes the major stages in the problem solving process. In this paradigm, we assume that no user interaction takes place once problem solving has commenced.

Problem Encounter. A user, wanting to solve a problem, goes to a terminal and contacts one of the surrogate clients. See Fig. 2 again. This triggers the latter to examine the requirements of the problem and then choose an appropriate agency through the *Agency Directory*[6]. It sends a mail containing the problem description to the selected agency.

There are many issues involved in this stage. The most important is the representation of the problem. This is very fundamental since the efficiency and

---

[5] A host is equivalent to a workstation.

[6] This is a repository that is maintained globally by a system agent.

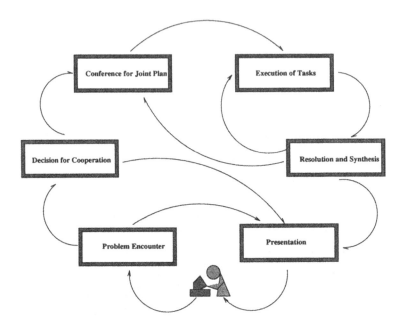

Fig. 3. Problem Solving Paradigm

correctness of the decisions made for planning depend so much on how the agents can elaborate from the description alone [1].

Decision for Cooperation. Meanwhile, each agency secretary checks out any messages from its mailbox. In case of a job request, it notifies the agency manager who later evaluates it. If the manager realizes that, given its current state, the agency is not capable to solve the problem then it will attempt to refer it to other agencies. It summons the secretary to multicast a *request-for-evaluation* mail to selected agencies. Replies are collected and among those who gave a positive response, one is selected based on a policy[7] and the problem is passed to it. On the other hand, if there none then mail are sent to agencies calling for a conference.

Conferencing for a Joint Plan. The agency managers that were called meet to draw a solution plan. There are a number of methods that were proposed for planning [11]. Basically, in joint planning the problem is decomposed into several tasks and distributed to the agents. Decomposition can be performed in

---

[7] The selection policy used can be arbitrarily chosen by the designer or implementor.

many ways too [5] [3] [14] [1]. The framework is quite liberal in adapting any planning strategy.

In the end, either a plan is derived or none at all. In the latter case, the surrogate client is informed immediately about the failure. Otherwise, a project is initiated formally and each participating agency manager is given its task plan. The task plan includes information about the task assignment, synchronization rules, and other constraints.

Execution of Tasks. Each agency manager submits the plan to its respective workgroup. More specifically, it communicates with the adaptor who in turn communicates with the workgroup. In doing so, the workgroup performs its own internal planning to solve the task plan after which they begin to work as individual agents. Due to the non-centralized control and task dependencies, their executions need to be coordinated with other workgroups [3] [6]. Cooperation and coordination are achieved through communication. We shall discuss about these in the next section.

ACACIA is a tightly committed system in that every agent is presumed responsible to fulfill its part and terminates only when done, when the current conditions make its achievement impossible, or when a termination is decided by the group. In case of adverse situations such as the death of an agent, stability is ensured by means of a *replacement* policy.

Resolution and Synthesis. One of the things that needed to be coordinated is knowing when the problem has actually been solved. At this point, the agency managers agree to meet and report to each other about their accomplishments. The requesting agency manager sends a *request-for-meeting* mail to all agency managers concerned. The agency managers tap the adaptors for a report while the latter talk to the workgroups to get a summary of their current states.

Conflicts and problems that arise in the meeting are resolved through negotiation. If all agencies completed successfully then the last stage is reached. Otherwise, it should be decided whether or not the process could be continued. If yes then another planning session might be called before their execution is resumed.

Presentation. Successful or not, the final result is given back to the requesting agency who later sends the result to the requesting surrogate client. Finally, the surrogate client gives the result back to the user client.

3.5 Cooperation Through Communication

We regard communication as the primary way of achieving cooperative work. In this section, we discuss three aspects: *primitives, mechanisms,* and *protocols.*

The primitives of communication specify the *language* used for exchanging messages. We use an internal language for coordination and data exchange[8] among the system agencies and all management groups. Since affairs inside the workgroup is considered private, we do not concern ourselves with that. Between the adaptor and the workgroup, however, a variant of KQML [7] is used to interface the two. Therefore, the management group and the workgroup are reconciled by the intermediate translation performed by the adaptor.

The mechanisms for communication specify the methods of exchanging messages. We have illustrated the wide use of mailboxes for relaying requests, inquiry and information. With this design, messages are serialized in a FCFS manner. On top of that, we also provided the facility to override this by using different levels of mail priorities such as *urgent, important,* and *ordinary.* The *Postal Agency* is the only means by which mail can be delivered. Mail delivery and collection are executed by a set of agents called the *postmen.* Each agency has two mailboxes, an incoming mail to which the postman can drop the mail, and an outgoing mailbox from which the postman can collect them. Still, a successful mail delivery does not guarantee an immediate attention from the receiver so we provided an optional instruction to the postman that interrupts the agency for immediate attention.

Within the workgroup, the agents cooperate using the mechanism defined by their respective framework. Meanwhile, inter-agency cooperation is done through a *distributed blackboard system* [10] [6]. Each agency maintains a local blackboard that carries information relevant only to it. Meanwhile, a global blackboard is maintained in parallel with these blackboards. This global blackboard is simply a collection of contents gathered from all local blackboards. It is updated by the secretary everytime a local blackboard is updated. All incoming and outgoing

---

[8] The language is a proprietary coordination language which we called *ACCORD.*

information are controlled by the respective secretaries. Similarly, agents in the workgroup can read from and write to their local blackboard through the adaptor who communicates with the secretary. In case of an update, the secretary sends the new information to the agencies that are affected by it, including the global blackboard.

By communication protocols, we refer to the control sequence of exchanging messages. Design patterns is an active area of research in object-oriented software engineering [9]. Here, we also talk about *communication patterns* in which we propose a similar idea. Certain classes of problems follow the same patterns of communications among their elements. By identifying these classes, we can define these coordination protocols and store them in a repository. They become part of the agents' knowledge base. Initially, a problem is matched with one of the existing communication patterns and its corresponding protocol is used. However if the matching fails, then the process proceeds as before. We call this collection of protocols the *Collaboration Protocols*. For instance, if the problem follows a *bidding* pattern then we know that several communication protocols exist in this interaction domain. Having chosen one, we can coordinate the actions of each participant with respect to others by first assigning them their roles. These assignments are known to everybody. A specification of their responsibilities are provided which includes information about the sources of needed data at some specific points in their computation and some constraints that they need to satisfy. In some cases, the specification may also instruct that a *code* or *token* be sent to another to signal that the latter can proceed in its processing. This strategy can also be applied partially if a certain stage in the problem solution satisfies some of the interaction patterns stored in the database. This implies that a number of different patterns may be used for one problem. This case-based coordination scheme improves the system performance since it facilitates the planning stage. Furthermore, the collaboration protocols can be updated and fine tuned anytime.

4 Runtime Environment

A MAS already has a defined runtime environment. This is not going to change since a MAS executes independently. Therefore, we only concern ourselves with the runtime system of the management groups and the system agencies.

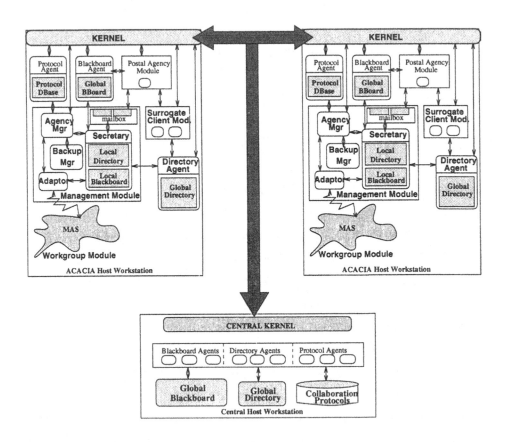

Fig. 4. ACACIA's Runtime Environment

The overall runtime system has one or more workstations that form the ACNET (ACACIA Network). First, there is a central host or workstation that contains the central ACACIA module. The module contains the central kernel which manages and oversees all other nodes in the ACNET, and the system agents together with their respective global data. Although the transient agencies will have their local versions of these data, i.e. in the local blackboard, the global copies are maintained for backup purposes or fallback versioning, tracing, consistency check and other system-related maintenance. Meanwhile, the *Collaboration Protocol* repository is being updated only by the system administrator.

To connect an agency to the ACNET, an ACACIA kernel has to be loaded in the hosting workstation. The kernel takes care of the many administrative and core system functions including the low-level communication routines in that host.

The management group is implemented as a Java module. Each of the agents we defined in this group is implemented as a Java active object [4]. The adaptor object communicates with its corresponding workgroup by behaving like a client to the MAS. This module also contains the implementation of the secretary agent who holds[9], as part of its knowledge base, the local blackboard and the local directory. The mailboxes which have their own set of interfaces are also being managed by the secretary within the module. See Figure 4. A *protocol agent*, a *blackboard agent* and a *directory agent* are active objects that stay with the kernel as well. Whenever the data in the central host are updated, these agents are informed and their copies are refreshed.

Each agency has another module that contains the active object implementation of the surrogate clients. They interface with user clients in the workstation where they are located. Each surrogate client object has methods for its mailbox and interface methods for the user client. The module also implements a windowing system with which the user can interact to the system on-line.

The postal agency module implements the *postmen*. Each agency has one postman that communicates with postmen from other agencies. It consults the directory agent to determine the addresses of these postmen. Communication is via message passing using sockets to interface with the transport layer. There is no special network topology designed for the agencies. Since each agency has a copy of the global directory, the agency manager can send and receive messages directly from any other agency manager via message passing as well.

A MAS can join the system by registering itself to a local ACACIA kernel. Registration is also done in KQML and can be performed directly by a user or

---

[9] By a *has-a* relationship in the OO sense.

by a special user agent. This special agent must be programmed by the user himself[10]. Once the MAS is connected, the system updates all copies of the global directories.

Leaving the system is done simply by revoking the registration status of the MAS from the local kernel. The latter, consequently, will discard all entries pertaining to that MAS in all system directories[11].

5 Conclusion

Combining heterogeneous agents to work together has its obvious advantages. In this paper, we presented a framework that can be used to unite different MAS together without having to re-code them. The framework is based mainly on agency collaboration. We showed how this framework can be used in an open distributed system. We also described briefly the runtime environment. Among the concepts we applied are the following: mailbox system for inter-agency communication, distributed blackboards for inter-agency cooperation, management level planning, agency-based user interfacing, case-based coordination through collaboration protocols, active object agent implementation, and the use of adaptors to link ACACIA with different MAS. Our most important contribution is the use of a high order collaboration framework, nesting all other existing frameworks, in which the granularity for cooperation shifted from the agent to the agency. The system has been implemented in Java JDK[12] 1.1 and is currently being extended to include mobility functions using the IBM Aglets[13] framework.

References

1. Bond, Alan H. and Gasser, Les,(editors) "An Analysis of Problems and Research in DAI", *Readings in Distributed Artificial Intelligence*, Morgan Kauffman Pub. Inc., San Mateo, California, 1988.

---

[10] The necessary information for registration will be detailed in a reference document.

[11] More details about the runtime system or ACACIA implementation will appear in future papers.

[12] Check http://java.sun.com

[13] Check http://www.trl.ibm.com.jp/aglets

2. Byrne, Ciara and Edwards, Peter, "Building Agent-Based Systems", Department of Computer Science, Univ. of Aberdeen, King's College, ABERDEEN, Scotland, UK. *AUCS/TR9405*.

3. Cammarata, Stephanie, McArthur, David and Steeb, Randall, "Strategies of Cooperation in Distributed Problem Solving", *Readings in Distributed Artificial Intelligence*, Alan H. Bond and Les Gasser (editor), Morgan Kauffman Pub. Inc., San Mateo, California, 1988.

4. Cardozo, E., Sichman, J.S., Demazeau, Y., "Using Active Object Model to Implement Multi-Agent Systems", *Proc. of the 5th IEEE Int. Conf. on Tools with Artificial Intelligence*, 1993, Boston, USA.

5. Davis, Randall and Smith, Reid G., "Negotiation as a Metaphor for Distributed Problem Solving", *Readings in Distributed Artificial Intelligence*, Alan H. Bond and Les Gasser (editor), Morgan Kauffman Pub. Inc., San Mateo, California, 1988.

6. Durfee, Edmund H., Lesser, Victor R. and Corkill, Daniel D., "Cooperation Through Communication in Distributed Problem Solving Network", *Distributed Artificial Intelligence*, Michael N. Huhns (editor), Pitman Publishing, London. 1987.

7. Finin, Tim, Fritzon, Rich and McKay, Don, "A Language and Protocol to Support Intelligent Agent Interoperability", *Proceedings of the CE and CALS Washington '92 Conference*, June 1992.

8. Franklin, Stan and Graesser, Art, "Is it and Agent or just a Program? A Taxonomy for Autonomous Agents", *On-line:http://www.msci.memphis/franklin*, March 5, 1996.

9. Gamma, E., Helm, R., Johnson, R. and Vlissides, J., **Design Patterns, Elements of Reusable Object-Oriented Software**, Addison-Wesley Pub. Co., 1995.

10. Hayes-Roth, Barbara, "A Blackboard Architecture for Control", *Readings in Distributed Artificial Intelligence*, Alan H. Bond and Les Gasser (editor), Morgan Kauffman Pub. Inc., San Mateo, California, 1988.

11. Katz, Matthew J. and Rosenschein, Jeffrey S., "Plans for Multiple Agents", *Distributed Artificial Intelligence Vol. II*, Les Gasser and Michael N. Huhns (editor), Pitman Publishing, London. 1989.

12. Orfali, R., Harkey, D. and Edwards, J., The Essential Distributed Objects, John Wiley and Sons, Inc., 1996.

13. Rosenschein, Jeffrey and Zotkin, Gilad, **Rules of Encounter, Designing Conventions for Automated Negotiation among Computers**, The MIT Press, Cambridge, Mass., 1994.

14. Smith, Reid G. and Davis, Randall, "Frameworks for Cooperation in Distributed Problem Solving", *Readings in Distributed Artificial Intelligence*, Alan H. Bond and Les Gasser (editor), Morgan Kauffman Pub. Inc., San Mateo, California, 1988.

15. Sycara, Katia P., "Multiagent Compromise via Negotiation", *Distributed Artificial Intelligence Vol. II*, Les Gasser and Michael N. Huhns (editor), Pitman Publishing, London. 1989.

16. Wooldridge, Michael and Jennings, Nicholas R., "Agent Theories, Architectures and Languages: A Survey", in Wooldridge and Jennings Eds., **Intelligent Agent**, Berlin:Springer-Verlag, 1-22.

A Multi-Agent Cooperative Reasoning System for Amalgamated Knowledge Bases

Lifeng He[1]*, Yuyan Chao[2], Shohey Kato[1], Tetsuo Araki[3], Hirohisa Seki[1] and Hidenori Itoh[1]

[1] Nagoya Institute of Technology, Nagoya 466, Japan
[2] Nagoya University, Nagoya 464, Japan
[3] Fukui University, Fukui 910, Japan

Abstract. We propose a multi-agent cooperative reasoning system for amalgamated knowledge bases. A multi-agent cooperation environment, where inconsistency is allowed, can be presented by an amalgamated knowledge base. Our reasoning method is an extension of the magic sets technique [2] for amalgamated knowledge bases, augmented with the capabilities of handling amalgamated atoms. Through rewriting a given amalgamated knowledge base, our method offers the advantages associated with top-down as well as bottom-up evaluation. Especially, our reasoning method makes unnecessary the expensive reductant rules of inference introduced in [5], and the translation of a given amalgamated knowledge base into its regular representation as in [1]. We consider how to make the bottom-up computation for amalgamated atoms, describe the extended magic sets translation rules, and discuss some related problems.

keywords: multi-agent cooperation, reasoning system, inconsistency, amalgamated knowledge bases, magic sets

1 Introduction

Recently, reasoning about multi-agent cooperation environments has attracted much attention in AI (e.g., [7], [11]). In multi-agent cooperation environments, agents need sometimes during reasoning information that is distributed among several agents (therefore, may be different, and even inconsistent). For example, in a multi-agent system, an agent A will draw a conclusion to move an object O to some location L_1, while another agent B will conclude that O should be moved to another location L_2. Thus, it is necessary to reason under inconsistency in such a multi-agent system.

* This research is supported in part by the Japanese Ministry of Education and the Artificial Intelligence Research Promotion Foundation.

Kifer and Subrahmanian proposed GAPs (Generalized Annotation Programs) for reasoning with inconsistency [6], and Subrahmanian presented an amalgamation theory [9] for integrating multiple GAPs into a single *amalgamated knowledge base* (*AKB* for short). With AKBs, inconsistencies, temporal information and unprecise information can be handled in a uniform way.

There were two reasoning methods for AKBs. One is incorporating *reductant rule of inference* into SLD-style reasoning procedure, which can be done similarly as in [6] and [5] with some extensions. As there are infinite reductants for a given AKB, it is difficult and expensive to find those suitable reductants. Another method is the so-called MULTI-OLDT method [1]. Using this method, we have to translate a given AKB into its *regular representation* and resolve the *maximization problem* during reasoning process. Moreover, the operations of *table insertion* are quite complicated.

In this paper, we propose a reasoning method for such amalgamated knowledge bases. Our method is an extension of the so-called "magic sets" [2] technique for AKBs. It combines the advantages both top-down and bottom-up reasoning procedures.

In order to use magic sets technique for AKBs, we have to augment it with the capabilities to handle amalgamated atoms. To do that, as we shall see, we should consider not only the propagation of information for those variables occurring in ordinary predicates of amalgamated atoms, but also the propagation of information for those *annotated variables*.

We also discuss how to make bottom-up computation of amalgamated atoms, which is very important in magic sets method.

The organization of the rest of the paper is as follows. In the next section, we review generalized annotated programs and the amalgamation theory and give a motivating example. In section 3, we give the motivation of our research. Then, we consider the techniques about the bottom-up computation for amalgamated atoms in section 4 and discuss the extension of the magic sets method for AKBs in section 5. In section 6, we make some discussions. Lastly, we give our conclusions in section 7.

2 Preliminaries

2.1 Generalized Annotated Programs

Following [6] and [1], suppose that T is a set of truth values that forms a complete lattice under an ordering $\preceq$, where the maximal element of T is denoted to $\top$ and the minimal element of T to $\bot$. Then, *annotation terms* are defined as follows: (1) any member of T is an annotation term, (2) any variable ranging over T is an annotation term (such a variable is called an annotated variable), and (3) if f is a function symbol of arity $n \geq 1$ on T (called annotation functions[4]) and $t_1, \ldots, t_n$ are annotation terms, then $f(t_1, \ldots, t_n)$ is an annotation term.

---

[4] Same as [6] and [1], we suppose that all annotation function symbols can be interpreted in only one fixed way.

Furthermore, if A is a usual atom and μ is an annotation term, then $A : \mu$ is called an *annotated atom*. Lastly, *generalized annotated programs* (abbreviated to *GAPs* hereafter) are defined as sets of *annotated clauses* which have of the form:

$$A : \rho \leftarrow C_1 : \mu_1, \ldots, C_n : \mu_n$$

where $A : \rho$ is an annotated atom and $C_i : \mu_i$ $(1 \leq i \leq n)$ is an annotated atom such that μ_i contains no annotation function.

Intuitively, the above annotated clause means that "A has truth value at least ρ if C_1 has truth value at least μ_1 and ... C_n has truth value at least μ_n".

In [6], a formal model theory, proof theory and fixpoint theory for GAPs were developed. An *interpretation I* assigns an element of $\mathcal{T}$ to each ground annotated atom. I *satisfies* a ground annotated atom $A : \mu$ iff $\mu \preceq I(A)$. The satisfaction of any formula is defined in usual way.

2.2 The Amalgamation Theory

Now, we review the amalgamation theory [9]. A *local database* consists of GAPs. Suppose that $D_1, \ldots, D_n$ are local databases over $\mathcal{T}$. Then, the **DNAME** lattice is the power set $2^{\{1,\ldots,n,\mathbf{m}\}}$, where $\mathbf{m}$ refers to a *mediatory database (mediator)*. Variables ranging over $2^{\{1,\ldots,n,\mathbf{m}\}}$ are called **DNAME** variables. If $A : \mu$ is an annotated atom over $\mathcal{T}$, V is a **DNAME** variable and $D \subseteq \{1, \ldots, n, \mathbf{m}\}$, then $A : [D, \mu]$ and $A : [V, \mu]$ are called *amalgamated atoms*. Intuitively, for example, $A : [D, \mu]$ means that the truth value of predicate A is μ in the set of the databases D. And an *amalgamated clause* is defined to:

$$A : [D, \rho] \leftarrow C_1 : [D_1, \mu_1], \ldots, C_n : [D_n, \mu_n]$$

where $A : [D, \rho], C_1 : [D_1, \mu_1], \ldots, C_n : [D_n, \mu_n]$ are amalgamated atoms and μ_i $(1 \leq i \leq n)$ is a annotation term containing no function symbol.

Intuitively, the above amalgamated clause means that "if the databases in set D_i $(1 \leq i \leq n)$ jointly imply that the truth value of C_i is at least μ_i, then the databases in set D jointly imply the truth value of A is at least ρ".

In the above amalgamated clause, when $n = 0$, it is called an *amalgamated fact*. On the other hand, an amalgamated atom to be proved is called a *goal* [5].

Lastly, an *amalgamated knowledge database* is a set of amalgamated clauses. Moreover, suppose that $D_1, \ldots, D_n$ are GAPs. A *mediatory database*, $\mathcal{M}$, is a set of amalgamated clauses such that every clause in $\mathcal{M}$ is of the form:

$$A : [\{\mathbf{m}\}, \rho] \leftarrow C_1 : [D_1, \mu_1], \ldots, C_n : [D_n, \mu_n]$$

where $D_i \subseteq \{1, \ldots, n, \mathbf{m}\}$. Intuitively, it means: "If the databases in set D_i, $1 \leq i \leq n$, jointly imply that the truth value of A_i is at least μ_i, then the mediator will conclude that the truth value of A is at least ρ."

Every clause C in a local database D_i of the form

---

[5] Requiring a goal to be an atom is not a significant restriction, since a conjunctive goal $G_1 \wedge \ldots \wedge G_n$ can be converted into the rule $G_1 \wedge \ldots \wedge G_n \rightarrow G$ and the goal G.

$$A : \rho \leftarrow C_1 : \mu_1, \ldots, C_n : \mu_n$$

can be replaced by a corresponding amalgamated clause, denoted by $AT(C)$:

$$A : [\{i\}, \rho] \leftarrow C_1 : [\{i\}, \mu_1], \ldots, C_n : [\{i\}, \mu_n].$$

We use $AT(D_i)$ to denote the set $\{AT(C)|C \in D_i\}$. The *amalgam* of $D_1, \ldots, D_n$ via a *mediator* $\mathcal{M}$ is the amalgamated knowledge database $\mathcal{M} \cup \bigcup_{i=1}^{n} AT(D_i)$.

An **A**-*interpretation*, $\mathbf{J}$, for an amalgamated knowledge database is a mapping from the set of ground atoms of our base language, $\mathbf{B}_L$, to the set of functions from $\{1, \ldots, n, \mathbf{m}\}$ to $\mathcal{T}$, where $\mathbf{m}$ is a mediatory database. Thus, for each $A \in \mathbf{B}_L$, $\mathbf{J}(A)$ is a mapping from $\{1, \ldots, n, \mathbf{m}\}$ to $\mathcal{T}$. For example, $\mathbf{J}(A)(i) = \mu$ means that the truth value of A is at least μ in i. An A-interpretation , $\mathbf{J}$, satisfies the ground amalgamated atom $A : [D, \mu]$ iff $\mu \preceq \bigsqcup_{i \in D}(\mathbf{J}(A)(i))$, where $D \subseteq \{1, \ldots, n, \mathbf{m}\}$ and $\bigsqcup$ denotes "least upper bound (lub)". The concepts of **A**-model and **A**-consequence are defined in the usual way. All the other symbols are interpreted in the same way as for ordinary $\mathcal{T}$-valued interpretations with the caveat that for quantification, **DNAME** variables are instantiated to subsets of $\{1, \ldots, n, \mathbf{m}\}$ and annotated variables are instantiated to members of $\mathcal{T}$.

Same as in [9] and [6], we assume that any annotation function is monotonic. Then, according to the semantics defined, if an annotated variable occurs only in the head of an amalgamated clause, it can be replaced by the top element of $\mathcal{T}$, and if an annotated variable occurs only in an atom in the body of a clause, it can be replaced by the bottom element of $\mathcal{T}$, i.e., the atom containing it can be removed from the clause. On the other hand, if D is a **DNAME** variable, then $A : [D, \mu]$ means that for any $D \subseteq \{1, \ldots, n, \mathbf{m}\}$, A has the truth value μ. Therefore, if a **DNAME** variable occurs only in the amalgamated atom of the head of a clause, it can be replaced by Φ, where $\Phi \subset D$ for any $D \subseteq \{1, \ldots, n, \mathbf{m}\}$. If a **DNAME** variable occurs only in the body of a clause, it can be replaced by Ω, where $\Omega = \{1, \ldots, n, \mathbf{m}\}$. Thus, throughout this paper, we assume, without loss of generality, that any $\mathcal{T}$ (**DNAME**) variable occurring in the head of a clause also occurs in the body, and so is the converse. Especially, any amalgamated fact contains neither $\mathcal{T}$ variable nor **DNAME** variable.

2.3 A Motivating Example

Example 1. Suppose $\mathcal{T}$ is the lattice $\{\bot, \mathbf{f}, \mathbf{t}, \top\}$ in Fig. 1. This lattice has been used extensively in reasoning about knowledge bases which contain inconsistent information [8]. Intuitively, $\bot$ represents "unknown", $\mathbf{t}$ and $\mathbf{f}$ mean *true* and *false* respectively, whereas $\top$ represents the truth value "inconsistent".

Consider two mobile agents, a_1 and a_2, that are working in a common workspace. Each of these two agents has access to three databases. One describes the information about the weight of objects, the second describes the information about the volume of objects, the last one is a mediator database, which controls the cooperation of the two agents. Each of these three AKBs is expressed over the lattice FOUR, i.e., $\mathcal{T} = \{\bot, \mathbf{f}, \mathbf{t}, \top\}$. An example can be given as follows.

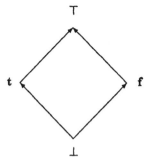

Fig. 1. The four-valued lattice $\{\bot, \mathbf{f}, \mathbf{t}, \top\}$.

DB1:

$$move(a_1, X) : [\{1\}, \mathbf{t}] \leftarrow weight(X, W) : [\{1\}, \mathbf{t}] \wedge (W \leq 80) : [\{1\}, \mathbf{t}]$$
$$move(a_1, X) : [\{1\}, \mathbf{f}] \leftarrow weight(X, W) : [\{1\}, \mathbf{t}] \wedge (W > 80) : [\{1\}, \mathbf{t}]$$
$$move(a_2, X) : [\{1\}, \mathbf{t}] \leftarrow weight(X, W) : [\{1\}, \mathbf{t}] \wedge (W \leq 40) : [\{1\}, \mathbf{t}]$$
$$move(a_2, X) : [\{1\}, \mathbf{f}] \leftarrow weight(X, W) : [\{1\}, \mathbf{t}] \wedge (W > 40) : [\{1\}, \mathbf{t}]$$

DB2:

$$move(a_1, X) : [\{2\}, \mathbf{t}] \leftarrow volume(X, V) : [\{2\}, \mathbf{t}] \wedge (V \leq 2) : [\{2\}, \mathbf{t}]$$
$$move(a_1, X) : [\{2\}, \mathbf{f}] \leftarrow volume(X, V) : [\{2\}, \mathbf{t}] \wedge (V > 2) : [\{2\}, \mathbf{t}]$$
$$move(a_2, X) : [\{2\}, \mathbf{t}] \leftarrow volume(X, V) : [\{2\}, \mathbf{t}] \wedge (V \leq 5) : [\{2\}, \mathbf{t}]$$
$$move(a_2, X) : [\{2\}, \mathbf{f}] \leftarrow volume(X, V) : [\{2\}, \mathbf{t}] \wedge (V > 5) : [\{2\}, \mathbf{t}]$$

DB3 (a mediator database):

$$cooperation(X) : [\{m\}, \mathbf{f}] \leftarrow move(a_1, X) : [\{1\}, \mathbf{t}] \wedge move(a_1, X) : [\{2\}, \mathbf{t}]$$
$$cooperation(X) : [\{m\}, \mathbf{f}] \leftarrow move(a_2, X) : [\{1\}, \mathbf{t}] \wedge move(a_2, X) : [\{2\}, \mathbf{t}]$$
$$cooperation(X) : [\{m\}, \mathbf{t}] \leftarrow move(a_1, X) : [\{1, 2\}, \top]$$
$$\wedge move(a_2, X) : [\{1, 2\}, \top]$$

Intuitively, DB1 says that agent a_1 (a_2) can move any object whose weight is below $80kg$ ($40kg$) and can not move any object weightier than that. DB2 says that agent a_1 (a_2) can move any object whose volume is below 2 (5) cubic meter and can not move any object bigger than that. It is obvious that there may be inconsistency between DB1 and DB2. For example, suppose that a given object o is $60kg$ (i.e., $weight(o, 60) : [\{1\}, \mathbf{t}]$ is added to DB1) and 4 cubic meter (i.e., $volume(o, 4) : [\{2\}, \mathbf{t}]$ is added to DB2). a_1 can move it from DB1 but can not move it from DB2. Conversely, a_2 can not move it from DB1 but can move it from DB2. In order to resolve such conflicts, we wish that the two agents can cooperate to move o. This is just the role of the mediator database, DB3. If an object can be moved by some agent from both DB1 and DB2, no cooperation of the two agents is necessary. Otherwise, if an object can not be moved by either agent a_1 or agent a_2 singly, a cooperation is taken.

3 Why is the bottom-up computation necessary?

Suppose that a set of truth values $T = \{\perp, f, t, \top\}$ is given. Let P be the following AKB:

1. $p : [\{1\}, V] \leftarrow q(X) : [\{1\}, V]$
2. $q(a) : [\{1\}, t]$
3. $q(b) : [\{1\}, f]$

and a goal G be $p : [\{1\}, \top]$.

In order to prove $q(X) : [\{1\}, \top]$, Kifer and Lozinskii [5] introduced the so-called *reductant rule of inference* into SLD-style reasoning procedure. By this method, we have to find some suitable reductants of P before using resolution. In the above example, a reductant of P,

$$p : [\{1\}, \sqcup(V_1, V_2)] \leftarrow q(X_1) : [\{1\}, V_1], q(X_2) : [\{1\}, V_2]$$

has to be established. As there are infinite reductants for a given AKB, it is extremely difficult and expensive to find those suitable ones. For example, for any i,

$$p : [\{1\}, \sqcup(V_1, V_2)] \leftarrow q(X_1) : [\{1\}, V_1], \ldots, q(X_i) : [\{1\}, V_i]$$

is a reductant of the above P.

Adali and Subrahmanian introduced another method to solve this problem [1]. They first translate a given program P and a query Q into their *regular representations*, then use the so-called MULTI-OLDT method to do the query processing. One disadvantage of MULTI-OLDT method is that we have to transform amalgamated clauses to their regular representations and resolve the maximization problem during the reasoning process. Another disadvantage is that the table operations are quite complicated.

On the other hand, forward reasoning will generate all facts derivable from a given program. For example, using the forward chaining, the amalgamated atom set generated by the above AKB is constructed as follows:

$$\begin{aligned}
\{\phi\} &\Rightarrow \{q(a) : [\{1\}, t]\} \\
&\Rightarrow \{q(a) : [\{1\}, t], q(b) : [\{1\}, f]\} \\
&\Rightarrow \{q(a) : [\{1\}, t], q(b) : [\{1\}, f], p : [\{1\}, t]\} \\
&\Rightarrow \{q(a) : [\{1\}, t], q(b) : [\{1\}, f], p : [\{1\}, t], p : [\{1\}, f]\} \\
&= \{q(a) : [\{1\}, t], q(b) : [\{1\}, f], p : [\{1\}, \top]\}.
\end{aligned}$$

As $p : [\{1\}, \top]$ can be generated by P, so $p : [\{1\}, \top]$ can be derived by P.

It is well known that pure forward chaining lacks *goal-directedness*. A lot of amalgamated facts irrelevant to the amalgamated fact to be proved might be generated during the proof processing. For example, suppose that $P' = \{P \cup r : [\{1, 2\}, \top]\}$ and the goal G is the same as before. Then, $r : [\{1, 2\}, \top]$, which is irrelevant to Q, is also generated. Therefore, the reasoning only based on the forward reasoning may be very inefficient.

In order to solve this problem, we extend the usual magic sets method [2], which offers all the advantages associated with top-down as well as bottom-down evaluation, for AKBs.

4 Bottom-up Computation for Amalgamated Atoms

In this section, we discuss some problems concerning with bottom-up computation in our reasoning method, which is necessary when we make the extension of magic sets method for AKBs.

Suppose that $\mathcal{M}$ is an amalgamated fact set. We first consider how to decide whether an amalgamated atom $A : [D, \mu]$ is satisfiable in $\mathcal{M}$, and when μ is an annotated variable, how to obtain the maximal value of μ such that $A : [D, \mu]$ is satisfiable in $\mathcal{M}$.

Definition 1. Given an amalgamated fact set, $\mathcal{M}$, and an amalgamated atom $A : [D, \mu]$, suppose that $A_1 : [D_1, \mu_1], \ldots, A_n : [D_n, \mu_n]$ are all amalgamated atoms in $\mathcal{M}$ such that there is a substitution σ such that for all i, $1 \le i \le n$, $A\sigma = A_i\sigma$ and $D_i \subseteq D\sigma$. If μ is not an annotated variable then $A\sigma : [D\sigma, \mu]$ is *satisfiable* in $\mathcal{M}$ iff $\mu \preceq \sqcup(\mu_1, \ldots, \mu_n)$. Otherwise, i.e., μ is an annotated variable, $A\sigma : [D\sigma, \mu]$ is *satisfiable* in $\mathcal{M}$ and the *maximal value* of μ, μ_{max}, is $\sqcup(\mu_1, \ldots, \mu_n)$.

Example 2. Suppose $\mathcal{T} = \{\bot, \mathbf{f}, \mathbf{t}, \top\}$ and $\mathcal{M} = \{p(a) : [\{1\}, \mathbf{t}], p(a) : [\{2\}, \mathbf{f}]),$ $p(b) : [\{2\}, \mathbf{t}]\}$. $p(X) : [\{1, 2\}, V]$ is satisfiable in $\mathcal{M}$ when $X = a$ (where $V_{max} = \top$) or $X = b$ (where $V_{max} = \mathbf{t}$). On the other hand, $p(b) : [\{1, 2, 3\}, \top]$ is not satisfiable in $\mathcal{M}$.

Next, we consider how to insert an amalgamated fact to extend an amalgamated fact set. In our case, an amalgamated fact set is constructed from an empty set and extended by inserting amalgamated facts one by one.

Definition 2. An amalgamated fact $A : [D, \mu]$ is said to be an *instance* of another amalgamated fact $A' : [D', \mu']$ iff there is a substitution σ such that $A = A'\sigma$, $D' \subseteq D$ and $\mu \preceq \mu'$.

Definition 3. ($\mathcal{M}$ extension operations) Suppose that $\mathcal{M}$ is an amalgamated fact set and $A : [D, \mu]$ is an amalgamated fact unsatisfiable in $\mathcal{M}$ to be inserted into $\mathcal{M}$. Then M is extended according to the following three steps.

1) (the maximizing operation) We first find the maximal value of V, ξ, for $A : [D, V]$ in $\{A : [D, \mu]\} \cup \mathcal{M}$. Suppose that $A_1 : [D_1, \mu_1], \ldots, A_n : [D_n, \mu_n]$ are all amalgamated facts in $\mathcal{M}$ such that for each i ($1 \le i \le n$) there is a substitution σ_i such that $A = A_i\sigma_i$ and $D_i\sigma \subseteq D$, then $\xi = \sqcup(\mu, \mu_1, \ldots, \mu_n)$.
2) (the contracting operation) Next, remove all instances of $A : [D, \xi]$ from $\mathcal{M}$.

3) (the inserting operation) Lastly, extend $\mathcal{M}$ by inserting $A : [D, \xi]$.

Example 3. Suppose $\mathcal{T} = \{\bot, \mathbf{f}, \mathbf{t}, \top\}$. Let $\mathcal{M} = \{p(X) : [\{1\}, \mathbf{f}], p(a) : [\{1, 2\}, \top]\}$ and $p(a) : [\{1\}, \mathbf{t}]$ be the atom to be inserted into $\mathcal{M}$. The maximal value of V for $p(a) : [\{1\}, V]$ in $\{p(a) : [\{1\}, \mathbf{t}] \cup \mathcal{M}$ is $\sqcup(\mathbf{t}, \mathbf{f}) = \top$. On the other hand, $p(a) : [\{1, 2\}, \top]$ is an instance of $p(a) : [\{1\}, \top]$, it is removed from $\mathcal{M}$. The extended amalgamated fact set is $\{p(X) : [\{1\}, \mathbf{f}], p(a) : [\{1\}, \top]\}$.

5 Magic Sets Method for AKBs

In this section, we first review the magic sets method for Horn clauses in first-order problems. Then, we extend it to AKBs.

5.1 The Review of Magic Sets Method

The magic sets method [2] is a technique for rewriting logical rules so bottom-up evaluation offers all the advantages associated with top-down as well as bottom-up evaluation.

Suppose that

$$p(\mathbf{X}) \leftarrow p_1(\mathbf{X}_1) \wedge \ldots \wedge p_m(\mathbf{X}_m)$$

is a rule. By the top-down reasoning method, it means that from the goal $p(\mathbf{X})$ derive the goals $p_1(\mathbf{X}_1), \ldots, p_m(\mathbf{X}_m)$. While the bottom-up interpretation is that derive the fact $p(\mathbf{X})$ from the facts $p_1(\mathbf{X}_1), \ldots, p_m(\mathbf{X}_m)$. Combining the two methods, we can interpret it as follows:

> From the goal $p(\mathbf{X})$ derive the goal $p_1(\mathbf{X}_1)$, from the goal $p(\mathbf{X})$ and the fact $p_1(\mathbf{X}_1)$ derive the goal $p_2(\mathbf{X}_2)$, ..., from the goal $p(\mathbf{X})$, the fact $p_1(\mathbf{X}_1)$, ..., and the fact $p_m(\mathbf{X}_m)$, derive the fact $p(\mathbf{X})$.

The above idea can be formulated by the following translation rule, where m_p is called a magic predicate and s_i is called a supplementary predicate.

$$m\_p(\mathbf{X}) \rightarrow m\_p_1(\mathbf{X}_1)$$
$$m\_p(\mathbf{X}) \rightarrow s_1(\mathbf{Y}_1)$$
$$s_1(\mathbf{Y}_1) \wedge p_1(\mathbf{X}_1) \rightarrow m\_p_2(\mathbf{X}_2)$$
$$s_1(\mathbf{Y}_1) \wedge p_1(\mathbf{X}_1) \rightarrow s_2(\mathbf{Y}_2)$$

$$\vdots$$

$$s_{m-1}(\mathbf{Y}_{m-1}) \wedge p_{m-1}(\mathbf{X}_{m-1}) \rightarrow m\_p_m(\mathbf{X}_m)$$
$$s_{m-1}(\mathbf{Y}_{m-1}) \wedge p_{m-1}(\mathbf{X}_{m-1}) \rightarrow s_m(\mathbf{Y}_m)$$
$$s_m(\mathbf{Y}_m) \wedge p_m(\mathbf{X}_m) \rightarrow p(\mathbf{X})$$

In the above translated rules, $\mathbf{Y}_i$ is a term which contains all variables in the head, i.e., $p(\mathbf{X})$, and those variables that occur before p_i, i.e., $p_1, \ldots, p_{i-1}$, and also occur from p_i, i.e., $p_i, \ldots, p_m$.

The magic sets translation rule for a goal, i.e., an atom to be proved, $g(\mathbf{Z})$, is as follows.

$$m\_g(\mathbf{Z}).$$

Example 4. Consider the following Horn clause set,

$$q(X_1, X_3) \leftarrow p_1(X_1, X_2), p_2(X_2, X_3), p_3(X_3)$$
$$p_1(a, X_4)$$
$$p_2(b, X_5)$$
$$p_3(c)$$

with the goal $q(a, c)$. The translated rules are shown as follows.

$$m\_q(X_1, X_3) \rightarrow m\_p_1(X_1, X_2)$$
$$m\_q(X_1, X_3) \rightarrow s_1(X_1, X_3)$$
$$s_1(X_1, X_3) \wedge p_1(X_1, X_2) \rightarrow m\_p_2(X_2, X_3)$$
$$s_1(X_1, X_3) \wedge p_1(X_1, X_2) \rightarrow s_2(X_1, X_2, X_3)$$
$$s_2(X_1, X_2, X_3) \wedge p_2(X_2, X_3) \rightarrow m\_p_3(X_3)$$
$$s_2(X_1, X_2, X_3) \wedge p_2(X_2, X_3) \rightarrow s_3(X_1, X_3)$$
$$s_3(X_1, X_3) \wedge p_3(X_3) \rightarrow q(X_1, X_3)$$
$$m\_p_1(a, X_4) \rightarrow p_1(a, X_4)$$
$$m\_p_2(b, X_5) \rightarrow p_2(b, X_5)$$
$$m\_p_3(c) \rightarrow p_3(c)$$
$$m\_q(a, c)$$

The generation of the atom set by the magic sets method is as follows.

$$M_0 = \{\phi\}$$
$$M_1 = M_0 \cup \{m\_q(a, c)\}$$
$$M_2 = M_1 \cup \{m\_p_1(a, X_2)\}$$
$$M_3 = M_2 \cup \{s_1(a, c)\}$$
$$M_4 = M_3 \cup \{p_1(a, X_2)\}$$
$$M_5 = M_4 \cup \{m\_p_2(X_2, c)\}$$
$$M_6 = M_5 \cup \{s_2(a, X_2, c)\}$$
$$M_7 = M_6 \cup \{p_2(b, c)\}$$
$$M_8 = M_7 \cup \{m\_p_3(c)\}$$
$$M_9 = M_8 \cup \{s_3(a, c)\}$$
$$M_{10} = M_9 \cup \{p_3(c)\}$$
$$M_{11} = M_{10} \cup \{q(a, c)\}$$

Therefore, $q(a, c)$ is proved (since $q(a, c)$ is generated).

5.2 The Extension of Magic Sets Method for AKBs

We now start describing the extension of magic sets method for AKBs. Since we must deal with amalgamated atoms, there are two key distinctions between our framework and that of [2].

- We need consider not only the propagation of the information for the variables contained in predicates of amalgamated atoms, but also the propagation of the information for the annotated variables and the **DNAME** variables.
- Checking whether an amalgamated atom is satisfiable in an amalgamated fact set and how to extend an amalgamated fact set by asserting an amalgamated fact are significantly more complicated operations than in [2].

Without loss of generality, an amalgamated clause in the given AKB can be represented in the following form:

$$p_0(\mathbf{X}_0) : [D_0, f(V_1, \ldots, V_m)] \leftarrow p_{11}(\mathbf{X}_{11}) : [D_{11}, V_1], \ldots, p_{1a_1}(\mathbf{X}_{1a_1}) : [D_{1a_1}, V_1],$$
$$\ldots, p_{m1}(\mathbf{X}_{m1}) : [D_{m1}, V_m], \ldots, p_{ma_m}(\mathbf{X}_{ma_m}) : [D_{ma_m}, V_m],$$
$$p_{n1}(\mathbf{X}_{n1}) : [D_{n1}, \mu_1], \ldots, p_{nc}(\mathbf{X}_{nc}) : [D_{nc}, \mu_c] \qquad (*)$$

where $V_1, \ldots, V_m$ are annotated variables and $\mu_1, \ldots, \mu_c \in \mathcal{T}$ are annotated constants.

When checking whether an amalgamated atom $A : [D, \mu]$ can be proved by a given AKB, we can derive all amalgamated facts $A : [D_1, \mu_1], \ldots, A : [D_n, \mu_n]$ from the AKB such that for all $1 \leq i \leq n$, $D_i \subseteq D$ and then check whether $\mu \preceq \sqcup(\mu_1, \ldots, \mu_n)$. Therefore, the above clause is selected to prove an amalgamated atom $A : [D, \mu]$ iff there is a substitution σ that $p_0(\mathbf{X}_0)\sigma = A\sigma$ and $D_0\sigma \subseteq D\sigma$.

Now, suppose that the above clause $(*)$ is selected. In order to prove its head, we should show that all its body amalgamated atoms can be proved. Similar to usual case [2], we prove them one by one from left to right. Obviously, this proof need not be continued if some body amalgamated atom can not be proved.

Next, suppose that for all $1 \leq k \leq c, p_{nk}(\mathbf{X}_{nk})\sigma : [D_{nk}\sigma, \mu_k]$ and for all $1 \leq i \leq m$ and $1 \leq j \leq a_i$, $p_{ij}(\mathbf{X}_{ij})\sigma : [D_{ij}\sigma, \nu_{ij}]$ are derived from the given AKB, where σ is a substitution and ν_{ij} is the maximal truth value of V_i such that $p_{ij}(\mathbf{X}_{ij})\sigma : [D_{ij}\sigma, V_i]$ is derivable. Then, the maximal value of V_i such that $p_{i1}(\mathbf{X}_{i1})\sigma : [D_{i1}\sigma, V_i], \ldots, p_{ia_i}(\mathbf{X}_{ia_i})\sigma : [D_{ia_i}\sigma, V_i]$ can be simultaneously derivable is the greatest lower bound of $\nu_{i1}, \ldots, \nu_{ia_i}$, denoted by $\xi_i = \sqcap(\nu_{i1}, \ldots, \nu_{ia_i})$. Lastly, according to the monotonous property of annotation terms, the maximal value of $f(V_1, \ldots, V_n)$ such that $p_0(\mathbf{X}_0)\sigma : [D_0\sigma, f(V_1, \ldots, V_n)]$ is derivable from the given AKB is $f(\xi_1, \ldots, \xi_n)$.

The techniques processing predicates and necessary information are similar as in [2], but we have to consider more in that supplementary predicates contain not only the binding information about the relevant variables included in $A_0, A_1, \ldots, A_n$, but also the binding information about the annotated variables and the **DNAME** variables.

Concluding above discussions, the translation procedures for an amalgamated clause, an amalgamated fact and a goal (an amalgamated fact to be proved) are given as follows, where $m\_p_{\alpha\beta}$ is the magic predicate of $p_{\alpha\beta}$, $s_{\alpha\beta}$ is a supplementary predicate of the predicate $m\_p_{\alpha\beta}$, and ν is a supplementary argument for recording the values of annotated variables. A special predicate $sat(A : [D, \mu])$ is also introduced, which is true if there is a substitution σ such that $A\sigma : [D\sigma, \xi]$

is satisfiable in the constructed amalgamated fact set, where ξ is the maximal value such that $A\sigma : [D\sigma, V]$ is satisfiable in the constructed amalgamated fact set, and $\xi \succeq \mu$ if μ is an annotated constant, $\xi \succ \perp$ if μ is an annotated variable.

(1) The translation procedure for the amalgamated clause $(*)$

$$m\_p_0(\mathbf{X}_0, D'), D_0 \subseteq D' \to m\_p_{11}(\mathbf{X}_{11}, D_{11})$$
$$m\_p_0(\mathbf{X}_{11}, D'), D_0 \subseteq D' \to s_{11}(\mathbf{Y}_{11}, \top)$$

$$\vdots$$

$$s_{1i}(\mathbf{Y}_{1i}, \nu_{1(i-1)}), sat(p_{1i}(\mathbf{X}_{1i}) : [D_{1i}, V_{1i}]) \to m\_p_{1(i+1)}(\mathbf{X}_{1(i+1)}, D_{1(i+1)})$$
$$s_{1i}(\mathbf{Y}_{1i}, \nu_{1(i-1)}), sat(p_{1i}(\mathbf{X}_{1i}) : [D_{1i}, V_{1i}]) \to s_{1(i+1)}(\mathbf{Y}_{1(i+1)}, \sqcap(\nu_{1(i-1)}, V_{1i}))$$

$$\vdots$$

$$s_{1a_1}(\mathbf{Y}_{1a_1}, \nu_{1(a_1-1)}), sat(p_{1a_1}(\mathbf{X}_{1a_1}) : [D_{1a_1}, V_{1a_1}]) \to s_1(\mathbf{Y}_{1a_1}, \sqcap(\nu_{1(l-1)}, V_{1a_1}))$$
$$s_1(\mathbf{Y}_{1a_1}, V_1) \to m\_p_{21}(\mathbf{X}_{21}, D_{21})$$
$$s_1(\mathbf{Y}_{1a_1}, V_1), \to s_{21}(\mathbf{Y}_{21}, \top)$$

$$\vdots$$

$$s_{mb}(\mathbf{Y}_{ma_m}, \nu_{m(a_m-1)}), sat(p_{ma_m}(\mathbf{X}_{ma_m}) : [D_{ma_m}, V_{ma_m}])$$
$$\to s_m(\mathbf{Y}_{ma_m}, \sqcap(\nu_{m(a_m-1)}, V_{ma_m}))$$
$$s_m(\mathbf{Y}_{ma_m}, V_m) \to m\_p_{n1}(\mathbf{X}_{n1}, D_{n1})$$
$$s_m(\mathbf{Y}_{ma_m}, V_m) \to s_{n1}(\mathbf{Y}_{n1})$$

$$\vdots$$

$$s_{nj}(\mathbf{Y}_{nj}), sat(p_{nj}(\mathbf{X}_{nj}) : [D_{nj}, \mu_j]) \to m\_p_{n(j+1)}(\mathbf{X}_{n(j+1)}, D_{n(j+1)})$$
$$s_{nj}(\mathbf{Y}_{nj}), sat(p_{nj}(\mathbf{X}_{nj}) : [D_{nj}, \mu_j]) \to s_{n(j+1)}(\mathbf{Y}_{n(j+1)})$$

$$\vdots$$

$$s_{n(c-1)}(\mathbf{Y}_{n(c-1)}), sat(p_{n(c-1)}(\mathbf{X}_{n(c-1)}) : [D_{n(c-1)}, \mu_{c-1}]) \to m\_p_{nc}(\mathbf{X}_{nc}, D_{nc})$$
$$s_{n(c-1)}(\mathbf{Y}_{n(c-1)}), sat(p_{n(c-1)}(\mathbf{X}_{n(c-1)}) : [D_{n(c-1)}, \mu_{c-1}]) \to s_{nc}(\mathbf{Y}_{nc})$$
$$s_{nc}(\mathbf{Y}_{nc}), sat(p_{nc}(\mathbf{X}_{nc}) : [D_{nc}, \mu_c]) \to p_0(\mathbf{X}_0) : [D_0, f(V_1, \ldots, V_m)]$$

where D' is a **DNAME** variable, $\mathbf{Y}_{\alpha\beta}$ is the tuple of variables such that the variables appear among the head of the clause (including those annotated variables and the **DNAME** variable if any), and the variables which appear before $p_{\alpha\beta}(\mathbf{X}_{\alpha\beta})$ and also appear from $p_{\alpha\beta}(\mathbf{X}_{\alpha\beta})$.

(2) The translation procedure for an amalgamated fact
An amalgamated fact $p(\mathbf{X}) : [D, \mu]$ is translated into:

$$m\_p(\mathbf{X}, D'), D \subseteq D' \to p(\mathbf{X}) : [D, \mu]$$

where D' is a **DNAME** variable.

(3) The translation procedure for a goal (an amalgamated fact to be proved)
A goal $p(\mathbf{X}) : [D, \mu]$ is translated into:

$$true \to m\_p(\mathbf{X}, D)$$
$$m\_p(\mathbf{X}, D), sat(p(\mathbf{X}) : [D, \mu]) \to satisfiable(p(\mathbf{X}) : [D, \mu])$$

Example 5. Let P (where $\mathcal{T} = \{\bot, \mathbf{f}, \mathbf{t}, \top\}$) be:

$$p_0(a) : [\{1\}, V_1] \leftarrow p_1(X) : [\{1,2\}, V_1], p_2(Y) : [\{1,2\}, \mathbf{t}]$$
$$p_2(Z) : [\{2\}, V_2] \leftarrow r_1(Z) : [\{1,2\}, V_2], r_2(Z) : [\{1\}, V_2]$$
$$p_1(b) : [\{2\}, \mathbf{t}]$$
$$p_1(c) : [\{1\}, \mathbf{f}]$$
$$r_1(e) : [\{1\}, \top]$$
$$r_2(e) : [\{1\}, \mathbf{t}]$$

and the goal be $p_0(W) : [\{1,2\}, \top]$.

The magic sets derived by the translation procedures are:

$$m\_p_0(a, D_1), \{1\} \subseteq D_1 \rightarrow m\_p_1(X, \{1,2\})$$
$$m\_p_0(a, D_1), \{1\} \subseteq D_1 \rightarrow s_{11}^1(V_1, \top)$$
$$s_{11}^1(V_1, \top), sat(p_1(X) : [\{1,2\}, V_{11}]) \rightarrow s_1^1(V_1, \sqcap(\top, V_{11}))$$
$$s_1^1(V_1, V_1) \rightarrow m\_p_2(Y, \{1,2\})$$
$$s_1^1(V_1, V_1) \rightarrow s_{21}^1(V_1)$$
$$s_{21}^1(V_1), sat(p_2(Y) : [\{1,2\}, \mathbf{t}]) \rightarrow p_0(a) : [\{1\}, V_1]$$
$$m\_p_2(Z, D_2), \{2\} \subseteq D_2 \rightarrow m\_r_1(Z, \{1,2\})$$
$$m\_p_2(Z, D_2), \{2\} \subseteq D_2 \rightarrow s_{11}^2((Z, V_2), \top)$$
$$s_{11}^2((Z, V_2), \top), sat(r_1(Z) : [\{1\}, V_{21}]) \rightarrow m\_r_2(Z, \{1\})$$
$$s_{11}^2((Z, V_2), \top), sat(r_1(Z) : [\{1\}, V_{21}]) \rightarrow s_{12}^2((Z, V_2), \sqcap(\top, V_{21}))$$
$$s_{12}^2((Z, V_2), \nu_{10}^2), sat(r_2(Z) : [\{2\}, V_{22}]) \rightarrow s_1^2((Z, V_2), \sqcap(\nu_{10}^2, V_{22}))$$
$$s_1^2((Z, V_2), V_2) \rightarrow p_2(Z) : [\{2\}, V_2]$$
$$m\_p_1(b, D), \{2\} \subseteq D_3 \rightarrow p_1(b) : [\{2\}, \mathbf{t}]$$
$$m\_p_1(c, D), \{1\} \subseteq D_4 \rightarrow p_1(c) : [\{1\}, \mathbf{f}]$$
$$m\_r_1(e, D), \{1\} \subseteq D_5 \rightarrow r_1(e) : [\{1\}, \top]$$
$$m\_r_2(e, D), \{1\} \subseteq D_6 \rightarrow r_2(e) : [\{1\}, \mathbf{t}]$$
$$true \rightarrow m\_p_0(W, \{1,2\})$$
$$m\_p_0(W, \{1\}), sat(p_0(W) : [\{1,2\}, \top]) \rightarrow satisfiable(p_0(W) : [\{1,2\}, \top])$$

The amalgamated fact set generated by the magic sets method is shown as follows.

$$M_0 = \{\phi\}$$
$$M_1 = M_0 \cup \{m\_p_0(W, \{1,2\})\}$$
$$M_2 = M_1 \cup \{m\_p_1(X, \{1,2\}), s_{11}^1(V_1, \top)\}$$
$$M_3 = M_2 \cup \{p_1(b) : [\{2\}, \mathbf{t}], p_1(c) : [\{1\}, \mathbf{f}]\}$$
$$M_4 = M_3 \cup \{s_1^1(V_1, \mathbf{t}), s_1^1(V_1, \mathbf{f})\}$$
$$M_5 = M_4 \cup \{m\_p_2(Y, \{1,2\}), s_{21}^1(\mathbf{t}), s_{21}^1(\mathbf{f})\}$$
$$M_6 = M_5 \cup \{m\_r_1(Y, \{1,2\}), s_{11}^2((Y, V_2), \top)\}$$
$$M_7 = M_6 \cup \{r_1(e) : [\{1\}, \top]\}$$

$$M_8 = M_7 \cup \{m\_r_2(e, \{1\}), s_{12}^2((e, V_2), \top)\}$$
$$M_9 = M_8 \cup \{r_2(e) : [\{1\}, t]\}$$
$$M_{10} = M_9 \cup \{s_1^2((e, V_2), t)\}$$
$$M_{11} = M_{10} \cup \{p_2(e) : [\{2\}, t]\}$$
$$M_{12} = M_{11} \cup \{p_0(a) : [\{1\}, \top]\}$$
$$M_{13} = M_{12} \cup \{satisfiable(p_0(a) : [\{1, 2\}, \top])\}$$

That is, $p_0(a) : [\{1, 2\}, \top]$ can be derived from the given AKB.

The correctness of our method is shown by the following theorem, whose proof is omitted due to the lack of space and can be found in [4].

Theorem 4. *Suppose that P is an AKB and G is a goal, P^* and G^* are their translated magic sets rules respectively. Then G can be proved by P iff satisfiable(G) can be generated by $G^* \cup P^*$.*

6 Discussions

Sometimes, we need to find the maximal truth value V such that an atom A can be derived from a set D of local databases, i.e., find the maximal truth value V such that $A : [D, V]$ is derivable from the given AKB. For example, suppose that agent a_1 can move o according to DB_1 ($move(a_1, o) : [\{1\}, t]$) and can not move o according to DB_2 ($move(a_1, o) : [\{2\}, f]$). Now, we want to know what is the maximal value such that $move(a_1, o) : [\{1, 2\}, V]$ can be derived. If the maximal value V is true, then a_1 will move o by itself, if the maximal value V is $\top$, a_1 will ask other agents for cooperation.

This problem is surprisingly simple in our case. Let the goal be $A : [D, V]$. When proof processing terminates, using $sat(A : [D, V])$, we can get the the maximal truth value of V. Of course, there is only one maximal truth value if there is not any variable in A. Otherwise there may be a corresponding maximal truth value for each case.

Example 6. Let $T = \{\bot, f, t, \top\}$. Suppose that the amalgamated fact set constructed by a given AKB is $M = \{p(a) : [\{1, 2\}, t], p(b) : [\{1\}, f]\} \cup M'$, where M' does not contain the predicate p. The maximal truth value of V for the goal $\leftarrow p(X) : [\{1, 2, 3\}, V]$ is t when $X = a$ and f when $X = b$.

Moreover, agents may have a hard deadline within which to reason and perform its tasks. This requires that a reasoning method must be interruptible, i.e., whenever interrupting the reasoning processing, the "best" answer obtained so far can be gotten. Our method can satisfy this request. Whenever the reasoning processing is interrupted, we can use $sat(A : [D, V])$ to find the approximate maximal truth value for V from the amalgamated fact set obtained so far. For example, in Example 6, if there is only $p(a) : [\{1, 2\}, t]$ in $\mathcal{M}$ when the goal processing is interrupted, then the maximal truth value of V for $p(X) : [\{1, 2, 3\}, V]$ is t, where $X = a$.

Our reasoning system for AKBs has currently been implemented in SICStus Prolog on Sun SPARCstation5/85MHz.

7 Conclusions

We have presented a reasoning method for amalgamated knowledge bases, which is very useful for multi-agent cooperation environments. Our method, an extension of the magic sets method, has the advantages associated with top-down as well as bottom-up evaluation. We have discussed how to insert an amalgamated fact to extend an amalgamated fact set and have shown the correctness of our method. Our reasoning method can be used interruptibly and approximately. We have implemented our reasoning system in SICStus Prolog.

As for the future work, we will introduce parallel processing into our system to enhance the efficiency and use our method to solve practical problems in multi-agent cooperation environments. We will also try to extend our method for reasoning about disjunctive amalgamated knowledge bases.

References

1. S. Adali and V.S. Subrahmanian, 'Amalgamating Knowledge Bases, III: Algorithms, Data Structures, and Query Processing', *Journal of Logic Programming*, Vol.28, NO.1, pp45-88, 1997.
2. A. Bancilhon, D. Maier, U. Sagiv and J.D., Ullman, 'Magic Sets and Other Strange Ways to Implement Logic Programs', *Proceedings of Fifth ACM SIGMOD-SIGACT-SIGART symp. on Principles of Database Systems*, pp.1-15, 1986.
3. H.A. Blair and V.S. Subrahmanian, 'Paraconsistent Logic Programming', *LNCS* 287, Dec. 1987.
4. L. He, 'The Correctness of the Extended Magic Sets Method for AKBs', *Technical Report*, Itoh Lab., Nagoya Institute of Technology, Japan, 1996.
5. M. Kifer and E. Lozinskii, 'A Logic for Reasoning with Inconsistency', *J. of Automated Reasoning* 9, pp.179-215, 1992.
6. M. Kifer and V.S. Subrahmanian, 'Theory of Generalized Annotated Logic Programming and Its Applications', *J. of Logic Programming*, 12, 4, pp.335-368, 1992.
7. U.W. Schwuttke and A.G. Quan, 'Enhancing Performance of Cooperating Agents in Real-Time Diagnostic System', *Proceedings of IJCAI*, pp.332-337, 1993.
8. V.S. Subrahmanian, 'Paraconsistent Disjunctive Databases', *Theoretical Computer Science Journal*, 1992.
9. V.S. Subrahmanian, 'Amalgamating Knowledge Bases', *ACM Trans. on Database Systems*, 19,2, pp.291-331, 1994.
10. J.D. Ullman, 'Principles of Database and Knowledge-Base Systems', *Computer Science Press*, Rockville, Maryland, 1989.
11. G. Weiß, 'Learning to Coordinate Action in Multi-Agent System', *Proceedings of IJCAI*, pp.311-316, 1993.

Detecting Conflicts in Multi-Agent Systems[1]

Love Ekenberg

IIASA, International Institute for Applied Systems Analysis,
A-2361 Laxenburg, AUSTRIA
email: ekenberg@iiasa.ac.at

Abstract. When a set of autonomous agents are going to decide on a global plan, it may be difficult to determine whether the set of common goals is non-empty. Furthermore, even if the combined plan is consistent, it may be hard to determine the set of common goals. We present a formal framework for the analysis of conflicts in sets of autonomous agents restricted in the sense that they can be described by first-order formulae and transaction mechanisms. In this framework, we allow for enrichment of agent systems with correspondence assertions, expressing the relationship between different entities in the formal specifications of the agents. Thereafter the specifications are analysed with respect to conflictfreeness. If two specifications are conflictfree, the formulae of one specification together with the set of correspondence assertions do not restrict the models of the other specification, i.e. the agent system does not restrict the individual agents. The approach takes into account static as well as dynamic aspects of the concept of conflictfreeness.

Keywords Multi-agent system, conflict detection, conceptual schema, theorem proving

1 Motivation

Different principles have been suggested for resolving conflicts in multi-agent systems, where a conflict situation could be one in which the negotiation set is empty, i.e. the ultimate goals of the individual agents are incompatible [11]. However, a basic problem in this context is that in many cases it is hard to determine whether the set of agents has conflicting goals [9]. It may be that the agents involved (or in a centralised domain, a co-ordinating agent) can not detect whether the system actually is in conflict; in particular if there are no restrictions on the interactions or communication processes between them. Moreover, even if the consistency of the system can be proved, it may be difficult to determine the consistent subsets of goals.

In the sequel, we suggest a set of concepts and procedures for determining whether an agent system is in conflict. The approach taken is that *parts* of multi-agent designs can often be formulated as processes (in the sense of algorithms).

---

[1]This work was supported by STINT (the Swedish Foundation for International Cooperation in Research and Higher Education) and the NUTEK (Swedish National Board for Industrial and Technical Development) project CISIS.

Consequently, we do not take into account such aspects as beliefs, intentions, free will, wants, or consciousness. This does not mean that we express a firm standpoint in this matter. The purpose is rather to demonstrate how some aspects of conflicts in systems of autonomous agents can be formally analysed using a simple language such as first-order logic.

Thus, we investigate agent systems restricted in the sense that the dynamic behaviour of the agents involved can be considered as a transition system. Such a system could be specified in some kind of process based language. To enable the various methods for determining conflicts in specifications to be used, and to allow analysis of the integrated model, the relevant set of agent specifications are transformed into first-order formulae integrated with a transition model.[2] The process is illustrated in Fig. 1.

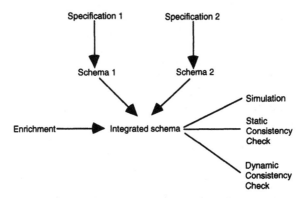

Fig. 1. Transformation, integration, enrichment, and analysis

Assume that there are initially only two specifications to be analysed. Aiming at facilitating logical analysis, they are first transformed into schemata which can be analysed separately. Thereafter they are merged, allowing them to be enriched with further invariants. At this stage the resulting schema can be analysed for static and dynamic consistency. This paper focuses on the integration step.

It should be emphasised that the process-oriented approach does not require a deterministic perspective. A model could include a set of processes communicating with each other as well with the environment. In this context the information exchange could contain complex information structures that the agents, for instance, may analyse with respect to different decision rules.

In [5], an approach using integration assertions is chosen to demonstrate how different aspects of integration of such models formulated in first-order logic can be analysed. This approach makes the integration process simpler and easier to understand than the traditional restructuring approach. In [7], it is shown how this

---

[2]A treatment of the details of such a transformation is beyond the scope of this paper. [3] demonstrates how this can be done in the case of SDL88 [2].

can be extended to handle general dynamic aspects of a schema. Based on this work, we describe a framework for the analysis of conflicts.

2 Representation in First-Order Logic

In the framework described, agent process specifications are transformed to formulae in first-order logic with a transaction mechanism. Such a structure will be referred to as a conceptual schema.[3] Needless to say, any suitable representation could have been used instead, but conceptual schemata provides a suitable and widespread formalism for these objects. Furthermore, as will be described below, the representation in first-order logic has some convenient features from a theorem proving perspective.

In the definitions below, we assume an underlying *language* L of first-order formulae.[4] By a *diagram* for a set R of formulae in a language L, we mean a Herbrand model of R, extended by the negation of the ground atoms in L that are not in the Herbrand model. Thus, a diagram for L is a Herbrand model extended with classical negation.[5]

Definition 1

A *schema* S is a structure $\langle R, ER \rangle$ consisting of a *static part* R and a *dynamic part* ER. R is a finite set of closed first-order formulae in a language L. ER is a set of *event rules*. Event rules describe possible transitions between different states of a schema and will be described below. *L(R)* is the *restriction of L to R*, i.e. L(R) is the set $\{ p \mid p \in L, \text{ but p does not contain any predicate symbol, that is not in a formula in R} \}$. The elements in R are called *static rules* in L(R). *A static integration assertion expressing the schema S_2 in the schema S_1* is a closed first order formula: $\forall x \, (p(x) \leftrightarrow F(x))$, where p is a predicate symbol in $L(S_2)$ and $F(x)$ is a formula in $L(S_1)$. ■

The intuition behind static integration assertions is that they express static relations between objects in the two schemata.

---

[3] As was mentioned above, the viewpoint taken is that significant aspects of agent behaviour actually can be represented as processes.

[4] As we will explain below, this assumption is not necessary, since the concepts can be more generally defined.

[5] For our purposes, this is no loss of generality by the well-known result that a closed formula is satisfiable iff its Herbrand expansion is satisfiable. For a discussion of this expansion theorem and its history, see, e.g. [4].

Example

Assume that the static parts of the two schemata S_1 and S_2 are the following: [6]

$$R_1 = \{\neg r(a) \vee r(b), r(c) \leftrightarrow r(a)\}$$
$$R_2 = \{p(a) \rightarrow p(b), p(c) \vee \neg p(b)\}$$

The diagrams for schema S_1 are then:

$$\{r(a), r(b), r(c)\}$$
$$\{\neg r(a), r(b), \neg r(c)\}$$
$$\{\neg r(a), \neg r(b), \neg r(c)\}$$

The diagrams for schema S_2 are:

$$\{p(a), p(b), p(c)\}$$
$$\{\neg p(a), p(b), p(c)\}$$
$$\{\neg p(a), \neg p(b), p(c)\}$$
$$\{\neg p(a), \neg p(b), \neg p(c)\}.$$

A possible integration assertion for the schemata is:

$$\forall x(p(x) \leftrightarrow r(x)) \quad \blacksquare$$

The dynamic part of a schema requires a definition of the concept of event rules which is given its semantics through the event concept. Intuitively, an event is an instance of an event rule, i.e. a transition from one diagram to another one. An event rule may be initialised from the environment of the agent system or from another agent included in the system. Initialised event rules map on possible events that may change the state of an instance of a specification. Below, L denotes a language.

Definition 2

An *event rule* in L is a structure $\langle P(z), C(z) \rangle$. $P(z)$ and $C(z)$ are first-order formulae in L, and z is a vector of variables in the alphabet of L.[7] In terms of conceptual modelling, $P(z)$ denotes the precondition of the event rule, and $C(z)$ the post condition. $\blacksquare$

---

[6] To simplify the presentation, a, b, and c are constants. As can be seen from definition 1, the static part of a schema may have a more general form.

[7] The notation A(x) means that x is free in A(x).

Definition 3

The set of *basic events* for a schema $\langle R, ER \rangle$ is a relation $E \subseteq D \times D$, where D is the set of diagrams for R. An element (σ, ρ) belongs to E iff

(i) $\rho = \sigma$, or
(ii)   there is a rule $\langle P(z), C(z) \rangle$ in ER, and a vector **e** of constants in L, such that $P(e) \in \sigma$ and $C(e) \in \rho$. In this case we will also say that the *basic event* (σ, ρ) *results* from the event rule.[8] ∎

Note that E not necessarily is a function. Intuitively, this means that an event rule is non-deterministic: if an instance of the precondition of an event rule belongs to a diagram σ, the event rule results in events (σ, ρ) for every diagram ρ, such that the corresponding post condition belongs to ρ. Thus, the approach to the dynamics of a schema differs from the traditional transactional approach in the database area, where an event deterministically specifies a minor modification of a state [1]. Depending of the particular information processor used, this event concept can be restricted in a variety of ways.

Example (cont.)

The event rules for the schema S_1 are:

$$Er_{1a} = \langle r(a), r(b) \rangle$$
$$Er_{1b} = \langle \neg r(a), (\neg r(b) \wedge \neg r(c)) \rangle$$
$$Er_{1c} = \langle (\neg r(a) \wedge r(b)), r(a) \rangle$$

Let:

$$\sigma_1 = \{r(a), r(b), r(c)\}$$
$$\sigma_2 = \{\neg r(a), \neg r(b), \neg r(c)\}$$
$$\sigma_3 = \{\neg r(a), r(b), \neg r(c)\}$$

Then the set of basic events for schema is:

$$\{(\sigma_1, \sigma_1), (\sigma_2, \sigma_2), (\sigma_3, \sigma_3), (\sigma_1, \sigma_3), (\sigma_3, \sigma_1), (\sigma_3, \sigma_2)\}. \quad \blacksquare$$

A description of a schema is a structure consisting of all diagrams for a schema, together with all possible transitions that are possible with respect to the basic events for the schema.

Definition 4

The *description of a schema S* is a digraph $\langle D, E \rangle$, where D is the set of diagrams for S, and E is the set of basic events (i.e. arcs in the digraph) for S. ∎

---

[8]In [7] an approach using event messages is described. However this concept is not necessary in a framework not presupposing a particular information processor.

Example (cont.)

Fig. 2 illustrates a description of schema S_1. The arrows in the figure represent basic events and the circles represent the diagrams for the schema. ■

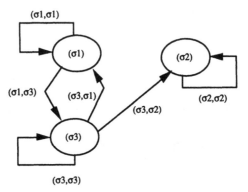

Fig. 2 The description of a schema

Using thresholds and other criteria for selecting reasonable paths only, the state space may be reduced. However, in general real-world applications the possible state space will probably remain very large when taking choice mechanisms into consideration. Therefore, when analysing the processes in a multi-agent system with respect to conflicts, it is often intractable to determine which combination of states that actually may occur by generating all the possible combinations and checking them one by one. An approach to this problem is presented in the following sections.

3 Conflict Detection

Intuitively, two schemata are in conflict with respect to a set of static integration assertions if one of them together with the integration assertions restrict the set of diagrams for the other one. This means, for instance, that if the set of goals for an agent A_1 and the set of goals for an agent A_2 are (partly) incompatible, they are in conflict since the ultimate goals (or ultimate states) of both agents cannot simultaneously be fulfilled, i.e. they restrict each other in this sense. We will say that S_2 and S_1 are conflictfree w.r.t. IA iff for each diagram σ in D_1, there exists a diagram τ in D_2, such that $\sigma \cup \tau$ is a diagram for IA. However, to emphasise the independence of a particular underlying language, we formulate the concept of conflictfreeness somewhat more generally.

Definition 5

Let IA be a set of static integration assertions expressing S_2 in S_1, and let the schemata be expressed as connected digraphs $\langle D_i, E_i \rangle$, where $E_i \subseteq D_i \times D_i$. Define a relation $R \subseteq D_1 \times D_2$. (There is no need to assume that the D_is are diagrams in the sense described above.) The definition of conflictfreeness between S_1 and S_2 then becomes an instance of R in the following sense: *S_2 and S_1 are conflictfree w.r.t. IA iff $\forall \sigma \in D_1$ $\exists \tau \in D_2$ $\sigma R \tau$, where $\sigma R \tau$ iff $\sigma \cup \tau \models$ IA. Otherwise S_2 and S_1 are in conflict w.r.t. IA.* ■

Example (cont.)

Reconsider the example above. The two schemata S_1 and S_2 are in conflict w.r.t. $\forall x(p(x) \leftrightarrow r(x))$. The diagram for S_1:

$$\{r(a),r(b),r(c)\}$$

can be extended to:

$$\{r(a),r(b),r(c),p(a),p(b),p(c)\}$$

which is a diagram for the integration assertion. Similarly the diagram:

$$\{\neg r(a),\neg r(b),\neg r(c)\}$$

can be extended to:

$$\{\neg r(a),\neg r(b),\neg r(c),\neg p(a),\neg p(b),\neg p(c)\}$$

However, the third diagram below cannot be extended in this way.

$$\{\neg r(a),r(b),\neg r(c)\}$$

The diagrams for schema S_2 are:

$$\{p(a),p(b),p(c)\}$$
$$\{\neg p(a),p(b),p(c)\}$$
$$\{\neg p(a),\neg p(b),p(c)\}$$
$$\{\neg p(a),\neg p(b),\neg p(c)\}$$

Since none of:

$$\{\neg r(a),r(b),\neg r(c),p(a),p(b),p(c)\}$$
$$\{\neg r(a),r(b),\neg r(c),\neg p(a),p(b),p(c)\}$$
$$\{\neg r(a),r(b),\neg r(c),\neg p(a),\neg p(b),p(c)\}$$
$$\{\neg r(a),r(b),\neg r(c),\neg p(a),\neg p(b),\neg p(c)\}$$

is a diagram for $\forall x(p(x) \leftrightarrow r(x))$, the schemata are in conflict w.r.t the integration assertion. On the other hand, the schemata are conflictfree w.r.t.

$$\forall x(p(a) \leftrightarrow (r(x) \leftrightarrow r(c)))$$

The possible extended diagrams are then:

$$\{r(a),r(b),r(c),p(a),p(b),p(c)\}$$
$$\{\neg r(a),\neg r(b),\neg r(c),p(a),p(b),p(c)\}$$
$$\{\neg r(a),r(b),\neg r(c),\neg p(a),\neg p(b),\neg p(c)\}$$
$$\{\neg r(a),r(b),\neg r(c),\neg p(a),\neg p(b),p(c)\}$$
$$\{\neg r(a),r(b),\neg r(c),\neg p(a),p(b),p(c)\} \blacksquare$$

Note that the check for conflictfreeness may be both too strong and to weak, since not all states in a schema need to be compatible with other states in another schema. In some cases only states including ultimate goals need consideration. If two schemata S_1 and S_2, representing the agents A_1 and A_2, are in conflict, and the conflicting states contain ultimate goals of the agents, then there is a real conflict with respect to the goals. In case of goal-conflict detection, the relation R in the above definition could be modified in the following respect. (The definition does not take into account that several states may contain the same goal.)

Definition 6

Let IA and $\langle D_i, E_i \rangle$ be as above, and let G_i denote the set of states containing goals of the agent represented by S_i. S_2 and S_1 are conflictfree w.r.t. IA iff $\forall \sigma \in G_1 \ \exists \tau \in G_2 \ \sigma R \tau$, where $\sigma R \tau$ iff $\sigma \cup \tau \models IA$. Otherwise S_2 and S_1 are in conflict w.r.t. IA. ∎

As the definition of conflictfreeness is formulated above, the general problem of determining conflictfreeness is undecidable. With the (in most cases) reasonable assumption that there is a finite number of relevant objects in the agent system as well as in its environment, a language with a finite number of constants may be used. In that case we have a problem in second order propositional logic that is Π_2^P-complete. This follows from the characterisation of the complexity class Π_k^P and the observation that the criterion of conflictfreeness for two schemata is an expression in second order logic: $\forall \sigma \in D_1 \ \exists \tau \in D_2 \ \sigma R \tau$.[9] By restricting the formulae in IA as suggested in [7], we receive a problem that is NP-complete. Naturally, even this appears computationally demanding, but in actual fact, interesting classes of NP-complete problems can be solved within a reasonable time. A very competitive candidate for a theorem prover is proposed in [10].

4 Extending the Event Concept

The definition of conflictfreeness does only take into consideration the static aspects of the agent behaviour, i.e. how the static properties of one agent affect the static properties of another. Next, we introduce more general dynamic aspects in our framework by defining sequential combinations of event rules.

Definition 7

Given a schema $\langle R, ER \rangle$ and a set $\{V_1, V_2, ..., V_k\}$ of event rules in ER. The *sequential combination* of $V_1, V_2, ..., V_{k-1}$ and V_k is denoted by
$\langle [P_1(z_1), C_1(z_1)] ; ...; [P_k(z_k), C_k(z_k)] \rangle$, or shorter, $V_1 \nabla ... \nabla V_k$. ∎

The semantics for sequential combinations of event rules is given by the concept of instances of event rules.

---

[9]For a detailed treatment of the different complexity classes, see, e.g., [8], p. 96.

Definition 8

Given a schema $S = \langle R, ER \rangle$ and a set $\{V_1, \ldots, V_k\}$ of event rules in ER. The following notation will be used:

(i) $\Lambda(S, V_i)$, is the set of basic events for S resulting from V_i, $i = 1, \ldots, k$.

The *combined instances of* $V_1 \, \nabla \ldots \nabla V_k$ is defined by:

(ii) $\Lambda(S, V_1 \, \nabla \ldots \nabla V_k) = \{(\sigma, \rho) \mid$ there is a τ, such that $(\sigma, \tau) \in$
$\Lambda(S, V_1 \, \nabla \ldots \nabla V_{k-1})$ and $(\tau, \rho) \in \Lambda(S, V_k)\}$, $k \geq 2$. ■

Example (cont.)

Two of the event rules for the schema S_1 are:

$$Er_{1a} = \langle r(a), r(b) \rangle$$
$$Er_{1b} = \langle \neg r(a), (\neg r(b) \wedge \neg r(c)) \rangle$$

Then:

$$\Lambda(S_1, Er_{1a} \, \nabla Er_{1b}) = \{(\{r(a), r(b), r(c)\}, \{\neg r(a), \neg r(b), \neg r(c)\})\}. ■$$

We may now generalise the event concept by defining an event as either a basic event or an instance of the combined extension of a schema.

Definition 9

Given a schema $S = \langle R, ER \rangle$. The *combined extension of S* $\Lambda(S)$ is the union of $\Lambda(S, V)$ for all sequential combinations V of event rules in ER. ■

Definition 10

Given a schema $S = \langle R, ER \rangle$. An *event* for S is an ordered pair $(\sigma, \rho) \in \Lambda(S)$. ■

Example (cont.)

Thus, using the same notation as in Fig. 2:

$$\Lambda(S_1) = \{(\sigma_1, \sigma_1), (\sigma_2, \sigma_2), (\sigma_1, \sigma_3), (\sigma_3, \sigma_1), (\sigma_3, \sigma_2), (\sigma_1, \sigma_2)\}. ■$$

We will also use a notation for the diagrams that an event traverses.

Definition 11

Let $S = \langle R, ER \rangle$ be a schema, and let $V = V_1 \, \nabla \ldots \nabla V_k$ be a sequential combination of event rules in ER.

(i)   The *event path extension for V*, $\Pi(S, V)$, is the set of sequences of diagrams for S, $(\sigma_1, \sigma_2, \ldots, \sigma_{k+1})$, such that $(\sigma_i, \sigma_{i+1}) \in \Lambda(S, V_i)$.

(ii)   The *event path extension for S*, $\Pi(S)$, is the union of $\Pi(S, V)$ for all sequential combinations V of event rules in ER. ■

Fig. 3 exemplifies these concepts in a part of a description of a schema S. The dots represent diagrams and the arcs represent basic events. The labelled basic events correspond to the labelled instance of $\Pi(S)$ below the graph. (σ_1, σ_5) is an instance of $\Lambda(S)$ through the same sequence of basic events.

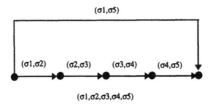

Fig. 3 Basic events, events and event paths

Example (cont.)

Let S_1 be the schema as before, and let $V = Er_{1a} \nabla Er_{1b}$. Then:

$$\Pi(S, V) = \{(\{r(a),r(b),r(c)\}, \{\neg r(a),r(b),\neg r(c)\}, \{\neg r(a),\neg r(b),\neg r(c)\})\}. \ \blacksquare$$

Using these concepts, we extend the framework to include dynamic integration assertions.

5 Dynamic Enrichment

This section generalises the concepts from section 3, by giving semantics for some dynamic aspects of schemata. Testing for static conflictfreeness is in general not enough. For instance, assume that schemata S_1 and S_2, representing the agents A_1 and A_2, are conflictfree in the static sense. Consider an event (σ', τ') in the description of S_2. Since the schemata are conflictfree, there are elements σ and τ in the description of S_1, such that $\sigma \cup \sigma'$ and $\tau \cup \tau'$ are diagrams for IA. However, it may still be the case that there is no path from σ to τ in the description of S_1, and consequently no possibility for schema S_1 to be in state τ when starting from state σ. Consequently, even if conflictfreeness prevails, the agents may still restrict each other when the dynamic behaviour of the agents are considered.

To avoid such a situation the schemata should be checked for dynamic conflictfreeness. The idea behind this concept can be illustrated as follows: If the schemata S_1 and S_2, representing the agents A_1 and A_2, are dynamically conflictfree, then for every event in the schema S_2 representing a transition from a state σ' to a state τ', there is a corresponding sequence of events in the schema S_1. This sequence starts from a state of S_1 not in conflict with σ' and terminates in a state not in conflict with τ'.

Needless to say, to determine dynamic conflictfreeness in this sense is a very demanding problem from a computational viewpoint, but sometimes it is possible to reduce the amount of combined instances that should be investigated by explicitly expressing which parts of a specification should have a similar behaviour as parts of another specification. The following shows how this can be done in the case where one event rule corresponds to a sequential combination of event rules.[10]

Definition 12

Let $S_1 = \langle R_1, ER_1 \rangle$ and $S_2 = \langle R_2, ER_2 \rangle$ be two schemata. An *identifying dynamic integration assertion expressing the schema S_2 in the schema S_1* is an expression ([V], [U_1, ..., U_n]), where V is an event rule in ER_2 and U_1, ..., U_n are event rules in ER_1. ■

We may restrict the semantics of an identifying dynamic integration assertion as in the following definition.

Definition 13

Let S_1 and S_2 be two schemata, and let ID = ([V], [U_1, ..., U_n]) be an identifying dynamic integration assertion expressing the schema S_2 in S_1. *ID is adequate for S_1, S_2, and IA*, if:

(i)   For all $(\sigma', \tau') \in \Lambda(S_2, V)$, there is a sequence of events
      $(\sigma_1, \sigma_2, ..., \sigma_n, \sigma_{n+1}) \in \Pi(S_1, U_1 \nabla...\nabla U_n)$,
      such that $\sigma_1 \cup \sigma'$ and $\sigma_{n+1} \cup \tau'$ are both diagrams for IA.

(ii)   For all $(\sigma_1, \sigma_2, ..., \sigma_n, \sigma_{n+1}) \in \Pi(S_1, U_1 \nabla...\nabla U_n)$, there is an event
      $(\sigma', \tau') \in \Lambda(S_2, V)$, such that $\sigma_1 \cup \sigma'$ and $\sigma_{n+1} \cup \tau'$ are both diagrams for IA.

If only (i) above is fulfilled, then we will say that ID is *semi-adequate* for S_1, S_2 and IA. When $(\sigma_1, \sigma_2, ..., \sigma_n, \sigma_{n+1})$ and (σ', τ') correspond in the way described in (i) or (ii), they are called *compatible* with ID. ■

Example (cont.)

Let:

$$S_1 = \langle \{\neg r(a) \vee r(b), r(c) \leftrightarrow r(a)\}, \{\langle r(a), r(b)\rangle, \langle \neg r(a), (\neg r(b) \wedge \neg r(c))\rangle\}\rangle$$
$$S_2 = \langle \{p(a) \rightarrow p(b), p(c) \vee \neg p(b)\}, \{\langle (p(a) \wedge p(b)), \neg p(b)\rangle\}\rangle$$
$$IA = \{ \forall x(p(a) \leftrightarrow (r(x) \leftrightarrow r(c)))\}$$
$$ID = \{[\langle (p(a) \wedge p(b)), \neg p(b)\rangle], [\langle r(a), r(b)\rangle, \langle \neg r(a), (\neg r(b) \wedge \neg r(c))\rangle]\}$$

Then:

$$\Lambda(S_2, \langle (p(a) \wedge p(b)), \neg p(b)\rangle) = \{(\{p(a),p(b),p(c)\}, \{\neg p(a),\neg p(b),p(c)\}),$$
$$(\{p(a),p(b),p(c)\}, \{\neg p(a),\neg p(b),\neg p(c)\})\}$$

As we have seen, the only member in:

$$\Pi(S_1, \langle r(a), r(b)\rangle \nabla \langle \neg r(a), (\neg r(b) \wedge \neg r(c))\rangle)$$

is:

$$\{(\{r(a),r(b),r(c)\}, \{\neg r(a),r(b),\neg r(c)\}, \{\neg r(a),\neg r(b),\neg r(c)\})\}$$

---

[10][7] discusses a more general concept of conflictfreeness.

However, neither:

$$\{\neg r(a),\neg r(b),\neg r(c)\} \cup \{\neg p(a),\neg p(b),p(c)\}, \text{ nor}$$
$$\{\neg r(a),\neg r(b),\neg r(c)\} \cup \{\neg p(a),\neg p(b),\neg p(c)\}$$

is a diagram for IA. Thus, ID is not semiadequate for S_1, S_2 and IA. This argument is illustrated in Fig. 4 below.

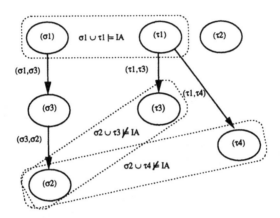

Fig. 4. ID is not semiadequate for S_1, S_2 and IA

In the Fig. 4 the following notations are used:

$$\sigma_1 = \{r(a),r(b),r(c)\}$$
$$\sigma_2 = \{\neg r(a),\neg r(b),\neg r(c)\}$$
$$\sigma_3 = \{\neg r(a),r(b),\neg r(c)\}$$
$$\tau_1 = \{p(a),p(b),p(c)\}$$
$$\tau_2 = \{\neg p(a),p(b),p(c)\}$$
$$\tau_3 = \{\neg p(a),\neg p(b),p(c)\}$$
$$\tau_4 = \{\neg p(a),\neg p(b),\neg p(c)\} \blacksquare$$

We modify our earlier definition of conflictfreeness and incorporate the requirement of adequacy by the following definition.

Definition 14

Let $S_1 = \langle R_1, ER_1 \rangle$ and $S_2 = \langle R_2, ER_2 \rangle$ be two schemata. Also, let IA be a set of static integration assertions expressing the schema S_2 in S_1, and let D be a set of IDs. S_1 and S_2 are *dynamically conflictfree* w.r.t. IA and D, if:

(i) S_1 and S_2 are conflictfree w.r.t. IA.

(ii) S_2 and S_1 are conflictfree w.r.t. IA.

(iii) All the IDs in D are semi-adequate for S_1, S_2, and IA. $\blacksquare$

Example (cont.)

Let S_1, S_2, IA, and ID be as in the examples before. As we have seen (iii) is not valid in this case. Since the ID is violated in this respect, S_1 and S_2 are not dynamically conflictfree w.r.t. IA and ID. ∎

As in the static case, a dynamic conflict does not necessarily mean that the ultimate goals of the agents are in conflict. This shortcoming can be remedied in a way similar to the static case.

It should also be noted that similar to the concept of static conflictfreeness, the concepts of dynamic conflictfreeness may be generalised independent of a specific underlying language such as first-order logic. Given two schemata S_1 and S_2 expressed as connected digraphs $\langle D_i, E_i \rangle$, where $E_i \subseteq D_i \times D_i$ and $R \subseteq D_1 \times D_2$ are relations as before. Further, let $E_i^j \subseteq D_i \times ... \times D_i$ (where the cartesian product operates on j D_is), let E_i^+ be the set of E_i^j, $j = 1,2,...,$ and let $T \subseteq E_1 \times E_2^+$. A generalised definition of semi-adequacy is then:

$$\forall(\sigma_1,\sigma_2) \in E_1 \ \exists(\tau_1,...,\tau_i) \in E_2^+ \ (\sigma_1,\sigma_2 T\tau_1,...,\tau_i \wedge \sigma_1 R\tau_1 \wedge \sigma_2 R\tau_i).$$

The main point is again that the relations R and T are general and do not by themselves require a specific underlying language. Similar to defining conflictfreeness as an instance of the relation R, it is straightforward to define the requirement of adequacy or more general concepts of dynamic conflictfreeness as instances of the relation T.[11]

5 Concluding Remarks

The work described in this paper is motivated by the difficulty in real-life situations to determine whether complex agent systems are in conflict. Even in situations where it is quite easy to determine whether the subset of common goals of the agents involved is non-empty, it may be difficult to determine this subset. Based on our earlier work, we have described a framework for the analysis of conflicts in multi-agent systems with respect to properties that can be formalised by first-order formulae, and also indicated that the assumption of a particular language is not necessary. The framework includes procedures for determining static as well as dynamic conflictfreeness. The main assumptions on the multi-agent systems analysable with the methods described here may seem to be quite strong, since they are supposed to be modelled as specifications restricted in several respects. However, the working process for analysing process related specifications by theorem proving means can as well be applied to more complex situations. A forthcoming paper will provide a more detailed treatment of how the framework described in this paper can be integrated in a multi-agent architecture to detect problematic cases of global inconsistency with respect to sets of certain measures over imprecise domains [6].

---

[11] In [7], the complexity properties of determining semi-adequacy of two schemata is described.

References

[1]   S. Abiteboul and V. Vianu, "Equivalence and Optimization of Relational Transactions," *Journal of ACM*, vol. 35, pp. 130–145, 1988.

[2]   CCITT, *CCITT Recommendation Z.100: Specification and Description Language SDL (Blue Book, Volume X.1-X.5)*: ITU General Secretariat-Sales Section, Places des Nations, CH-1211 Geneva 20, 1988.

[3]   G. Davies and L. Ekenberg, "Using First-Order Theorem Proving for Analysing Transaction Systems," Technical Report, Department of Computer and Systems Sciences, Stockholm University.

[4]   B. Dreben and W. D. Goldfarb, *The Decision Problem: Solvable Classes of Quantification Formulas*: Reading, Mass, Addison-Wesley, 1979.

[5]   L. Ekenberg and P. Johannesson, "Conflictfreeness as a Basis for Schema Integration," Proceedings of CISMOD-95, pp. 1–13, Lecture Notes in Computer Science, 1995.

[6]   L. Ekenberg, M. Danielson, and M. Boman, "From Local Assessments to Global Rationality," *International Journal of Intelligent and Cooperative Information Systems*, vol. 5, nos. 2 & 3, pp. 315–331, 1996.

[7]   L. Ekenberg and P. Johannesson, "A Formal Basis for Dynamic Schema Integration," Proceedings of 15th International Conference on Conceptual Modelling ER'96, pp. 211–226, Lecture Notes in Computer Science, 1996.

[8]   D. S. Johnson, "A Catalogue of Complexity Classes," in *Handbook of Theoretical Computer Science: Volume A*, J. van. Leeuwen, Ed. Amsterdam: Elsevier, 1990.

[9]   M. J. Katz and J. S. Rosenschein, "Verifying Plans for Multiple Agents," *Journal of Experimental and Theoretical Artificial Intelligence*, vol. 5, pp. 39–56, 1993.

[10]   G. Stålmarck, "System for Determining Propositional Logic Theorems by Applying Values and Rules to Triplets that are Generated from a Formula," US. Patent No. 5 276 897 1995.

[11]   G. Zlotkin and J. S. Rosenschein, "Incomplete Information and Deception in Multi-Agent Negotiation," Proceedings of 12th IJCAI, pp. 225–231, 1991.

Persuasion as a Form of Inter-Agent Negotiation*

Chris Reed[1], Derek Long[2], Maria Fox[2] and Max Garagnani[2]

[1] Department of Computer Science,
University College London,
Gower St.,
London
WC1E 6BT
C.Reed@cs.ucl.ac.uk
http://www.cs.ucl.ac.uk/staff/C.Reed

[2] Department of Computer Science,
Durham University,
South Road,
Durham
{D.P.Long, M.Fox,
M.Garagnani}@dur.ac.uk

Abstract. Agents in a multi-agent environment must often cooperate to achieve their objectives. In this paper an agent, B, cooperates with another agent, A, if B adopts a goal that furthers A's objectives in the environment. If agents are independent and motivated by their own interests, cooperation cannot be relied upon and it may be necessary for A to *persuade* B to adopt a cooperative goal. This paper is concerned with the organisation and construction of persuasive argument, and examines how a rational agent comes to hold a belief, and thus, how new beliefs might be engendered and existing beliefs altered, through the process of argumentation. Argument represents an opportunity for an agent to convince a possibly sceptical or resistant audience of the veracity of its own beliefs. This ability is a vital component of rich communication, facilitating explanation, instruction, cooperation and conflict resolution. An architecture is described in which a hierarchical planner is used to develop discourse plans which can be realised in natural language using the LOLITA system. Planning is concerned with the intentional, contextual and pragmatic aspects of discourse structure as well as with the logical form of the argument and its stylistic organisation. In this paper attention is restricted to the planning of persuasive discourse, or monologue.

Keywords: agent communication, argumentation theory, rhetoric, belief modelling, planning.

*This work has been partly funded by EPSRC grant no. 94313824.

1. Introduction

In this paper an architecture is presented for the autonomous construction of argument, outlining the components required for persuasive communication. Argument plays a crucial role in multi-agent worlds in which agents are motivated to pursue their own interests. The focus of this work is restricted to logical argument, and the assumption is made that agents will adopt, or reject, certain beliefs if they are presented with convincing reasons to do so. Rhetorical argument, which has been pursued in the context of multi-agent communication [20], is difficult to model because its success depends on the inability of the hearer to recognise the fallacy it depends upon. It is assumed in this work that agents can both construct and follow logical argument.

The architecture described here is intended as a model of communication between two artificial agents, although it also models a restricted form of inter-human communication and human-computer interaction. The realisation of the planned discourses must result in their expression in some language. In this work, natural language has been chosen as an example because generation of natural language texts from planned monologues has been explored successfully in the LOLITA system [18]. The proposed architecture is not inextricably bound to the use of natural language - the planning levels are independent of the language in which plans will be expressed and the intentional structures produced at these levels are sufficiently abstract to remain unchanged by a shift to some more simple and restrictive artificial language.

2. Overview

The architecture described in this paper is hierarchical in structure, reflecting the distinct, though inter-related, levels of structure within arguments. The part of argument synthesis which is concerned with the resolution of syntax, expression and morphology comprises the lowest level of the architecture and represents the interface to the LOLITA system. Above this lowest level sits functionality based upon Mann & Thompsons's Rhetorical Structure Theory [11], and then above this is a hierarchy of levels concerned with the planning and presentation of the discourse. The highest level of abstraction in the architecture is the Argument Objectives (AO) level which determines the overall form of argument to be constructed. Three forms are considered: an agent can *explain*, *inform* or *persuade*. Informing the hearer of a proposition simply involves stating the proposition without the support of argument. It is assumed that the hearer had no knowledge of the proposition prior to being informed. Explaining a proposition involves providing support for the proposition through argument, under the assumption that the hearer knew of the proposition but was undecided about its truth value prior to the explanation. Persuading a hearer to accept a proposition involves undermining the hearer's current beliefs in the falsity of the proposition and then the provision of support for belief in the truth of the proposition. It is assumed that the hearer believes in the converse before the persuasion takes place. As this account suggests, a four-valued model of belief is used in the architecture described here. An agent either believes, disbelieves, is unaware of or is undecided about a proposition. This model is described and justified in §3.

The persuade and explain argument forms are developed at the Argument Structure (AS) level which produces the logical form of the argument, employing purely intentional data structures, by the application of operators modelling logical inference rules. This form is then augmented and modified by the subordinate Eloquence Generation (EG) level which is concerned with properties of a speech such as its length, detail, meter, ordering of sub-arguments, grouping of sub-arguments, enthymeme contraction, use of repetition and so on. The architecture is summarised in Fig. 1. A collection of operators describing the actions which may be employed at the different levels in argument construction are supplied to a hierarchical planner which plans firstly an intentional structure (an abstracted model of the intended discourse), which is then supplemented with further details to form a deeper content structure, linking the intentions to rhetorical structures for realisation. These structures are supplemented with the addition of constraints on textual realisation, including vocabulary restrictions, rhythm and mood of text and so on. This is finally realised as text.

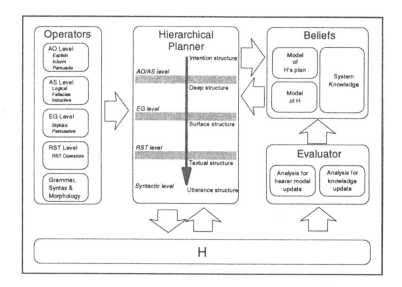

Fig. 1. System architecture overview

3. Belief Modelling

3.1. Issues

It has become clear that both AS and EG levels require access to the belief model of the audience, in addition, of course, to the beliefs of the system. The AS level needs to be able to assess in advance how different structures are likely to be received, and to take account of the beliefs of the audience in producing structure. The EG level employs the belief model to pitch an argument at the right level of detail, and to track the saliency of beliefs used during argumentation. A more detailed examination of the relationship between the higher levels and belief is described below in §4 and §5.

There are a number of issues involved in analysing belief. There are different kinds of belief. These will be referred to in this paper as factual beliefs, which are either testable (at least in theory) or are definitional (and include beliefs based on sensory experiences); opinions, which are based on moral and aesthetic judgement and are thus ultimately personal and unprovable (since there is no universally accepted and provably correct aesthetic-moral framework - and it is hard to conceive how there could be); and cultural beliefs, which are based upon sociocultural maxims (such as that which states that living into old age is desirable). This tripartite distinction has been based upon the views expressed implicitly by [3], when talking about general types of argument, but there are also numerous other divisions which could be detailed (see [1] for a number of examples). The way in which beliefs become manifest in argumentative dialogue - both their individual expression, and their interrelation - is chiefly dependent upon their class, so competent representation and recognition of these distinct belief types represents an important problem. A further discussion of these divisions and their implications is pursued in §3.2.

Another major problem is how to resolve two seemingly contradictory views generated by introspection, that of whether beliefs are best represented as dichotomous or scalar. Various problems associated with the concept of 'strength of belief' are discussed in [7]. A pragmatic resolution to this issue is in itself crucial to competent belief modelling.

A simple, but powerful, way to model beliefs is to say that an agent believes a proposition in a given context if that agent would be prepared to act on that proposition in that context. Action might take different forms reflecting different levels of commitment on the part of the agent to the implications of believing in the proposition. For example, action on the belief that lottery winnings should be distributed amongst the poor can range from simply claiming this belief to taking actions in the world which bring about the redistribution of individuals' winnings. Using this model, given a context, an agent can be said to believe, disbelieve or be undecided about a given proposition with respect to a given action.

In the current work, agents co-existing within an environment communicate in order to engage in co-operative activity. An agent, A, will attempt to persuade an agent, B, to adopt a certain goal. This objective can be achieved if A can persuade B to adopt beliefs which will result in B generating the goal A intends. In simple cases A will only need to make B believe that A wishes the goal to be adopted. This will occur in situations in which adoption of the goal will imply little planning and execution effort on the part of B, with no conflicts with B's existing goals. When achievement of the goal demands significant effort from B, or conflicts with B's existing goals, more complex beliefs might need to be induced. For example, B might need to be persuaded that achievement of the goal will result in benefits for B as well as for A. In the current work, monologue, and not dialogue, is being considered, and hence the contexts in which beliefs are held and the goal which A hopes that B will adopt are fixed so that beliefs can be treated as three-valued (believed, disbelieved or undecided), as proposed above.

Since A plans its monologue relative to its own model of B's beliefs, the beliefs that B actually holds are not accessible to A and cannot be considered relevant in the construction of A's monologue. Furthermore, it is possible for A to believe that B is ignorant of certain propositions, which precludes the possibility of B having any belief attitude (that is, any of the three values identified above) towards these propositions in A's model of B. In this case, A will believe B to be *unaware* of the proposition - a different relationship to belief, disbelief or indecision.

Another property of belief which is manifest in argument is that of saliency. Enthymeme contraction (where an implicit premise or conclusion is omitted) relies heavily upon saliency and so too does the process of focusing: keeping the argument to the point (Cf. the lower level focusing of [8]). The belief model used must therefore be able to competently handle the concept of saliency.

Argument modelling also relies on a treatment of the complex phenomenon of mutual belief: an argument is based upon common ground - a set of mutual beliefs (ie. which both parties hold, and which both parties also know the other to hold). Mutual belief is defined in terms of an infinite regress of nested beliefs. That is, A believes that A and B mutually believe a proposition, P, if A believes (i) P and (ii) that B believes P and (iii) that A and B mutually believe that A and B mutually believe P. The problem is to pragmatically choose a level of nesting beyond which 'mutual' belief is to be assumed. In making this choice, it is understood that no matter how many levels a system can cope with, it is always possible to construct a (highly convoluted) example which exceeds the capabilities of that system. From a psychological (and intuitive) point of view, choosing some arbitrary level of nesting by which to define mutuality seems rather implausible. In humans, it would appear that belief nesting is a resource bounded operation with no known limit, and it is possible to construct deeply nested examples which present remarkably little difficulty (such as the example in Fig. 2, below), though handling further complexity rapidly becomes extremely difficult and time consuming. It may be possible to utilise

In the classic Hitchcock film "North by Northwest", Cary Grant is the central character in a case of mistaken identity - he is mistaken for a goodguy agent by the evil James Mason. Towards the end, a scene occurs in which CG masquerades as the goodguy agent he is thought to be. As part of a goodguy ploy, he informs JM of his wish to defect, at which he is shot by EveMarie Saint, a goodguy agent working undercover as accomplice to JM. In her role as a villain, she needs to stop the defection, believing him to be a traitor to the goodguys. Thus with the proposition P that 'ES is a goodguy',

```
BEL(ES, P)                                  She knows she's a goodguy
BEL(CG, P)                                  He knows she's a goodguy ...
BEL(ES, BEL(CG, -P))                        ... but she doesn't realise that ...
BEL(CG, BEL(ES, BEL(CG, -P)))               ... and he knows she doesn't realise ...
BEL(Audience, BEL(CG, BEL(ES, BEL(CG, -P))))   ... or at least that's what the audience thinks!
```

After JM has left however, CG gets up - the shooting had been faked. CG and ES must have been in league with each other after all. At this point the belief held must be changed to

```
BEL(Audience, BMB(CG, ES, P))))             They both know she's a goodguy, and
                                            both know that they both know it.
```

Hitchcock envisaged the whole situation and realised that it was unusual and interesting. There were in total, five levels of nested beliefs.

Fig. 2. Deep nesting of beliefs

this evidence and allow for a similar process in an implementation, so that some default operator (say, BMB, following [4]) is employed using a naively shallow level of nesting, but, in the light of new evidence, this may be replaced (or supplemented) with a more sophisticated nesting and appropriate operator.

3.2. Grounding of Beliefs

The knowledge representation adopted as the basis for this system has as a fundamental unit the concept of an *event*. An event is a piece of information representing a proposition which is perceived to be a part of reality: for example, "the sky is blue". The constituent elements of an event are the subject, the predicate and the object. It is possible for the object to be absent as in "the bomb exploded". If necessary, further features can be added, such as the time or the location of the event. This form of knowledge representation constitutes the basis for the semantic network on which the LOLITA system depends [18]. An example of such a network is given below in Fig. 3. The representation is reified so that events can themselves be the subject of events, with transformation being possible of the links between events (which represent various possible relations, such as implication or causation) so that these are also accessible as events. The events encoded within the knowledge base of an agent represent the beliefs held by that agent. The events can be representations of (the agents beliefs about) another agent's beliefs, allowing one agent to model the beliefs of another. An account of the semantics of the basic framework of the representation can be found in [17].

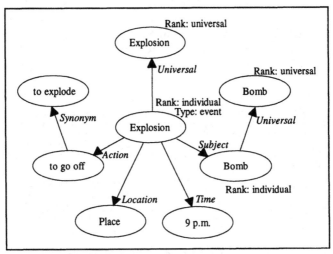

Fig. 3. "The bomb exploded"

In order to persuade another agent to adopt a belief, it is important to understand what might lead to the adoption. Beliefs are not held without reason: the reasons for an agent holding a belief are captured as the *supports* for that belief. In the LOLITA representation, this can be seen as a special event relationship holding between an event, E, and its supporter, E', namely: Supports(E', E). The presence of the pair of events in a network corresponding to the beliefs, or perceived beliefs, of an agent, E' and Supports(E', E), can be seen as sanctioning the inference that the event E holds.

The supports for a belief are of great importance, since it is the supports which allow an agent to decompose an argument into sub-arguments, through the identification of the supporting components which must be introduced into the main argument. Supporting relationships are established in the initial knowledge of the agent - the current work is not concerned with attempting to infer them from observations of the world or even from implicit relationships within the initial knowledge of the agent. The supports can be related to the event they support in different ways, but the two that have been considered so far are *implicational* relationships and *causal* relationships. In order for the recursive structure of events and their supports to terminate it is clear that there must be events which do not require support. These events are of great interest, since it is apparent that they represent premises of an argument and could prove difficult to persuade other agents to accept. It is therefore worth attempting to identify the nature of these events and determine why they might have no supports.

Events which have no supporting events are referred to in this work as *grounded* events. Grounded events can be grounded for several reasons. One key reason is that an agent will trust its own sensory input (which is not the same as the interpretation of that input). So, if the agent believes it has experienced some particular sensory experience, then the event representing that experience will be unsupported - it is grounded by virtue of the sensory experience itself. These events are a special case of a more general type of grounded event: the events which are grounded through external sources. In the case of sensory experience the external source is the sensory capacity of the agent itself, but, more generally, the source might be another agent. Of course, events which are sourced by another agent are (certainly for human agents, at least) only admitted into an agent's beliefs via its senses and it is possible to argue that the grounding of all events which have external sources must therefore be through sensory experiences. In practice it is not particularly helpful to distinguish the sensory event from the literal interpretation of that event when considering information provided by another agent: the question of the status of the content of the information (whether or not the content is accepted as a belief or not) is determined on the basis of an estimation of the reliability of the source agent, not on whether the senses that conveyed the message are considered reliable.

There is a further category of grounded events: some beliefs are held not because of a direct external source, but because of internal motivations and value-systems of an agent. An agent might believe that it is deemed punishable to carry out some action - this would be an externally sourced belief, grounded through the source from which it was obtained - but a belief that the action is wrong can only be based on the agent's own moral code. Events which are believed because of the agent's own value-system are considered to be grounded through that value-system. The distinction between events which are grounded through the agent's experience of the world and those which are grounded through the agent's value-system reflects the division of beliefs discussed earlier into factual beliefs and opinions.

Many beliefs are supported by a combination of grounded beliefs and causal relationships which reflect the way in which an agent believes the world works. For example, a belief that a ball is under a table might be supported by the grounded belief that the agent saw the ball roll slowly under the table and a (complex) belief that objects which are rolling slowly will quickly stop and stay where they come to rest. The first belief is grounded in sensory perception. The second belief (which might, in fact, be a structure of several interlocking beliefs) is a belief about the way that the world works. It is more difficult to assess the status of this belief: it is not grounded in experience, since a causal relationship cannot be experienced. It is unlikely to be sourced by a single information source: if it were, it might prove dangerously volatile, being susceptible to possible future revisions of the reliability of the source. Beliefs about the physical laws of the world in which an agent works are neither sourced by individual sensory experiences (although they can, of course, be undermined by single sensory experiences), nor is it likely that they are sourced by another agent. Further, these beliefs are not opinions - they do not reflect a value-judgement. Therefore, it must be possible for an agent to ground beliefs in one further way: beliefs about physical laws are grounded as hypotheses. That is, some beliefs are adopted because they represent working hypotheses from which deductions about the way the world will behave can be drawn, predictions made and control of the environment derived. In the tradition of falsificationism [13], these hypotheses survive until they can be bettered, or until demonstrated to be false.

Finally, there are beliefs which are a priori beliefs about the ontological status of the terms used in the construction of the beliefs. For example, agents will have beliefs about the meaning of elements such as part-of relationships. These beliefs are partly expressed in a declarative form, and, more importantly, partly procedurally, within the algorithms which manipulate the knowledge. Beliefs of this form will be assumed to be shared knowledge agreed upon by all parties to a monologue, since misunderstandings about the meaning of terms cannot be resolved in the scope of a monologue.

Having considered the various ways in which events can be grounded, it is now possible to consider the consequences of these alternatives for argument construction. Any unsupported event can be proposed to another agent by simply asserting it, in the hope that the agent will adopt it as an event sourced by the asserting agent. The adoption will depend on the assessment of the source agent's reliability on the information content according to the listening agent. In some cases this will prove adequate, but when adoption of the belief by the listening agent implies the generation and achievement of goals the reliability of the source agent might not be sufficient to lead to adoption of the belief. In this case, various strategies are possible according to the grounding of the event in the source agent's beliefs. If the event is grounded through being sourced by a third party, then an "appeal to authority" is possible, in which the third party is invoked as a source in the hope that this source will have the necessary reliability in the assessment of the listener to cause adoption of the belief. If the event is grounded through sensory experience then providing more detail of the context for the sensory experience can serve to improve the assessment of the reliability of the agent as a source, leading to acceptance of the veracity of the experience and the event it yields. If the event is a hypothesis about a physical law then an "appeal to the people" might be appropriate, if the law is a widely accepted one. Otherwise, demonstration of the predictive power of the law and a description of the testing to which it has been subjected will provide support for its adoption. Finally, opinions which rest purely on the value-system of the agent will prove the most difficult to persuade another agent to adopt. At present, these beliefs are handled by simply proposing them as premises to be accepted or rejected entirely at the listener's discretion. It is considered that argument founded on moral or ethical judgements are amongst the most difficult to uphold and the most bitterly contested of arguments.

4. Argument Objectives and Structure

The objectives of an argument will depend on the perceived beliefs of the hearer with respect to the belief that it is intended to convey. If the hearer is ignorant of the event, then simply informing the hearer of the event might be sufficient to have it adopted. If the hearer is aware of the event, but is undecided about whether to believe it, then it will be necessary to provide the hearer with supports from which to build a belief in the target event. Finally, if the hearer disbelieves the event then the objective of the argument will be to persuade the hearer to accept the event. If the hearer disbelieves the target event then the hearer must believe at least one event which is in contradiction with belief in the target event - this is an event-complement. This will be achieved by identifying supports that the hearer has for the beliefs in the event-complements (in the speaker's model of the hearer's beliefs) and systematically undermining these, before building supports for the belief that is intended to supplant the complementary belief originally held by the hearer. The new supports can be provided through explanation, unless the hearer believes in the complement of these events, in which case persuasive argument must again be employed. This coarse structure forms the foundation on which the argument structure can be built, and reflects the division into subarguments components developed in the AS level.

Through an analysis of a corpus of arguments drawn from a number of the sources mentioned in §2, the following structure has been identified:

(1) an argument consists of one or more premises and exactly one conclusion

(2) a premise can be a subargument (which itself consists of one or more premises and exactly one conclusion: the conclusion then stands as the premise in the superargument)

(3) a subargument is an integral unit whose components cannot be referred to from elsewhere, nor can the conclusion of a subargument rest upon premises extraneous to that subargument

(4) the only exception to (3) is where a conclusion in a distant subargument is restated locally as a premise

Analyses based on similar theories are performed in many texts: see for example, [25]. It is this structure which the AS level constructs, linking premises to conclusions through the use of two groups of operators: standard logical relations and inductively reasoned implications.

The first group comprises the standard rules of inference of classical logic. In the second group there are the inductive operators which are of three types: inductive generalisation, causal and analogical (eg. [10]). All three will have preconditions that are again tightly specified for context and belief, but with the additional constraint of the 'criteria of inductive strength', ie. the requirements for their application to produce an inductively strong argument.

A third group, not considered in this work, is the rhetorical fallacies, such as red herrings, straw men or false dichotomies. Although these fallacies have a role in natural language argument generation, they complicate the model of argument significantly, not least because of the necessary accompanying assumption that the audience does not have the powers of analysis to unmask the fallacies, leading to questions about the more general abilities of the audience to follow an argument where it is correctly structured. Further discussion of these fallacies can be found in [14].

5. Eloquence Generation

Although the EG level also employs a number of operators, the bulk of its functionality is based on the application of heuristics. The first task of the EG level is to control stylistic presentation, comprising a number of relatively low level modifications such as the vocabulary range, syntactic construction and the frequency of specific devices such as repetition. There are a large number of such factors detailed in the stylistic literature - see [16] for an overview, although these are intended to apply to human audiences with sophisticated appreciation of the stylistic phenomena. To date, such factors have been controlled by quite artificial and simplistic means, typically, the user setting a number of variables to particular values (eg. [22]). For the instantiations to be made and altered 'on-the-fly', the EG level must refer to a body of parameters, in addition to the belief model of the audience and context, all of which are modified dynamically. Within LOLITA, a powerful low-level plan realisation system exists which realises components of the semantic network as text, governed by stylistic parameters. This system is flexible and robust, allowing a wide-ranging control over text-generation while separating stylistic and content issues from the problems of grammatical correctness and syntactic construction [19].

One vitally important parameter affecting the argument is the relationship which the speaker wishes to create or maintain with the hearer. This relationship is established through stylistic rather than structural means, and is not necessarily divorced from other aims: if a hearer accepts the speaker's authoritative stance, for example, the speaker may be able to use the relationship to reinforce his statements (by increasing the hearer's assessment of the agent's reliability). Attempts at instigating different relationships between speaker and hearer account (at least in part) for a number of complex phenomena - humour, for example, is frequently used to establish the speaker as a friend (and therefore reliable and truthful). Such phenomena do not fall inside the scope of this work.

Some of the EG heuristics rely on the general principles of argument formation (though others make use of factors such as tone and rhythm). There are three possible statement orderings in an argument: pre-order (C P*), post-order (P* C), and hybrid order (P* C P*). The first is usually used where the P* are examples (in the case of factual conclusions: for opinions, the P* would often be analogies), especially when the hearer is being led to a hasty generalisation from the P* to the C. Pre-order is also used when the initial conclusion is deliberately provocative - the construction being used to draw attention to the argument (and consequently it is unusual to find a weak argument structured with the pre-order ordering). It can also be forced, should a premise not be accepted by the hearer, and require a sub-argument in its support. Post-order is the usual choice for longer, more complex or less convincing arguments (indeed some arguments are less convincing precisely because they are longer or more complex). It is also used for 'thin end of the wedge' argument and for grouping together premises which individually lend only very weak support to the conclusion. The hybrid construction is rarer, usually occurring when the speaker has completed an post-order argument which has not been accepted and therefore requires further support.

Finally, there are a number of features controlled by the EG level which lie somewhere between the stylistic and the rhetoric: artifices such as repetition and alliteration can prove extremely effective in constructing eloquent and compelling argument. It is interesting to note that almost all of EG heuristics are devices listed by classical texts as figures and tropes. Indeed this is a uniquely interesting property of the EG level: the emphasis it puts in utilisation of ideas posited in precomputational treatises, especially the classical texts of Cicero and Aristotle ([6], for example) and the ideas developed in the late middle ages and renaissance ([23] and [3] have been used as source material for much of the analysis). This fact poses unique challenges as well as affording unique advantages: on the one hand, the ideas are clear and unbiased, whilst on the other, may be difficult to transcribe to implementation.

6. Intention

Recent research has clearly shown that intention, or motivation, plays a crucial role in the generation of discourse, due to its key role in justification, explanation, failure recovery, self referential discourse and response to follow-up questioning [12], [26]. The framework proposed here employs intentions at every level of processing. At the highest level, intention is represented through the use of communicative goals (following Moore and Paris, [12]). An entire argument may ultimately rest upon a single intention such as believes(H, P). At the AS level, then, an abstract plan is produced which fulfils this top level goal. In contrast to Moore and Paris, communicative goals are not necessarily resolved into linguistic (ie. non-intention) goals. Rather, intentions can give rise both to linguistic structures and more refined intention structures. For example, the stylised description of the Modus Ponens operator, as used at the AS level, fulfils the postcondition believes(H, P) by introducing two new communicative goals, believes(H, X) and believes(H, implies(X, P)).

Modus Ponens

Shell:	Preconditions:	believes(H, X)
		believes(H, implies (X, P))
	Add:	believes(H, P)
	Delete:	disbelieves(H, P)

Fig 4. Modus Ponens Operator Shell

It would be a dangerous oversimplification to assume that the MP step of an argument is simply a matter of stating the two premises followed by the conclusion, as might be inferred from Fig. 4. At a high level, there do exist the intentions for the hearer to believe X and implies(X, P) - this is part of the 'intention structure' described in Fig. 1. However, that intention structure undergoes heavy modification before being communicated.

At the AS level, then, intentions are substrate to the planning process; they form goals which are used in pre- and post-condition lists. At the EG level, most intentions play a rather different role, due to the difference in processing styles between the AS and EG. In particular, planning at the EG level primarily involves the use of maintenance goals, which affect the plan structure in a heuristic manner (as opposed to the more conventional achievement goals planned for and fulfilled at the AS level). For example, a typical EG level heuristic (implemented as a maintenance goal intention) blocks plan fragments which tell the hearer something they already know. In the example above, where the AS level suggests (in the body of the MP operator) uttering X, implies(X, P) and P, the EG level might remove the first premise if the hearer belief model indicated that the hearer already believed X.

The RST level also needs to maintain a representation of intention, and the proposed framework facilitates the adoption of the approach put forward by [12], wherein intentions map on a one-to-one basis with presentational relations and on a many-to-many basis with subject matter relations.

The hierarchical nature of the planning process means that the final surface structure communicated to the hearer is fully justified in terms of high level intentions, so that should explanation, justification or recovery be required, the system has recourse back to appropriate intentions with which to replan.

7. Planning Discourse

If the structure of knowledge alone is considered when planning discourse, it would appear that the planning task is not particularly difficult. This is because, given the initial assumption that the agent is not to deliberately mislead its audience and that its knowledge is consistent (or, rather, that once an inconsistency is discovered no argument will proceed founded on the inconsistent knowledge), operators that describe the argument process have a monotonic behaviour. That is, operators can be applied to shift the beliefs of an audience in only one direction: from disbelief through uncertainty to belief, or, conversely, from belief towards disbelief.

The role that planning plays in discourse construction is in the development and maintenance of *coherence* as the discourse develops. A speaker must present the components of an argument in a way that allows related elements to be connected in the hearer's knowledge. An argument cannot proceed by giving pieces of information in a disconnected and arbitrary way. It is necessary to organise the argument in a way that emphasises its structure and allows the hearer to identify the inferential structure and draw the appropriate inferences. This observation is reflected in the design of planning operators for the discourse planning domain. Operators affect not only the models of the state of the knowledge of the hearer but also the model of the hearer's view of the monologue, including its current focus, direction and intended purpose.

The planner used by the system described here is a hierarchical planner based on the use of *operator abstraction* and *encapsulation* [5]. It works by constructing a hierarchy of abstract plans, connected together by a special operation called *refinement*. The hierarchical structure of the plan development process corresponds to the organisation of the AO, AS and EG levels within the argument-planning framework. Most of the planning effort is concentrated within the AO and AS levels, with plan-post-processing being carried out during eloquence generation, which involves resolving previously unconstrained orderings between subarguments and the addition of stylistic elements to the plan structure based on the contextual information inherited from the AO and AS levels encoded within the plan structure. Abstract plans developed initially at the AO level and refined during the AS planning phase, shape the development of the final discourse by imposing increasing structure on the inter-relationships between components of the developing discourse. An abstract plan can be seen as a skeletal discourse, in which the overall structure is in place but none of the details of the argument have been planned. Refinement to more detailed planning levels, which is only performed when an abstract plan has been completed (that is, has no outstanding goals), must preserve the structure provided by the abstract plan. As a consequence of this, many choices which might have been considered during planning of an argument at the detailed level can be pruned as they become inconsistent with the abstract plan. Abstraction therefore assists in the planning of a complex argument by converging on a detailed argument from above. There is a great deal of evidence in the literature that this form of abstraction can considerably improve the performance of a classical planner [2].

Planners based on operator abstraction are characterised by the use of abstract operators which achieve an abstract effect and can be refined into the more detailed components that contribute towards these effects. Abstract operators contain some internal structure indicating what goals have to be achieved, or actions added, to achieve these abstract effects. The first planner to use operator abstraction was NOAH, [15], in which a plan was constructed as a procedural network composed of nodes representing operators and goals, and arcs representing temporal relations. When an operator is applied, its internal structure, consisting of goals to be achieved and actions to be applied, is added immediately to the network. NOAH is widely used as a basis for discourse and dialogue planning [9], and similar approaches were also adopted in NONLIN, [21], and SIPE, [24]. In the system described here, operator abstraction is used together with encapsulation which prevents the internal structures of abstract operators from being revealed before the contexts in which they will be interpreted have been constructed. Here, abstract operators are added to a plan as if they were primitive and only refined to reveal their hidden structures when the plan itself is completed and ready to be refined.

Operators have a *shell* and a *body*. The shell is visible at the planning level in which the operator is applied, and contains the preconditions and effects of the operator. The body contains a partial order on a set of goals which, when achieved after refinement of the plan, will combine to achieve the effects of the abstract operator. When a plan is refined it is necessary to tie together the local contents of the individual bodies to ensure that they maintain any relationships between the abstract operators in the plan prior to refinement. Thus, if the operators P and Q were ordered so that P precedes Q in the abstract plan, and P achieves a precondition for Q and, after refinement, P has been replaced by the goals p1 and p2 and Q has been replaced by the goals q1 and q2, it is necessary to have some way of insisting that the effect of p2 must last beyond the point in time at which Q was applied in the abstract plan. This coordination is achieved by the refinement operation of the planner and involves only linear work in the size of the abstract plan. Bodies of abstract operators contain only goals: not including plan steps in the bodies of operators ensures a fully flexible exploitation of context after refinement, so that unnecessary plan steps are not introduced.

An important feature of the abstraction mechanism offered by the planner used here is that different levels of abstraction can be characterised by different granularities of description. This allows the world, and the effects upon it which an agent wishes to bring about, to be expressed in terms of coarse-grained categories and relationships. For example: in the Towers of Hanoi domain towers of discs can be moved from peg to peg, and these moves will refine into many disc-moving operations at a later point in the development of the plan. In the blocks-world, towers can be transformed into different towers in two steps - destruction of the existing tower and construction of the new tower. These two steps will eventually refine into many carefully ordered block unstacking and stacking operations. In the construction of argument a coarse-grained argument to persuade a hearer to accept a proposition P might take the following form: Identify supports for Not(P), undermine one or more supports, explain reasons for belief in supports for P, inform about the causal link between supports and P. Following many levels of refinement this will result in a detailed argument in support of P, ready for realisation in an expressive language. It is possible for propositions of different granularities to co-exist within a plan, since the planner does not follow a rigidly hierarchical pattern of development within the AO, AS and EG levels, and the planner is equipped with mechanisms to detect and control their interaction [5].

The following operator is intended to give an example of how the beliefs of a speaker and hearer can be used to direct the planning process in the construction of a persuasive argument. The operator is not complete, since it does not include information concerning the current focus of the argument. In addition, the operator description language used by the hierarchical planner rests on a semantics based on information loss following the application of abstract operators. This makes operators syntactically more complex than this example and explanation of the complete encoding of a domain in this language is beyond the scope of this paper.

Persuade(H::agent, E::event)

Shell:	Preconditions:	disbelieves(H, E)
		supports(E'::event, E)
		disbelieves(H, supports(E', E))
	Add:	believes(H, E)
	Delete:	disbelieves(H, E)
		disbelieves(H, supports(E', E))
Body:	Goals:	t1: believes(H, E')
		t2: believes(H, supports(E', E))
		t3: believes(H, E)
	Ordering:	t1 < t3, t2 < t3

Fig 5. Persuade Operator

In this example, all propositions are evaluated with respect to the speaker's beliefs. The operator is abstract and contains sub-goals in its body. The preconditions are not sub-goals but conditions: the operator cannot be applied unless the speaker believes the preconditions in the state of application. The goals in the body are ordered with respect to one another. These goals and the ordering between them are revealed when the abstract plan containing this operator is refined. The operator shows how sub-goals involved in the achievement of an effect can be encapsulated so that the details of achieving them do not arise until the context in which they can be most usefully considered has been created. The principle upon which the hierarchical planning approach described in this paper is built is that, by postponing decisions, many of the choices that would normally arise in resolving them can be excluded. This is partly achieved by the ability to order goals in the bodies of abstract operators which are unordered when they appear as preconditions in STRIPS-style operators.

A similar persuade operator can be applied when the hearer disbelieves E' itself, but possibly accepts that E' supports E. If the hearer disbelieves E' then the hearer can be inferred to believe NOT(E'), since failure to believe in either E or E' implies that the hearer is undecided about both. An operator is required to undermine the hearer's beliefs in NOT(E') so that the hearer will be ready to accept reasoned arguments for belief in E'. This operator works by identifying the hearer's supports for E' and making the hearer undecided about them. This can be done at each stage either by undermining the hearer's belief in the supporting event or by undermining the supporting connection between two events. The process terminates more quickly if the supporting link is broken. If the hearer's beliefs in the events themselves are tackled the process can involve recursive invocation of the undermining process.

The persuade, explain and inform operators, of which this one is a simplified example, are applied at the AO level of the planning process. Operators embodying the principles of logical argument, such as Modus Ponens, are introduced at the AS level once the foundational and intentional structure of the argument is in place. The operations performed at the EG level are not encoded as planning operators since this level is a post-processing phase.

8. Conclusion

This paper has described an architecture for constructing extended arguments from the highest level of pragmatic, intention-rich goals to a string of utterances, using a core hierarchical planner employing operators embodying the principles of argument construction. The planner is responsible for all levels of the construction and organisation of the argument. The output of the planner is a detailed discourse plan complete with annotations to indicate emphasis, mood, rhythm, and other features characterising effective argument. This structure is given as input to the text generation level of the system. This component of the architecture is required to realise the abstract intentional structures into natural language utterances and is provided by LOLITA, a large scale, domain independent natural language system, in which a natural language generation algorithm is already implemented, [19], which subsumes responsibility for solving certain low-level text generation planning problems. The work described in this paper is still in progress and is currently concentrated on the representation of discourse operators for use by the hierarchical planner, the development of techniques applied at the EG level and the effects on argument construction of the speaker's partial knowledge of the hearer's beliefs. Future work will include the extension of the current framework to consider dialogue planning between motivated agents.

References

[1] Ackermann, R.J. *Belief and Knowledge*, Anchor, New York (1972)
[2] Baccus F. & Yang Q. The expected value of hierarchical problem-solving, in *Proceedings of the National Conference on Artifical Intelligence* (1992)
[3] Blair, H. *Lectures on Rhetoric and Belles Lettres*, Charles Daly, London (1838)
[4] Cohen, P.R., Levesque, H.J. "Rational Interaction as the Basis for Communication" in Cohen, P.R., Morgan, J., Pollack, M.E., (eds), *Intentions in Communication*, MIT Press, Boston (1990) 221-255
[5] Fox, M. & Long, D.P. "Hierarchical Planning using Abstraction", *IEE Proc on Control Theory and Applications* **142** (3) (1995) 197-210
[6] Freese, J.H. (trans), Aristotle *The Art of Rhetoric*, Heinmann, London (1926)
[7] Galliers, J.R. "Autonomous belief revision and communication" in Gardenfors, P., (ed), *Belief Revision*, Cambridge University Press, Cambridge (1992) 220-246
[8] Grosz, B., Sidner, C.L "Plans for Discourse" in Cohen, P.R., Morgan, J. & Pollack, M.E., (eds), *Intentions in Communication*, MIT Press, Boston (1990) 418-444
[9] Hovy, E. H. "Automated Discourse Generation Using Discourse Structure Relations", *Artificial Intelligence* **63** (1993) 341-385
[10] Long, D., Garigliano, R. *Reasoning by Analogy and Causality: A Model and Application*, Ellis Horwood (1994)
[11] Mann, W.C., Thompson, S.A. "Rhetorical structure theory: description and construction of text structures" in Kempen, G., *Natural Language Generation: New Results in AI, Psychology and Linguistics*, Kluwer (1986) 279-300
[12] Moore, J.D., Paris, C.L. "Planning Text for Advisory Dialogues: Capturing Intentional and Rhetorical Information", *Computational Linguistics* **19** (4) (1994) 651-694

[13] Popper, K.R. *The Logic of Scientific Discovery*, Hutchinson Education (1959)

[14] Reed, C.A., Long, D.P. & Fox, M. "An Architecture for Argumentative Dialogue Planning", in Gabbay, D. & Ohlbach, H.J. *Practical Reasoning*, Lecture Notes in AI Vol. 1085, Springer Verlag (1996) 555-566

[15] Sacerdoti, E.D. *A structure for plans and behaviour*, Elsevier, North Holland (1977)

[16] Sandell, R. *Linguistic Style and Persuasion*, Academic Press, London (1977)

[17] Shiu, S., Luo, Z., Garigliano, R. "A type theoretic semantics for SemNet", in Gabbay, D. & Ohlbach, H.J. *Practical Reasoning*, Lecture Notes in AI Vol. 1085, Springer Verlag (1996) 582-595

[18] Smith, M.H., Garigliano, R., Morgan, R.C. "Generation in the LOLITA system: An engineering approach" in *Proceedings of the 7th International Workshop on Natural Language Generation*, Kennebunkport, Maine (1994)

[19] Smith, M.H. *Natural Language Generation in LOLITA*, PhD Thesis, Durham University (1996)

[20] Sycara, K. "Argumentation: Planning Other Agent's Plans" in *Proceedings of the International Joint Conference on Artificial Intelligence* (1989) 517-523

[21] Tate, A. *Project planning using a hierarchic non-linear planner*, Technical Report, Department of Artifical Intelligence, University of Edinburgh (1976)

[22] Vreeswijk, G. "IACAS: an implementation of Chisolm's Principles of Knowledge", *Proceedings of the 2nd Dutch/German Workshop on Nonmonotonic Reasoning*, Utrecht, Witteveen, C. et al. (eds) (1995) 225-234

[23] Whately, R. *Logic*, Richard Griffin, London (1855)

[24] Wilkins D. *Practical planning: Extending the classical AI paradigm*, Addison-Wesley (1988)

[25] Wilson, B.A. *The Anatomy of Argument*, University Press of America, Washington (1980)

[26] Young, R.M., Moore, J.D. "DPOCL: A principled approach to discourse planning" in *Proceedings of the 7th International Workshop on Natural Language Generation*, Kennebunkport, Maine (1994) 13-20

Methodologies of Solution Synthesis in Distributed Expert Systems

Minjie Zhang

Department of Computer Science
Edith Cowan University, Perth, WA 6027, Australia
m.zhang@eagle.ac.cowan.edu.au

Chengqi Zhang

Distributed Artificial Intelligence Center (DAIC)
Department of Mathematics, Statistics and Computing Science
University of New England, Armidale, N.S.W. 2351, Australia
chengqi@neumann.une.edu.au

Abstract. In this paper, several methodologies for designing synthesis strategies in distributed expert systems are investigated. They are analytic methods, inductive methods, and analogical methods. Firstly, synthesis problems are formally described. Secondly, the measurements for synthesis strategies are formally defined. After that, all methodologies are analyzed thoroughly and corresponding examples are introduced. Furthermore, all methodologies are compared and we conclude that they compensate each other.

1 Introduction

A distributed expert system (DES) consists of different expert systems (ESs) which are connected by computer networks. In a DES, each expert system (ES) can work individually for solving some specific problems, and can also cooperate with other ESs when dealing with complex problems [2].

Due to the limited knowledge and the ability of problem solving of single ESs and the uncertainty features of tasks, some tasks need to be allocated to more than one ESs (multi-allocation) so as to increase the reliability of solutions. If more than one ES solves the same task, each ES could obtain a solution. It is important to synthesize these multiple solutions to the same task (called *inputs*) from different ESs in order to obtain the desired final solution to the task (called *outputs*). For example, experts in grant agency (e.g. ARC council) normally distribute any grant proposal to 3-5 domain experts to assess the proposal, then they make a final decision (score) of the proposal based on the scores and comments from different domain experts.

Some synthesis strategies have been developed. These strategies include: uncertainty management strategy developed by Khan [3], a synthesis strategy for heterogeneous distributed expert systems (DESs) introduced by Zhang [7], and computational synthesis strategies for both conflict and non-conflict cases proposed by Zhang [9, 12]. These strategies were mainly based on the mathematical analysis of the characteristics of the inputs.

In recent years, we have developed some synthesis strategies [11, 13] using neural network. These strategies were based on a number of samples with both inputs and corresponding outputs. Such samples are called *patterns*. For example, if enough patterns are known, a neural network can be trained to find relationships between inputs and outputs.

In current literatures, there are two methodologies to be used for designing synthesis strategies to solve synthesis problems. They are analytic methods, and inductive methods. In this paper, we will propose another methodology, which is called analogical methods. Different kinds of strategies are good in different kinds of problems. between inputs and outputs can be summarized by an analytic method. Especially this method is perfect for the case if the outputs are derived from some formulas based on inputs. Inductive methods can solve some complicated synthesis problems when the enough patterns exist and an inductive function can be found. A complicated synthesis problem means, in this paper, that the relationship between inputs and outputs is either so complicated or there is no mathematical formula which can represent it.

However, the current researches haven't dealt with the following issues very well. they are:

(1) The synthesis problems have not been formally described;

(2) The measurements for synthesis strategies have not been formally defined;

(3) The methodologies of designing synthesis strategies in DESs have not been investigated; and

(4) Consequently, they are not clear that the relationship among different methodologies, and the ways to choose the best methodology for different kinds of synthesis problems.

The purpose of this paper is to clarify the above issues. The remainder of this paper is organized as follows. In Section 2, the synthesis problem is formally described. In Section 3, the measurements for synthesis strategies are formally defined. In Section 4, several methodologies for designing synthesis strategies are proposed and corresponding examples are given. In Section 5, different kinds of methodologies are compared. Finally, in Section 6, this paper is concluded and further work is outlined.

2 Description of synthesis problems

Let's see an example first. Suppose there are three ESs (e.g. ES_1, ES_2, ES_3) to decide the identity of the organism for a specific patient. ES_1 says that it is pseudomonas with uncertainty 0.36 and proteus with uncertainty -0.9, ES_2 says that it is pseudomonas with uncertainty 0.5 and serratia with uncertainty 0.4, and ES_3 says that it is serratia with uncertainty 0.1 and proteus with uncertainty 0.85. Because ES_1 doesn't mention serratia, we believe that ES_1 has no idea about it. We can represent this unknown by using uncertainty 0 in the EMYCIN model [4]. Then the above solutions are represented in Table 1.

In Table 1, -0.9 signifies 'quite unlikely', 0.85 signifies 'quite likely', and 0 signifies 'unknown'. The authority indicates the level of reliability of the solution

	Pseudomonas	Serratia	Proteus	Authority
ES_1	0.36	0	-0.9	0.9
ES_2	0.5	0.4	0	0.8
ES_3	0	0.1	0.85	0.9

Table 1. The uncertainties for each attribute value obtained by different ESs.

from an ES. The higher the authority, the more reliable the solution. It can be assigned for each ES from human experts or generated based on the historical performance of ESs. The purpose of the synthesis of solutions here is to decide the final uncertainty of pseudomonas, serratia, and proteus according to Table 1.

We now formally describe the problems. Suppose there are n ESs in a DES to evaluate the values of an attribute of an object (e.g. in a medical DES, the identity of an organism infecting a specific patient). The solution for an ES_i can be represented as

$(< object >< attribute > (V_1\ CF_{i1}\ A_i)\ (V_2\ CF_{i2}\ A_i)\ ...\ (V_m\ CF_{im}\ A_i))$

where V_j $(1 \leq j \leq m)$ represents jth possible value, CF_{ij} $(1 \leq i \leq n, 1 \leq j \leq m)$ represents the uncertainty for jth value from ES_i, A_i represents the authority of ES_i, which is the confidence level from ES_i for the solution offered by ES_i. m indicates that there are m possible values for this attribute of the object. For example, there are 6 possible values for the face-up of a die.

From the synthesis point of view, all ESs are concerned with the same attribute of an object. So we will only keep the attribute values, uncertainties, and authorities in the representation. The representation of m possible values with uncertainties from n ESs can be represented as a matrix in Table 2.

	$Value_1$	$Value_2$	...	$Value_m$	Authorities
ES_1	CF_{11}	CF_{12}	...	CF_{1m}	A_1
ES_2	CF_{21}	CF_{22}	...	CF_{2m}	A_2
...	...	...	...	...	...
ES_n	CF_{n1}	CF_{n2}	...	CF_{nm}	A_n

Table 2. The matrix representation of multiple solutions

The synthesis strategy is responsible for obtaining final uncertainties of the vector $(CF_{*1}\ CF_{*2}\ ...\ CF_{*m})$ based on Table 2 where * indicates the synthesis result from corresponding values with the subscriptions of $1, 2, ..., n$.

Definition 1: The inputs of a synthesis strategy are the matrix representation of multiple solutions from different ESs.

Definition 2: The outputs of a synthesis strategy are the final uncertainties of the vector $(CF_{*1}\ CF_{*2}\ ...\ CF_{*m})$ after synthesis of the input matrix.

Definition 3: A pattern is a pair of an input matrix and a corresponding output vector.

It can be said a synthesis strategy is responsible for obtaining right outputs form inputs.

3 The measurements for synthesis strategies

Firstly, we would like to formally define synthesis strategies as follows:

Definition 4: A perfect synthesis strategy f can be defined as:

$$\forall X_i \in X, f(X_i) = Y_i \tag{1}$$

where X_i represents a matrix $(n * (m + 1))$ of multiple solutions to a problem from different ESs (an output), Y_i represents a vector (m) of the desired final solution after synthesis from X_i (an input), and X is the set of all X_i. As we described above, we always know the set X (all input matrixes). Y_i is our desired final solution after synthesis from X_i. Questions here are (1) how do we know whether Y_i is our desired final solution for any X_i and (2) for how many X_i we know corresponding Y_i? For the first question, it is reasonable to define Y_i as synthesis solution for any X_i from human experts. Refer to the example in Section 1, X_i is the scores of a proposal set from different domain experts and Y_i is the final score of the proposal from experts in grant agency based on X_i. For the second question, if for any X_i, we know Y_i, we have nothing to do about synthesis of solutions. In fact, only for a limited number of X_i, we know corresponding Y_i and f is defined as a psuedo function to map these limited X_i to corresponding Y_i perfectly.

The goal of synthesis strategies is to find a mapping function (strategy) f' in which, for any X_i, $f'(X_i) = Y_i'$ should be very closed to Y_i.

The better synthesis strategy is defined as one strategy which can map any X_i to the corresponding Y_i with less errors.

Definition 5: The specific error $\delta_{f'}(X_i)$ for a synthesis strategy f' for X_i is defined as

$$\delta_{f'}(X_i) = |Y_i - f'(X_i)| = |Y_i - Y_i'| = \{|\delta_1|, |\delta_2|, ..., |\delta_m|\} \tag{2}$$

where m is the number of possible values for an attribute.

Definition 6: The specific mean error $\bar{\delta}_{f'}(X_i)$ for a synthesis strategy f' from X_i is defined as

$$\bar{\delta}_{f'}(X_i) = \frac{|\delta_1| + |\delta_2| + ... + |\delta_m|}{m} \tag{3}$$

Definition 7: The The specific maximum error $\bar{\delta}_{max}(X_i)$ for the synthesis strategy f' from X_i is defined as

$$\delta_{max}(X_i) = max\{|\delta_1|, \delta_2|, ..., |\delta_m|\} \qquad (4)$$

Definition 8: The general mean error $\bar{\delta}_{f'}$ for the synthesis strategy f' from all X_i is defined as

$$\forall X_i \in X, \bar{\delta}_{f'} = \frac{\sum_{i=1}^{N} \bar{\delta}_{f'}(X_i)}{N} \qquad (5)$$

Supposing the number of elements in the set X is N.

Definition 9: The general maximum error for the synthesis strategy f' from all X_i is defined as

$$\forall X_i \in X, \delta_{max} = max\{\delta_{max}(X_1), \delta_{max}(X_2), ..., \delta_{max}(X_N)\} \qquad (6)$$

Thus, the strategy f' is said to be better than g' if $\bar{\delta}_f < \bar{\delta}_g$. The best synthesis strategy f is defined as $\bar{\delta}_f = 0$. Such measurement for a synthesis strategy is known as 'quantitatively measured'.

In practice, it is nearly impossible to define the best f. The above definition is meaningful only when you know a certain amount of Y_i from X_i. Otherwise, $\bar{\delta}_{f'}$ cannot be calculated for a strategy f'. If such a situation occurs, a synthesis strategy can be measured qualitatively (reasonably well) by the necessary conditions [10].

4 Methodologies for designing synthesis strategies

In the literatures, there are two methodologies to define f'. One is the method through the analysis of characteristics of the input X_i thoroughly [12] to define f' (analytic methods) and the other is from a number of X_is and the corresponding Y_is to define f' (inductive methods). In this paper, we will propose another method, analogical method, for defining synthesis strategies. We will analyse these methodologies in the following.

4.1 Analytic methods

4.1.1 The principles of analytic methods

An analytic method is a methodology which can be used to define a synthesis strategy from X to Y (refer to Definition 4) by analysing the characteristics of X. These characteristics may include relationships among original evidence sets [10] from ESs which derive the input matrix, the factors which affect the desired final solution, and the weights for all factors. For example, this method can be used to synthesize committee members' opinions to select the best movie in a movie festival; to synthesize the individual comments from examiners to decide whether a project should be funded; and to synthesize multiple opinions from different experts to decide whether a new product should be produced. This method is useful for areas in which the individual solution from each expert can be described by uncertainties, or numbers, and relationships between X_i and Y_i are not so complicated. In particular, this method is useful for areas in which patterns are difficult to obtain.

Popular mathematical theories to implement analytic methods could be 'decision theory', 'evidential theory' [5], 'probability theory' [1], and so on. Generally, there are five levels to be explored in this kind of methods:

- analytic of the characteristics of the evidence to derive an input X_i (such as conflict cases and non-conflict cases [10]);
- analytic of input X_i itself (such as all experts give consistently positive solutions, or negative solutions, or some experts give positive solutions while other experts give negative solutions);
- analytic of the factors which affect Y_i (such as, average of individual solutions, the consistency among individual solutions, confidence of each expert, and so on);
- how to weight each factor; and
- how to combine different factors.

We have developed a synthesis strategy [9] to demonstrate how an analytic method was used. The brief description is shown in Subsection 4.1.2 in this paper.

For this method, patterns are not absolutely necessary. If there are some patterns, they can be used to test strategies, and then give some clues to generate better strategies. If the patterns are difficult to obtain, or too few patterns are available, we will test the strategies to see whether they satisfy the necessary conditions [10]. For example, one typical necessary condition is that the final solution after synthesis should not be negative if all individual solutions are positive.

4.1.2 A synthesis strategy developed by analytic methods

In this subsection, we discuss a computational strategy which was developed by analytic methods.

This computational synthesis strategy is used to solve synthesis problems for conflict cases [9]. The design principle of this strategy is to (1) analyze the characteristics of input matrix X (uncertainties from different ESs) in conflict cases, (2) design a mathematical model to solve inconsistency problems based on the mean value and uniformity of uncertainties from ESs, and (3) use evidential theory to solve contradiction problems. The above procedures are typically main steps of analytic methods.

Different cases of belief conflicts

Suppose there are n ESs in a DES to evaluate an attribute with m possible values, the range of uncertainty of ESs is in $[-1, 1]$ and the set of uncertainties given by different ESs is $U_j = \{CF_{ij}\}$, where $j = 1, 2, ..., m$ and $i = 1, 2, ..., n$. U_j represents jth column only of a matrix X_k. Belief conflicts can be divided into two cases:

Case 1: Inconsistency

All of the ESs in a DES believe that the proposition is partially true (or partially false) and the difference is their uncertainties. This situation can be described as: $\forall CF_{ij} \in U_j, CF_{ij} \geq 0$, which means the proposition is partially true, (or $\forall CF_{ij} \in U_j, CF_{ij} \leq 0$, which means the proposition is partially false), where 0 represents the unknown in the EMYCIN inexact reasoning model [4].

Case 2: Contradiction

The opinions of all ESs in a DES are contradiction. Some of the ESs believe the proposition is partially true but others believe not. This case can be represented in the following way: $\exists CF_{lj} \in U_j, CF_{lj} < 0$ and $\exists CF_{kj} \in U_j, CF_{kj} > 0$.

The principle of the strategy

The key idea of this strategy is to classify conflicts cases into inconsistency and contradiction. For each case, there is a corresponding algorithm to solve the problem.

This strategy includes five steps:

(a) If the range of uncertainties of a proposition is not in [0,1], the uncertainties of the proposition are transformed from that range to the range of [0, 1] by using the heterogeneous transformation functions [7]. For example, if an ES uses the EMYCIN model, the range of $[-1, 1]$ should be transformed into the range of [0, 1].

(b) After transformation, the sum of uncertainties may not satisfy the precondition in the Probability model [1]. If such a case happens, the normalization function is used to normalize uncertainties in the Probability model.

(c) If the conflict degree $(max\{CF_{ij}\} - min\{CF_{ij}\})$ is great, the cluster strategy is used to classify the uncertainties into several subsets. In each subset, the conflict degree should satisfy a certain requirement. At least, it should fall in the case of inconsistency.

(d) For each subset, the *synthesis strategy for inconsistency* is used to obtain the final uncertainty among uncertainty values if there is more than one uncertainty value in a subset of uncertainties. The synthesis strategy for inconsistency calculates one column only from the input matrix (refer to Table 2) each time.

Here the basic idea of the synthesis strategy for inconsistency is briefly introduced.

Suppose that FCF denotes a final uncertainty value, $MEAN$ is the mean value of all uncertainties (CF_{ij}) in a subset where $i = 1, 2, ..., n$, and $UNIFORMITY$ is the deviation of uncertainty values, the FCF will depend on both $MEAN$ and $UNIFORMITY$ of uncertainties. One method of calculating $MEAN$ and $UNIFORMITY$ is as follows:

$$MEAN = \sum_{i=1}^{k} CF_{ij} * \frac{A_i}{\sum_{j=1}^{k} A_j}$$

where A_i is the authority of ES_i.

$$UNIFORMITY = \sum_{i=1}^{k} |CF_{ij} - MEAN| * \frac{A_i}{\sum_{j=1}^{k} A_j}$$

The formula of calculating FCF is:

$$FCF = \begin{cases} \gamma * MEAN - \beta_1 * UNIFORMITY & \text{if } MEAN \geq p_0 \\ \gamma * MEAN + \beta_2 * UNIFORMITY & \text{if } MEAN < p_0 \end{cases}$$

where γ, β_1, and β_2 are constants. We have derived $\gamma = 1$, $\beta_1 = \beta_2 = \frac{1}{2}$ [9].

(e) If there is more than one subset after cluster, the *synthesis strategy for contradiction* is used to obtain the final uncertainty for the whole set of uncertainties. In this case, evidential theory [5] is used to form the synthesis strategy for contradiction.

Suppose S is a finite set, $S = \{s_1, s_2, ..., s_m\}$ where $s_1, s_2, ..., s_m$ are propositions and m is the number of possible values for an attribute. 2^s denotes the set of all subsets of S. Suppose Sp_k and Sp_l are two basic support functions over the same set 2^s. $Sp_k(s_i)$ and $Sp_l(s_i)$ are used to measure the uncertainty of proposition s_i by ES_k and ES_l, respectively where $k, l = 1, 2, ..., n$. The synthesis function is defined as follows:

$$Sp(s_i) = \frac{Sp_k(s_i)Sp_l(s_i) + Sp_k(s_i)Sp_l(s) + Sp_k(s)Sp_l(s_i)}{Sp_k(s)Sp_l(s) + \sum_{i=1}^{m}(Sp_k(s_i)Sp_l(s_i) + Sp_k(s_i)Sp_l(s) + Sp_k(s)Sp_l(s_i))}$$

In the above functions, $Sp_l(s_i)$ and $Sp_l(s)$ are given by:

$$Sp_l(s_i) = \frac{Sp_l'(s_i)}{Sp_l'(s) + \sum_{i=1}^{m} Sp_l'(s_i)}$$

$$Sp_l(s) = \frac{Sp_l'(s)}{Sp_l'(s) + \sum_{i=1}^{m} Sp_l'(s_i)}$$

$$Sp_l'(s_i) = F_1(F_2(CF_{li}) * A_l)$$

$$Sp_l'(s) = F_1(F_2(1 - \sum_{i=1}^{m} CF_{li}) * A_l)$$

where CF_{li} is the uncertainty for the ith possible value from the ES_l (refer to Table 2), A_l is the authority for ES_l, F_1 is the transformation function from the EMYCIN model to the Probability model, and F_2 is the inverse function of F_1 [8]. The same method can be used to define $Sp_k(s_i)$ and $Sp_k(s)$.

The principle of the synthesis strategy for contradiction is to calculate final uncertainties based on the whole input matrix. Each time only two rows are used.

In the steps (d) and (e), both uncertainties of a proposition from different ESs, and the authorities for each ES are considered.

Figure 1 shows the working procedure of this computational strategy.

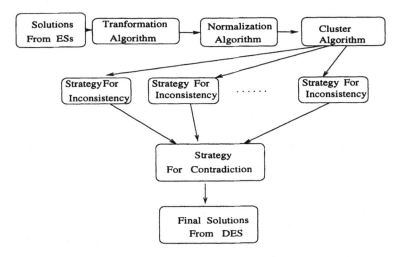

Fig. 1. The procedure of conflict resolution by an analytic method

4.2 Inductive methods

4.2.1 The principles of inductive methods

The idea of inductive methods is different from the idea of analytic methods. An inductive method is a methodology which can be used to find the general relationship between X and Y based on sufficient patterns.

The principle of inductive methods is from specific to general. Suppose $\forall i (1 \leq i \leq N) f(X_i) = Y_i$, in which f is a synthesis strategy, X_i is the input matrix of multiple solutions, and Y_i is the known synthesis solution from X_i, we believe that f also works well for any $X_j (j > N)$ although we cannot guarantee that it is always true.

It is obvious that the first condition of using this method for a strategy is that enough patterns must be known (this requirement differs from the analytic methods above). The more patterns, the better. The second condition is that the patterns are distributed fairly randomly. The third condition is that the $\bar{\delta}$ of the strategy is closed to 0, or the strategy 'converges' in neural network terms.

For some synthesis problems, if the relationship between inputs and outputs is linear, we can use mathematical models to find this relationship such as "The Least Square Method". However, it doesn't work well for complicated problems. Another tool to implement inductive methods is neural network. We have developed two synthesis strategies using neural network technique [11, 13]. The character of these strategies are based on patterns of both inputs and corresponding outputs to find the best mapping functions from inputs to corresponding outputs.

A neural network is a good mechanism to simulate some complicate relationships. The general structure of a neural network includes an input layer, a hidden layer, and an output layer. Three layers are connected by a certain method based on requirements. A neural network can be generated by a number of learning patterns. A pattern includes an input pattern and an output pattern. Generally, neural networks can be trained by supervised training. That means the input and output patterns are known during training. The output patterns offer hints as to the correct output for a particular input pattern. During training, the hidden layer continuously adjusts the weight to reduce the difference between desire outputs and actual outputs. The smaller the difference between desire outputs and actual outputs is, the better.

A neural network implements inductive methods by the following way: (1) After certain times of training, if the neural network can accommodate all of the training patterns and testing patterns, we believe that the relationship (mapping function) between inputs and outputs has been found; (2) the neural network can work well for untested cases; and (3) Once the relationship is found, actual outputs Y' comes from the mapping function. If it is easy to get enough training patterns, and a neural network converge, a neural network is a good method to solve synthesis problems. In the following subsection, an neural network strategy will be discussed.

4.2.2 A synthesis strategy developed by inductive methods

In this subsection, we demonstrate one neural network strategy which works based on the principle of inductive methods.

The basic principles

The basic principles of a neural network strategy are: the inputs of the neural networks are the matrix of multiple solutions from ESs (refer to Table 2); the outputs of neural networks should be the desired final solutions after synthesizing multiple solutions. If a neural network can converge for all of patterns after training, this neural network can act as an inductive function.

Now we introduce the structure of a neural network strategy working in conflict cases [11]. This method is to investigate whether a neural network can

be trained to converge for solving belief conflicts if enough patterns are given. The works should be done include to collect enough numbers of patterns from the real world, to set up a neural network architecture, to decide an activation function, and to train this neural network by adjusting the weights of links to accommodate all patterns. Currently, 200 artificial patterns have been created, which cover various possibilities, in which 180 patterns were chosen as training patterns and a further 20 patterns were used to test the neural network.

The architecture

Generally, the input layer is a matrix with $n * m$ nodes, where n is the number of expert systems in a DES and m is the number of possible values for the attribute. The output layer is a vector with m elements. For a DES, the number of ESs (n) is relatively stable. However, the possible number of values (m) for each attribute varies from case to case. It is not practical to train a different neural network every time when the number of values is changed. In this strategy, we proposed a method to build a fixed neural network architecture for conflict resolutions to adapt the problem with variable numbers of inputs and outputs.

Suppose k is the maximum number of values of all attributes in a DES. The idea is to set up a neural network with $n * k$ input nodes and k output nodes. The training patterns can be $n * 2$ inputs with 2 outputs, $n * 3$ inputs with 3 outputs, ..., and $n * k$ inputs with k outputs. If the number of values for some attributes is less than k, the default values "0" are chosen to substitute these absent values as inputs and corresponding outputs. If the neural network after training can accommodate all (enough number of) patterns, we believe that this neural network can work well for untested cases.

We choose $n = 4$, $k = 6$. The input layer has $4 * 6$ nodes and output layer has 6 nodes. The hidden layer consists of 49 nodes. The neural network is fully connected. The learning algorithm is backpropagation. Figure 2 shows the architecture of this neural network.

Result analysis

The neural network was trained by 90,000 cycles. If we still use $\bar{\delta}$ to represent the general mean error and δ_{max} to represent the general maximum error from all testing data (refer to Definition 8 and Definition 9 in Section 3 for the meaning of $\bar{\delta}$ and δ_{max}), Figure 3 figures out the distribution of test errors of all test data from test patterns (untrained patterns).

The mean error $\bar{\delta} = 0.036$ and for 93% of test data, $\delta_{max} < 0.07$. This result indicates that a neural network synthesis strategy is a good inductive method to solve synthesis problems if enough training patterns are available.

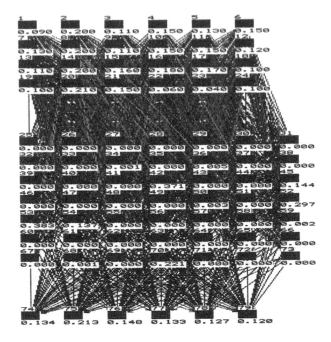

Fig. 2. The architecture of the dynamic neural network

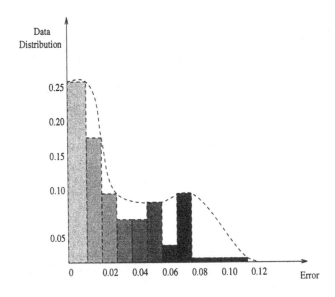

Fig. 3. The distribution of the test errors

4.3 Analogical methods

An analogical method here is a methodology which can be used to find Y_j from X_j by comparing X_j to similar known patterns X_i. Then, Y_j should be similar to Y_i. This method is useful for application in areas with limited patterns. Based on the characteristics of the analogical methods, we believe that a good application example could be the synthesis of experts' decision about whether a new product should be produced. The reasons are that (a) it is hard to find many patterns for similar cases to enable use of inductive methods, (b) a few patterns do exist for similar cases, and (c) this is difficult to analyse by mathematical formulas.

Case-based reasoning [6] is a good tool to implement analogical methods because the principle of case-based reasoning is to find similarity between cases. In case-based reasonings, the key factors are:

(a) which attributes for each case should be considered,
(b) how should each attribute be represented,
(c) how should the similarity between each attribute be defined,
(d) how should the similarity between two cases (consider all attributes) be calculated,
(e) how should cases be indexed in case bases, and
(f) how should inference engines be defined.

This methodology can compensate for both inductive and analytic methodologies. Inductive methodology needs many patterns but analogical methodology needs some patterns. Analytic methodology is difficult to solve complicated problems, but analogical methodology could do better. We will develop real strategies using case-based reasoning to demonstrate the above claims.

5 Comparison among different methodologies

In this section, we compare three different methods.

Three methodologies compensate each other in the following ways:

- **Performance**
  - Analytic methods can work well for some simple problems. Especially this method is perfect for the case if the desired final solutions are derived from some formulas based on inputs.
  - Inductive methods can be used to solve complicated problems. So far neural network mechanism is a good way to implement inductive function. For complicated cases, inductive methods are better than analytic methods because it can simulate complicated relationships quite closely if it converges.
  - Analogical methods can be used to compensate with both analytic methods and inductive methods. If both analytic methods and inductive methods cannot work for some situations, analogical methods can be considered such as case-based reasoning to find similar cases for the mapping functions.

- **Requirements**
  - Analytic methods need no patterns virtually. In analytic methods, only one requirement is that the relationship between inputs and outputs can be summarized by an analytic method.
  - Inductive methods need a lot of patterns. The additional requirements are: (1) these samples should be distributed randomly and covers most of cases, and (2) a mapping function should exist (neural network should be converged for the problems).
  - The requirements for analogical methods are between analytic methods and inductive methods. This kind of methods only needs certain number of patterns.
- **Complexity**
  - The complexity of analytic methods is less than that of inductive methods. In this kind of method, the relationship between inputs and outputs is concise and the calculation is inexpensive.
  - The complexity of inductive methods is the biggest among three methods. The selection of suitable samples is a big job. To find a final mapping function is time consuming such as training of a neural network.
  - The complexity of analogical methods is also between analytic methods and inductive methods since this kind of methods require less samples than inductive methods.

After comparison, our conclusion is that they compensate each other. Based on different kinds of synthesis problems and available information, different methodologies should be used to design synthesis strategies.

6 Conclusion

In this paper, methodologies for designing synthesis strategies in DESs are proposed. They are analytic methods, inductive methods, and analogical methods. Three methods have been analyzed. A computational strategy by using analytic methods and a neural network strategy which is an example of inductive methods are introduced for solving synthesis problems in conflict synthesis cases. Three methodologies are compared.

This work gives clear idea of potential ways for ongoing research in synthesis of solutions and also offer a guideline for developing synthesis strategies in DESs by using different methodologies.

Further work is to develop strategies by analogical methods for the synthesis of solutions first, then apply different methodologies in real application domains, and investigate how to combine different methodologies.

References

1. R. Duda, P. Hart and N. Nilsson (1976). Subjective Bayesian Method for Rule-based Inference System, *AFIPS*, **Vol. 45**, pp. 1075-1082.

2. E. Durfee, V. Lesser, and D. Corkill (1989). Trends in Cooperative Distributed Problem Solving, *IEEE Transactions on Knowledge and Data Engineering*, **Vol. KDE-1**, No. 1, pp. 63-83.

3. N. A. Khan and R. Jain (1985). Uncertainty Management in a Distributed Knowledge Based System, *Proceedings of 9th International Joint Conference on Artificial Intelligence*, California, pp. 318-320.

4. W. Van Melle (1980). A Domain-Independent System That Aids in Constructing Knowledge-Based Consultation Programs, *Ph.D. Dissertation, Report STAN-CS-80-820*, Computer Science Department, Stanford University, CA.

5. G. Shafer (1976). *A Mathematical Theory of Evidence*, Princeton University Press, Princeton and London.

6. K. Sycara (1987). Planning for Negotiation: A Case-Based Approach, *Proceedings of Darpa Knowledge-Based Planning Workshop*, pp. 11.1-11.10.

7. C. Zhang (1992). Cooperation Under Uncertainty in Distributed Expert Systems. *Artificial Intelligence*, **Vol. 56**, pp. 21-69.

8. C. Zhang (1993). Heterogeneous Transformation of Uncertainties of Propositions among Inexact Reasoning Models, *IEEE Transactions on Knowledge and Data Engineering*, **Vol. KDE-6**, pp. 353-360.

9. M. Zhang and C. Zhang (1994a). A Comprehensive Strategy for Conflict Resolution in Distributed Expert Systems, *Australia Journal of Intelligent Information Processing Systems*, **Vol. 1**, No. 2, pp. 21-28.

10. M. Zhang and C. Zhang (1994b). Synthesis of Solutions in Distributed Expert Systems. *Artificial Intelligence - Sowing the Seeds for the Future*, edited by Chengqi Zhang, John Debenham and Dickson Lukose, World Scientific Publishers, Singapore, pp. 362-369.

11. M. Zhang and C. Zhang (1995a). A Dynamic Neural Network Mechanism for Solving Belief Conflict in Distributed Expert Systems, *Proceedings of 6th Australian Conference on Neural Networks*, Australia, pp. 105-108.

12. M. Zhang and C. Zhang (1995b). Synthesis Strategies in Non-conflict Cases in Distributed Expert Systems, *AI'95*, edited by X. Yao, World Scientific Publishers, Singapore, pp. 195-202.

13. M. Zhang and C. Zhang (1996). Neural Network Strategies for Solving Synthesis Problems in Non-conflict Cases in Distributed Expert Systems, *Distributed Artificial Intelligence: Architecture and Modeling*, LNAI **Vol 1087**, Lecture Notes in Artificial Intelligence, Springer Verlag Publishers, pp. 174-188.

Implementing an Automated Reasoning System for Multi-Agent Knowledge and Time

Lifeng He[1]*, Yuyan Chao[2], Shohey Kato[1], Tetsuo Araki[3], Hirohisa Seki[1] and
Hidenori Itoh[1]

[1] Nagoya Institute of Technology, Nagoya 466, Japan
[2] Nagoya University, Nagoya 464, Japan
[3] Fukui University, Fukui 910, Japan

Abstract. We present an implementation of an automated reasoning system for multi-agent knowledge and time, which can be used to describe multi-agent environments. Our reasoning procedure is based on a so-called semantic method. That is, suppose that a multi-agent environment is given by a multi-agent knowledge and time modal logic formula set U. To see whether a multi-agent knowledge and time modal logic formula F can be derived from U, all formulas in U and the negation of F are first translated, according to the possible worlds semantics, into a semantically equivalent first-order formula set, from which we then derive a set of first-order clauses. Thus, F logically follows from U iff there is a refutation in the translated clause set. Since we have to use some transitive axioms and deal with inequalities when reasoning about the set of translated first-order clauses, we augment a general purpose first-order theorem proof procedure ME (the Model Elimination) [11] with the capabilities of using transitive axioms and dealing with inequalities. Theory resolution is incorporated into our reasoning procedure for using transitive axioms efficiently. We present our implementation and show some experimental results.

Keywords: multi-agent environment, system implementation, automated reasoning, knowledge and time

1 Introduction

Recently, reasoning about multi-agent environments has attracted much attention in AI, e.g., [9], [17]. In multi-agent cooperation, coordination and planning environments, the reasoning process of each agent depends on his current knowledge which is changing as time goes on. Therefore research on automated reasoning about multi-agent knowledge and time becomes a very important issue in distributed AI [6],[14].

Although lots of work has been reported on the theoretical framework of reasoning about knowledge and time (e.g., [8]), there has been relatively little

* This research is supported in part by the Japanese Ministry of Education and the Artificial Intelligence Research Promotion Foundation.

work reported on practical automated reasoning procedure for reasoning about multi-agent knowledge and time. For example, a simulator for a multi-agent system is proposed in [2], but it is known to be incomplete.

In this paper, we consider a simple modal logic called *MAKT* to model multi-agent knowledge and time, propose its automated reasoning procedures and present the implementation.

Our reasoning procedure for MAKT is based on the so-called semantic method [13]. That is, suppose that a multi-agent environment is given by a modal logic formula set U. To see whether F can be derived from U, all formulas in U and the negation of F are first translated, according to the possible worlds semantics, into a semantically equivalent first-order formula set, from which we then derive a set of clauses. F logically follows from U iff there is a refutation in the translated clause set.

Since we have to deal with transitive axioms and inequalities when reasoning about the derived set of first-order clauses, we cannot directly utilize a general purpose first-order theorem proof procedure such as ME (the Model Elimination) [11]. We therefore develop a special theorem prover based on Me, called *METAI* (ME with Transitive Axioms and Inequalities). Theory resolution [15] is incorporated for reasoning with transitive axioms appropriately.

The organization of the rest of the paper is as follows. In the next Section, we introduce the syntax and the possible worlds semantics of our logic for multi-agent knowledge and time and give a motivating example. In Section 3, we explain our translation procedure, by which an arbitrary modal logic formula for multi-agent knowledge and time can be translated into its corresponding first-order formula. We also prove that our translation procedure is sound and complete. In Section 4, we consider how to extend ME to METAI and implement METAI. Section 5 shows some experimental results of our system. We also compare the METAI procedure with the case where another general purpose proof procedure SATCHMO [10] is utilized instead of ME procedure. We make some concluding remarks in Section 6.

2 The Syntax and the Possible Worlds Semantics of MAKT

2.1 The Syntax of MAKT

The *language* of MAKT for m agents consists of a countable collection of symbols and all formulas defined over it. The countable collection of symbols is classified into the following groups:

(i) *time variables* denoted by $t, t_1, t_2, \cdots$;
(ii) *time constants* denoted by $0, 1, \cdots, T, T_i, \cdots$, where $T, T_i \in \mathcal{N} = \{0, 1, 2, \cdots\}$;
(iii) *agent constants* denoted by $a_1, \ldots, a_m$;
(iv) *an agent variable* denoted by l, where $l \in \{a_1, \ldots, a_m\}$;
(v) *proposition symbols* denoted by $p, q, r, \cdots$;

(vi) a *modal operator* denoted by K;

(vii) a *time order relation*, which is $\leq$;

(viii) *logical connectives*, which are: $\neg$ (negation) and $\wedge$ (conjunction);

(iv) a *quantifier*, which is: $\forall$ (for all);

(x) *parentheses*, which are: (and).

For the sake of convenience, we also use logic connectives $\vee$, $\rightarrow$ and an existential quantifier $\exists$ in our language.

The formation rules for MAKT formulas are defined as follows:

- if p is a proposition symbol, then p^{t+T} (especially, p^t or p^T) is a formula (called an atomic formula);
- if ϕ is a formula and a_i is an agent, then $K_{a_i}^\tau \phi$ and $\forall l K_l^\tau \phi$ are formulas, where τ is a time constant or a time variable;
- if ϕ is a formula, then $\forall (T \leq t)\phi$ ($\forall t\phi$ if $T = 0$) is a formula;
- if ϕ, ψ are formulas, then $\neg\phi$, $\phi \wedge \psi$ are formulas.

Example 1. A cooperation of agents in a common workshop can be described by the following MAKT formula, where w (c, f) means *work* (*communication, finished*), respectively. We also assume that w can be done only by cooperation.

$$\forall t_1 \forall t_2 (c^{t_1} \wedge \exists l K_l^{t_1} w^{t_2} \rightarrow f^{t_1+3} \vee f^{t_2+3}) \tag{1}$$

Formula (1) says if at time t_1, there is a communication between agents and some agent knows that a work moving objects to the designated place can be done from time t_2, i.e., w^{t_2}, then agents will cooperate to finish this work at time $t_1 + 3$ (if $t_2 \leq t_1$) or at time $t_2 + 3$ (if $t_1 \leq t_2$).

Now, suppose that agent a_1 knows w^{10} from time 2 and there is a communication between agents at time 8. That is, the following formula is added:

$$\forall (2 \leq t) K_{a_1}^t w^{10} \wedge c^8 \tag{2}$$

Now, we are interested in whether w can be finished by agent cooperation, i.e., whether

$$\exists t f^t \tag{3}$$

can be shown logically from formulas (1) and (2). □

2.2 The Possible Worlds Semantics of MAKT

Following Halpern and Vardi [8], we consider a possible worlds semantics for our MAKT. A possible worlds model of MAKT for m agents can be defined as a tuple:

$$(\mathcal{R}, \pi, \mathcal{X}_{a_1}, \ldots, \mathcal{X}_{a_m})$$

where $\mathcal{R}$ is a set of *runs*, each of which indicates a possible history of a given multi-agent system over time. We assume that each run proceeds in discrete time points, and thus (r,t) represents the t-th time point of run r. In addition, π assigns a truth value to each primitive proposition at every point (r,t), and $\mathcal{X}_l$ ($l \in a_1, \ldots, a_m$) is an equivalence relation on $\mathcal{R} \times \mathcal{N}$.

As a model of MAKT, we assume in this paper that each agent has unbounded memory and that time is synchronous. Then, for all $l \in \{a_1, \ldots, a_m\}$, the equivalence relation $\mathcal{X}_l$ in such a model has the following four properties [8]:

$$\forall rt \; (((r,t),(r,t)) \in \mathcal{X}_l) \quad (4)$$

$$\forall rtr' \; (((r,t),(r',t)) \in \mathcal{X}_l \to ((r',t),(r,t)) \in \mathcal{X}_l) \quad (5)$$

$$\forall rtr'r'' \; ((((r,t),(r',t)) \in \mathcal{X}_l) \wedge (((r',t),(r'',t)) \in \mathcal{X}_l) \to ((r,t),(r'',t)) \in \mathcal{X}_l) \quad (6)$$

$$\forall rtr' \; ((1 \le t) \wedge ((r,t),(r',t)) \in \mathcal{X}_l \to ((r,t-1),(r',t-1)) \in \mathcal{X}_l) \quad (7)$$

The first three properties indicate that, for each fixed t, $\mathcal{X}_l$ is reflexive, symmetric and transitive respectively [7], while the last one means that each agent keeps track of his whole history. In our case, the last property can be rewritten as follows, where T is an arbitrary time constant.

$$\forall rr't \; (((r,T),(r',T)) \notin \mathcal{X}_l \to \neg(T \le t) \vee ((r,t),(r',t)) \notin \mathcal{X}_l) \quad (7')$$

We denote by $M,(r_i,t_0) \models \phi$ that an MAKT formula ϕ is true at point (r_i,t_0) of a model M, whose definition is given inductively as follows:

- $M,(r_i,t_0) \models p^{t+T}$ iff $\pi(r_i,t+T,p) = true$;
- $M,(r_i,t_0) \models K_{a_i}^\tau \phi$ iff $M,(r,\tau) \models \phi$ for all (r,τ) such that $((r_i,\tau),(r,\tau)) \in \mathcal{X}_{a_i}$, where $1 \le i \le m$;
- $M,(r_i,t_0) \models \forall l K_l^\tau \phi$ iff $M,(r_i,t_0) \models K_l^\tau \phi$ for all $l \in \{a_1, \ldots, a_m\}$;
- $M,(r_i,t_0) \models \forall (T \le t)\phi$ iff $M,(r_i,t) \models \phi$ for all t such that $T \le t$;
- $M,(r_i,t_0) \models \phi \wedge \psi$ iff $M,(r_i,t_0) \models \phi$ and $M,(r_i,t_0) \models \psi$;
- $M,(r_i,t_0) \models \neg\phi$ iff $M,(r_i,t_0) \not\models \phi$.

Since time is synchronous in our case and MAKT is a subcase of $\text{LKT}_{(m)}$ presented in [8], the decidability of MAKT directly follows that of $\text{LKT}_{(m)}$ in the synchronous case.

3 Translation Procedure and Its Correctness

We show that it is possible, according to the possible worlds semantics, to translate any MAKT formula into its equivalent first-order formula. Thus, instead of checking whether an MAKT formula logically follows a given MAKT formula set U, we can show whether there is a refutation in $U' \cup \neg F'$, where U' (F') is the translated first-order form of U (F). This translation makes it possible for us to use a first-order theorem prover to construct an automated reasoning system for MAKT.

In order to translate an arbitrary MAKT formula into its equivalent first-order formula, we introduce predicate $X(r, r', t, h)$ to represent the possible worlds relation $((r, t), (r', t)) \in \mathcal{X}_h$. We also use the same inequality predicate symbol $\leq$ to represent the time order relation in the translated version. Moreover, we use the predicate symbol P to represent each corresponding propositional symbol p in an MAKT formula. Then, the translation procedure, tr, from an MAKT formula into its corresponding first-order formula at a given point (r_i, t_0) is defined inductively as follows:

$$tr(p^{t+T}, (r_i, t_0)) = P(r_i, t + T)$$
$$tr(K_{a_i}^{\tau} \phi, (r_i, t_0)) = \forall r(\neg X(r_i, r, \tau, a_i) \vee tr(\phi, (r, \tau)))$$
$$tr(\forall l K_l^{\tau} \phi, (r_i, t_0)) = \forall l \forall r(\neg X(r_i, r, \tau, l) \vee tr(\phi, (r, \tau)))$$
$$tr(\forall (T \leq t) \phi, (r_i, t_0)) = \forall t(\neg(T \leq t) \vee tr(\phi, (r_i, t)))(\forall t(tr(\phi, (r_i, t))) \text{ if } T = 0)$$
$$tr(\phi \wedge \psi, (r_i, t_0)) = tr(\phi, (r_i, t_0)) \wedge tr(\psi, (r_i, t_0))$$
$$tr(\neg \phi, (r_i, t_0)) = \neg tr(\phi, (r_i, t_0))$$

For all $l \in \{a_1, \ldots, a_m\}$, the four properties of $\mathcal{X}_l$, i.e., (4), (5), (6) and (7') can be translated as follows:

$$\forall rt X(r, r, t, l) \tag{8}$$
$$\forall rr't(X(r, r', t, l) \rightarrow X(r', r, t, l)) \tag{9}$$
$$\forall rr'tr''(X(r, r', t, l) \wedge X(r', r'', t, l) \rightarrow X(r, r'', t, l)) \tag{10}$$
$$\forall rr't(\neg X(r, r', T, l) \rightarrow \neg(T \leq t) \vee \neg X(r, r', t, l)) \tag{11}$$

Example 2. (Continued from Example 1)
By the translation procedure, the formulas (1), (2) and the negation of formula (5) in Example 1, are translated into the following corresponding first-order formulas respectively, where we assume $(0, 0)$ as the initial point.

$$\forall t_1 \forall t_2 (\neg C(0, t_1) \vee \forall l \exists r_1 (X(0, r_1, t_1, l) \wedge \neg W(r_1, t_2))$$
$$\vee F(0, t_1 + 3) \vee F(0, t_2 + 3)) \tag{12}$$
$$\forall t \forall r (\neg(3 \leq t) \vee \neg X(0, r, t, a_1) \vee W(r, 10)) \wedge C(0, 8) \tag{13}$$
$$\forall t(\neg F(0, t)) \tag{14}$$

$\square$

The correctness of our reasoning method can be shown by the following proposition.

Proposition 1. *Let F be an arbitrary MAKT formula and F' be its translated first-order formula at point (r, t) (i.e., $F' = tr(F, (r, t))$). Suppose that $\mathcal{R}_L$ is the set of the four properties of $\mathcal{X}_l$, i.e., (6)-(8),(9'), R_L is the set of their translated first-order forms, i.e., (10)-(13), and $INEQ$ is the set of inequality axioms. Then, F is $\mathcal{R}_L$ and $INEQ$ is valid if and only if $\neg R_L \vee \neg INEQ \vee F'$ is valid in the first-order sense.*

The proof of Proposition 1 is not very difficult. We first suppose that F is not $\mathcal{R}_L$ and $INEQ$ is valid and use the falsifying model and valuation to construct a first-order model to falsify $R_L \wedge INEQ \wedge \neg F'$. Second, we suppose that the translated first-order formula F' is not valid where $R_L \wedge INEQ$ is added as axioms and use the falsifying model and valuation to construct an MAKT model and valuation to falsify F. In each case, the set of possible worlds for MAKT is just the domain of the first-order interpretation. The translated set of $\mathcal{R}_L$ properties and $INEQ$ are always used as axioms when we deal with the translated first-order formula. We omit further details due to lack of space. Further details can be found in [13].

4 Implementation

This section considers the problems concerning the implementation of our automated reasoning system. ME (the Model Elimination) [11] is a general-purpose first-order proof procedure. As there are transitive axioms and time inequalities, ME cannot be directly utilized to check the satisfiability of the set of translated first-order clauses. In this section, we discuss how to extend ME to *METAI* by incorporating theory resolution [15], which can use the transitive axioms and deal with time inequalities properly.

4.1 The Review of the ME procedure

Suppose that S is the set of clauses to be refuted, and C, called center chain, is one clause in S. Generally, a clause has the form of $L_1 \vee \ldots \vee L_m$, where L_i $(1 \leq i \leq m)$ is a literal. The ME procedure consists of three operations: *extension* operation, *reduction* operation and *contraction* operation.

- The ME extension operation is, like the standard resolution operation, applied to the leftmost literal, L, of C and a matching literal[4], of some side clause in S, including C itself[5]. Instead of discarding L, it is converted to a marked literal L^*. For example, if $C = Q(x) \vee P(y)$ and a side clause $B = R(u) \vee \neg Q(a)$, then the result of the extension operation is $R(u) \vee Q^*(a) \vee P(y)$.
- The ME reduction operation is defined as follows: if the leftmost unmarked literal, L, of the center chain C is a matching literal of some marked literal K^* in C then, provided that σ is the matching substitution, the result of the reduction operation is $C\sigma$ with the leftmost literal deleted. For example, if $C = \neg Q(y) \vee P(y) \vee Q^*(a)$, then the result of the reduction operation is $P(a) \vee Q^*(a)$.

---

[4] Two literals are said to match if they have opposite signs and if there is a substitution that that makes their atoms identical. The matching substitution will be the most general unifier of the two atoms.

[5] Of course, before matching, the variables of the elected side clause must be renamed so that it has no variable in common with C.

- Lastly, the ME contraction operation is defined to simply delete all of the marked literals to the left of the leftmost unmarked literal. It is performed whenever possible after the extension and reduction operations.
- The procedure terminates successfully if an empty chain is obtained.

4.2 Handling Inequality Constraints

We have to deal with time inequalities occurring in a set of translated clauses. We assume the inequality axioms *INEQ* on the natural numbers, which include, among others, the following transitivity axioms:

$$t_1 \leq t_2, \ t_2 \leq t_3 \longrightarrow t_1 \leq t_3 \tag{15}$$

$$t_1 \leq t_2, \ t_2 < t_3 \longrightarrow t_1 < t_3 \tag{16}$$

$$t_1 < t_2, \ t_2 \leq t_3 \longrightarrow t_1 < t_3 \tag{17}$$

$$t_1 < t_2, \ t_2 < t_3 \longrightarrow t_1 < t_3 \tag{18}$$

We have to make some extensions of the ME procedure in order to use it in our cases. For example, the set of clauses $\{t_1 < 5 \vee P(t_1), \ t_2 < 2 \vee \neg P(t_2)\}$ is unsatisfiable (e.g., let $t_1 = t_2 = 7$), but we cannot show it by the ME procedure alone. Moreover, ordinary resolution in this case is quite inefficient. For example, it is obvious that there is no refutation based on $3 \leq T$ and the transitivity axiom $t_1 \leq t_2, t_2 \leq t_3 \longrightarrow t_1 \leq t_3$, but it is possible to derive an infinite number of consequences from them.

Therefore we use theory resolution [15] for reasoning about time inequalities in METAI. Theory resolution is an effective method for resolving these problems.

Our inequality theory includes, for example, the transitivity axioms, i.e., the axioms of (15) $\sim$ (18). With theory resolution, the use of a transitivity axiom is restricted to occasions where there are two predicates which can match the transitivity axiom.

Example 3. Suppose that the following set of inequality clauses is given, where T_1, T_2 are time constants.

1. $T_1 < 2 \vee 7 \leq T_2$
2. $T_2 < 4 \vee T_1 \leq 3$
3. $5 < T_1$

The satisfiability of the set of inequality clauses can be checked by theory resolution as follows.

4. $5 < 2 \vee 7 \leq T_2$ Theory resolution is applied to 1 with 3 using axiom (18)
5. $7 \leq T_2$ Simplification
6. $7 < 4 \vee T_1 \leq 3$ Theory resolution is applied to 5 with 2 using axiom (16)
7. $T_1 \leq 3$ Simplification
8. $5 < 3$ Theory resolution is applied to 7 with 3 using axiom (17)
9. □ Simplification

Therefore, the set of inequality clauses is shown to be unsatisfiable. $\square$

4.3 METAI: the Model Elimination with Transitive Axioms and Inequalities

Suppose that a multi-agent environment is given by an MAKT formula set $\mathcal{W}$ and $\mathcal{K}$ is an MAKT formula to be checked whether it can be derived from W. Moreover, suppose S is the set of clauses from the first order formula translated from $W \wedge \neg \mathcal{K}$. Furthermore, suppose that the initial center chain, C, is a clause obtained from the first order formula translated from $\neg\mathcal{K}$ (this makes the proof goal-directed). We denote a clause by $\mathcal{L} \vee \mathcal{I}$, where $\mathcal{L} = L_1 \vee \ldots \vee L_m$ is the disjunction of non-inequality literals, and $\mathcal{I} = I_1 \vee \ldots \vee I_n$ is the disjunction of inequality literals. We first give a preliminary definition.

Definition 2. A set of inequality clauses $\mathcal{S}_{\mathcal{I}} = \mathcal{I}_1 \wedge \ldots \wedge \mathcal{I}_m$ is *unsatisfiable* iff $\mathcal{S}_{\mathcal{I}} \cup INEQ \models \perp$.

METAI, the extension of Me, consists of five operations: the extension operation, the reduction operation, the contraction operation, the R-reasoning operation and the I-reasoning operation.

The extension operation, the reduction operation and the contraction operation are basically the same as in Me, except that they are only applied to members of $\mathcal{L}$ and instead of selecting the leftmost literal, we select the leftmost non-inequality literal in the center chain for those operations.

The R-reasoning operation is based on theory resolution with the transitive property of $\mathcal{X}_l$, i.e., $\forall r r' tr''(X_l(r, r', t) \wedge X_l(r', r'', t) \rightarrow X_l(r, r'', t))$. Suppose that the center chain is $X_l(r, r', t) \vee R_{est}$ and there is a side clause $R_{est1} \vee X_l(r', r'', t) \vee R_{est2}$. Then, the result of the $\mathcal{R}$-reasoning operation is $R_{est1} \vee R_{est2} \vee X_l(r, r'', t) \vee R_{est}$.

The I-reasoning operation is based on theory resolution with inequality theory. It is only applied to *pure* inequality clauses.

We also consider the following I-simplification operations applied to members of $\mathcal{I}$.

(1) If some $I \in \mathcal{I}$ is unsatisfiable, it is deleted from $\mathcal{I}$;
(2) If a variable occurring in some $I \in \mathcal{I}$ does not occur in any literal of $\mathcal{L}$, I is deleted from $\mathcal{I}$;
(3) Suppose that $I_j, I_k \in \mathcal{I}$. If I_k implies I_j, i.e., if I_j is false, then I_k is also false, and I_k is deleted from $\mathcal{I}$.

For example, applying the I-simplification operation to $P(3) \vee \neg Q^*(T) \vee T < 1 \vee T < 4 \vee 3 < 1 \vee t_3 < 7$, we obtain $P(3) \vee \neg Q^*(T) \vee T < 4$.

The contraction operation and the I-simplification operation are performed whenever possible after the extension, reduction and the R-reasoning operations.

The procedure terminates successfully iff $\mathcal{L}$ is empty and $\mathcal{I}$ is either empty or $\mathcal{I}_1 \wedge \ldots \wedge \mathcal{I}_n \wedge \mathcal{I}$ is unsatisfiable by the I-reasoning operation, i.e., $\mathcal{I}_1 \wedge \ldots \wedge \mathcal{I}_n \wedge \mathcal{I} \cup INEQ \models \perp$ by theory resolution, where $\mathcal{I}_i$ $(1 \leq i \leq n)$ is a clause only containing inequality literals in S or obtained earlier by METAI. Otherwise, select a new center chain and repeat the procedure.

Now, we show the correctness of METAI. The soundness of METAI is straightforward, since all operations of ME and theory resolution are sound. The completeness of METAI can be shown by the following theorem.

Theorem 3. *Let S be an unsatisfiable set of clauses. Then, $\square$ is derivable by METAI.*

We first show Theorem 3 holds in the ground case.

Theorem 4. *Let S be an unsatisfiable set of ground clauses. Then, $\square$ is derivable by METAI.*

Proof. If $\square \in S$, $\square$ is trivial and derived from S by METAI.

Otherwise, we prove Theorem 4 by induction on the complexity measure $c(S)$ [1], where $c(S) = (|S|, k(S))$, where $|S|$ is the number of clauses in S and $k(S)$ is the number of literals in S minus $|S|$. The ordering of $c(S)$ is defined by $c(S_1) \prec c(S_2)$ iff $|S_1| < |S_2|$ or $|S_1| = |S_2|$ and $k(S_1) < k(S_2)$.

Case $c(S) = (m, 0)$. Every clause in S must be a unit clause. Because S is unsatisfiable, it must include a minimally unsatisfiable subset S'.

Subcase 1: S' contains neither inequality predicate nor relation predicate. Either $|S'| = 0$, i.e., $\square \in S'$ or $|S'| = 2$, i.e., S' consists of two predicates A and $\neg A$. $\square$ can be derived as in ME.

Subcase 2: S' contains only relation predicates. Then $\square$ can be derived from $|S'|$ by using the ME operations and the R-reasoning operation.

Subcase 3: S' contains only inequality predicates, where $|S'| \geq 2$. By the complete procedure *theory resolution* for inequalities, $\square$ can be derived by METAI.

Case $c(S) = (m, n), n > 0$. Select a nonunit clause $C \in S$. Let $S^* = (S - \{C\})$. Decompose C into unit ground atom A and ground clause B, i.e., $C = A \vee B$. Both $S_A = S^* \cup \{A\}$ and $S_B = S^* \cup \{B\}$ are unsatisfiable. Since $c(S_A) \prec c(S)$ and $c(S_B) \prec c(S)$, by the induction hypothesis, $\square$ can be derived from both S_A and S_B by METAI.

Imitate the derivation of $\square$ from S_B, using C instead of B. The result will be a derivation of either $\square$ or A from S. In the latter case, there is a derivation of $\square$ from S by appending the derivation of $\square$ from S_A to the derivation of A from S.

Then, Theorem 3 can be immediately established by Theorem 4 and lifting theorem [4].

4.4 How METAI works

We explain how METAI works, using the previous example.

Example 4. (Continued from Example 2) The following set of clauses is obtained from translated formulas in Example 2, where R is a Skolem constant.

1. $\neg C(0, t_1) \vee X(0, R, t_1, l) \vee F(0, t_1 + 3) \vee F(0, t_2 + 3)$
2. $\neg C(0, t_3) \vee \neg W(R, t_4) \vee F(0, t_3 + 3) \vee F(0, t_4 + 3)$
3. $\neg(3 \leq t_5) \vee \neg X(0, r, t_5, a_1) \vee W(r, 10)$
4. $C(0, 8)$
5. $\neg F(0, t)$

The satisfiability checking of the above set of clauses is as follows, where $\mathcal{E}$ ($\mathcal{R}$, $\mathcal{C}, \mathcal{I}_s$) denotes the extension operation (the reduction operation, the contraction operation, the $\mathcal{I}$-simplification operation), respectively. The clause 5 is selected as the center chain.

6. $\neg C(0, t - 3) \vee X(0, R, t - 3, l) \vee F(0, t_2 + 3) \vee \neg F^*(0, t)$ $\mathcal{E}$ with 1
7. $X(0, R, 8, l) \vee F(0, t_2 + 3) \vee \neg F^*(0, 11)$ $\mathcal{E}$ with 4 & $\mathcal{C}$
8. $W(R, 10) \vee F(0, t_2 + 3) \vee \neg F^*(0, 11) \vee X^*(0, R, 8, a_1)$ $\mathcal{E}$ with 3 & $\mathcal{I}_s$
9. $\neg C(0, t_3) \vee F(0, t_3 + 3) \vee F(0, 13) \vee W^*(R, 10)$
        $\vee F(0, t_2 + 3) \vee \neg F^*(0, 11) \vee X^*(0, R, 8, a_1)$ $\mathcal{E}$ with 2
10. $F(0, 11) \vee F(0, 13) \vee W^*(R, 10) \vee F(0, t_2 + 3)$
         $\vee \neg F^*(0, 11) \vee X^*(0, R, 8, a_1)$ $\mathcal{E}$ with 4 and $\mathcal{C}$
11. $F(0, 13) \vee W^*(R, 10) \vee F(0, t_2 + 3)$
         $\vee \neg F^*(0, 11) \vee X^*(0, R, 8, a_1)$ $\mathcal{R}$
12. $F(0, t_2 + 3) \vee \neg F^*(0, 11) \vee X^*(0, R, 8, a_1)$ $\mathcal{E}$ with 5 and $\mathcal{C}$
13. $\square$ $\mathcal{R}$ & $\mathcal{C}$

Since there is a refutation in the translated clause set, it means that the given work can be finished by agent cooperation. $\square$

4.5 Discussions

Besides the ME procedure, there are other general first-order theorem provers, e.g., among others, a bottom-up model generation theorem prover SATCHMO [10], which could be utilized in our case in place of ME.

However, the application of SATCHMO here will not be so efficient because there exist inequalities. In SATCHMO, a clause is represented in the following implicational form:

$$A_1 \wedge \ldots \wedge A_m \rightarrow C_1 \vee \ldots \vee C_n$$

where $A_1, \ldots, A_m, C_1, \ldots, C_n$ ($m, n \geq 0$) are positive literals. The idea of the SATCHMO proof procedure is to try to construct a model for a given set of clauses $\mathcal{S}$, starting with an empty set as the initial model candidate set. The set of model candidates $\mathcal{M}$ is successively extended, if for any $M \in \mathcal{M}$ and any clause from S of the form: $A_1 \wedge \ldots \wedge A_m \rightarrow C_1 \vee \ldots \vee C_n$ $(m \geq 0, n \geq 1)$, if there exists a substitution θ such that $A_i\theta \in M$ $(1 \leq i \leq m)$ and $C_j\theta \notin M$ $(1 \leq j \leq n)$, then remove M from $\mathcal{M}$, and add $M \cup \{C_j\theta\}$ to $\mathcal{M}$ for every $j = 1, \ldots, n$. Therefore, if a clause is range-restricted (i.e., every variable in the consequence of the clause occurs in its antecedent), those literals added to a model candidate $(C_j\theta)$ are ground.

In our case, however, it is not so simple because of the existence of inequalities. Consider, for example, an MAKT formula $\forall (5 \leq t)(p^t \vee q^t)$, which is translated, at the initial point $(0,0)$, into the following clause:

$$5 \leq t \rightarrow P(0,t) \vee Q(0,t)$$

Although the above formula is range-restricted, we must consider all the cases such that $5 \leq t$ is satisfiable and none of $P(t,0)$ and $Q(t,0)$ is satisfiable in a current model candidate. Thus, an auxiliary predicate "$dom(t)$" has to be introduced, which can generate all the terms of the universe where a variable t varies. This approach usually causes inefficiency in the reasoning procedure, and we show some experimental results in the next section.

5 Experimental Results

Our automated reasoning procedure for MAKT is currently implemented in SICStus Prolog on a Sun SPARCstation5/85MHz. Many MAKT formulas have been checked for satisfiability and some of these results are shown in Table 1. The results 6_a, 6_b and 6_c in the table, for example, show that the running time of SATCHMOTAI (SATCHMO with Transitive Axioms and Inequalities) is greatly influenced by the number of inequalities in the clause, while the running time of METAI is almost not affected.

Among them, we explain the well-known "the three wise men problem" (e.g., [5], [16]). The problem description is as follows:

A king, who wishes to know which of his three wise men is the wisest, paints white dots on each of their foreheads. He tells them that at least one dot is white and asks each, after seeing the others' dots, to determine the color of his own dot and write down his conclusion. All of the wise men then exchange their conclusions and repeat the process until someone knows the color of their own dot.

The problem is easily expressed as an MAKT formula as follows. Let a_1, a_2 and a_3 be the three wise men. We denote by w_l^0 $(l \in \{a_1, \ldots, a_3\})$ that the color of l's dot is white.

Since time in our model is discrete, the reasoning process of each wise man is also assumed to be discrete, that is, his reasoning proceeds along the discrete time flow $t = \{0, 1, 2, \cdots\}$.

As the reasoning process of each wise man is exactly the same, we consider the reasoning process of, say, a_1.

Table 1. Some Experimental Results

$\mathcal{N}o.$	MAKT formulas	Results	Running Time ($msec$)	
			SATCHMOTAI	METAI
1	$\forall t_1 \forall t_2 ((c^{t_1} \wedge \exists l K_l^{t_1} w^{t_2}) \to f^{t_1+3} \vee f^{t_2+3})$ $\wedge \forall(2 \leq t) K_{a_1}^{t_3} w^{t_4} \wedge c^8 \to \exists t_5 f^{t_5}$	valid	1020	10
2	$K_{a_1}^1 (\forall(2 \leq t_1) p^{t_1} \vee K_{a_2}^2 q^4)$ $\to \forall(5 \leq t_2) K_{a_1}^{t_2} (p^3 \vee K_{a_2}^3 q^4)$	valid	5620	8
3	$K_{a_1}^1 (\forall(2 \leq t_1) p^{t_1} \vee q^4)$ $\to K_{a_1}^5 (\forall(1 \leq t_3) p^{t_3} \vee q^4)$	not valid	120	17
4	$K_{a_1}^2 K_{a_2}^3 (p^{10} \wedge K_{a_3}^5 q^2) \to K_{a_2}^6 K_{a_3}^7 q^2$	valid	185	7
5	$K_{a_1}^3 K_{a_3}^1 p^2 \to K_{a_3}^5 (\forall(1 \leq t) p^t \vee q^4)$	not valid	130	3
6_a	$K_{a_1}^4 K_{a_2}^2 (\forall(2 \leq t_2) p^{t_2} \vee \forall(3 \leq t_3) q^{t_3})$ $\to K_{a_2}^{10} (p^3 \vee q^6)$	valid	1281020	10
6_b	$K_{a_1}^4 K_{a_2}^2 (\forall(2 \leq t_2) p^{t_2} \vee q^6)$ $\to K_{a_2}^{10} (p^3 \vee q^6)$	valid	1130	10
6_c	$K_{a_1}^4 K_{a_2}^2 (p^3 \vee q^6) \to K_{a_2}^{10} (p^3 \vee q^6)$	valid	180	6
7	$K_{a_1}^2 (p^3 \wedge q^4) \wedge K_{a_2}^2 (p^3 \wedge q^4)$ $\to K_{a_1}^5 p^3 \wedge K_{a_2}^7 q^4$	valid	280	23
8	Three Wise Men Problem	valid	1040	30

- (at time $t = 0$) a_1 sees $w_{a_2}^0$ and $w_{a_3}^0$, which is expressed by $F_0 = K_{a_1}^0 (w_{a_2}^0 \wedge w_{a_3}^0)$, but he cannot know what color of his dot is.
- (at time $t = 1$) a_1 knows that neither a_2 nor a_3 knew the color of his dot at $t = 0$, which is expressed by $F_1 = K_{a_1}^1 (\neg K_{a_2}^0 w_{a_2}^0 \wedge \neg K_{a_3}^0 w_{a_3}^0)$, but a_1 cannot yet know the color of his dot.
- (at time $t = 2$) a_1 knows that neither a_2 nor a_3 knew the color of his dots at $t = 1$, which is expressed by $F_2 = K_{a_1}^2 (\neg K_{a_2}^1 w_{a_2}^0 \wedge \neg K_{a_3}^1 w_{a_3}^0)$. Then, the wise man a_1 does the following reasoning: if his dot is not white, a_2 and a_3 would know it at $t = 0$. When a_2 (a_3) knows at $t = 1$ that a_3 (a_2) does not know $w_{a_3}^0$ ($w_{a_2}^0$) at $t = 0$, a_2 (a_3) would know that the reason is that a_3 (a_2) sees $\neg w_{a_1}^0 \wedge w_{a_2}^0$ ($\neg w_{a_1}^0 \wedge w_{a_3}^0$), respectively. a_2 (a_3) would thus know $w_{a_2}^0$ ($w_{a_3}^0$) at $t = 1$, respectively. Therefore when a_1 knows at $t = 2$ that neither a_2 nor a_3 knew the color of his dot at $t = 1$, he would know the reason is that his dot is white. That is, a_1 would know $w_{a_1}^0$ at $t = 2$. This reasoning process is expressed by $F_3 = \forall(0 \leq t) K_{a_1}^t (w_{a_2}^0 \wedge w_{a_3}^0 \wedge \neg K_{a_2}^0 w_{a_2}^0 \wedge \neg K_{a_3}^0 w_{a_3}^0 \wedge \neg K_{a_2}^1 w_{a_2}^0 \wedge \neg K_{a_3}^1 w_{a_3}^0 \to w_{a_1}^0)$.

This reasoning process can be expressed in the following MAKT formula:

$$F_0 \wedge F_1 \wedge F_2 \wedge F_3 \longrightarrow K_{a_1}^2 w_{a_1}^0$$

Our automated reasoning system can prove the validity of the above formula as shown in Table 1.

6 Concluding Remarks

We have implemented an automated reasoning system for multi-agent environments. The reasoning method of our system has been shown to be sound and complete. We have then explained our automated reasoning prover, METAI, for the translated first-order clauses. METAI is based on ME, augmented with the capabilities of using transitive axioms and handling time inequalities. Some experimental results were also shown.

There are some other methods for constructing an automated reasoning system for modal logics. A famous one is the so-called tableau method [3]. Unfortunately, this method is difficult to be extended to multi modal logics, which is essential when complex reasoning tasks in multi-agent environments are given. Our method is easy to use, easy to extend, and can use developed techniques in first-order logics.

In this paper, we have confined ourselves mainly to propositional MAKT. The extension of the method to first-order MAKT will, however, be straightforward.

For future work, we will consider how to solve the competition of knowledge and renewing of knowledge. We will apply our method to solve practical problems and use the parallel processing to enhance the efficiency of our reasoning procedure.

References

1. R. Anderson and W.W. Bledsoe, 'A Linear format for resolution with merging and a new technique for establishing completeness', *J. ACM* **28**, pp193-214, 1970.
2. J. Akahani, 'A Multi-Agent System Simulator Based on Modal Logic', *Multi-Agent and Cooperative Computation'91*, pp.49-57, Modern Publisher, Japan, 1991.
3. L. Catach, 'TABLEAUX: A General Theorem Prover for Modal Logic', *Journal of Automated Reasoning* **7**: pp.489-510, 1991.
4. C.L. Chang and R.C.T. Lee, 'Symbolic Logic and Mechanical Theorem Proving', *Academic Press*, 1973.
5. J. Elgot-Drapkin, 'Step-Logic and the Three-wise-men Problem', *Proceedings of AAAI*, pp.412-417, 1991.
6. P.J. Gmytrsiewicz and E.H. Durfee, 'Elements of a Utilitarian Theory of Knowledge and Action', *Proceedings of IJCAI*, pp.396-402, 1993.
7. G.E. Hughes and M.J. Cresswell, 'An Introduction to Modal Logic', Methuen, London, 1968.
8. J.Y. Halpern and M.Y. Vardi, 'The Complexity of Reasoning About Knowledge and Time: Extended Abstract', *Proceedings of the Eighteenth Annual ACM Symposium on Theory of Computing*, pp.304-315, 1986.
9. S. Kraus and J. Wilkenfeld, 'Negotiations over Time in a Multi Agent Environment: Preliminary Report', pp.56-61, *Proceedings of IJCAI*, 1993.
10. R. Manthey and F. Bry, 'SATCHMO: a theorem prover implemented in Prolog', *Proceedings of 9th Conference on Automated Deduction*, 1988.
11. D.W. Loveland, 'Mechanical Theorem Proving by Model Elimination', *J. of the ACM* **15**, pp.236-251, 1968.

12. F. Lin and Y. Shoham, 'On the Persistence of Knowledge and Ignorance: A Preliminary report', In *the fourth Int. Workshop on Nonmonotonic Reasoning*, 1992.

13. C. Morgan, 'Methods for Automated Theorem Proving in Nonclassical Logics', *IEEE, Transactions on Computers*, vol.c-25, No.8, August 1976.

14. U.W. Schwuttke and A.G. Quan, 'Enhancing Performance of Cooperating Agents in Real-Time Diagnostic System', *Proceedings of IJCAI*, pp.332-337, 1993.

15. M. Stickel, 'Automated Deduction by Theory Reasoning', *Journal of Automated Reasoning*, 1(4):333-356, 1985.

16. X. Wang and H. Chen, 'On Assumption Reasoning in Multi-Reasoner System', *Proceedings of PRICAI*, pp.381-383, 1990.

17. G. Weiß, 'Learning to Coordinate Action in Multi-Agent System', *Proceedings of IJCAI*, pp.311-316, 1993.

Application of MAS in Implementing Rational IP Routers on the Priced Internet

Hongxia Yang[1] and Chengqi Zhang[2]

[1] School of Computer Science, Florida International University
Miami, FL 33199, USA
hyang03@fiu.edu
[2] Department of Mathematics, Statistics, and Computing Science
The University of New England, Armidale, NSW 2351, Australia
chengqi@neumann.une.edu.au

Abstract. Pricing and prioritizing the Internet access can be one of the potential measures to improve the efficiency of the Internet utilization and control the Internet congestion. In order to meet a diversity of user access requirements, the IP (Internet Protocol) routers can provide users with various priority service classes. This paper explores the application of multi-agent systems (MAS) in the implementation of rational IP routers on the priced Internet. The negotiation model for task decomposition and allocation, and the payment model are described. The strategies of achieving a more optimal global-level resource allocation and a rational and fair local-level resource allocation and scheduling for tasks with different priority are proposed. The strategies for price setting and adjustment are discussed. The consumer strategy is also addressed.

1 Introduction

The overuse of the Internet causes the low efficiency of the internet resource utilization. Most users today access the internet service almost "free" (supported by the universities, the government, or companies), and it is hard to see that they have any incentive to economize their use of the internet. As a result, the Internet is congested with quite a bunch of low value information, while high value information (even in quite a small quantity) that requires low delay has to contend with the great quantity of low value information for network resources.

One solution to the congestion of the internet is to extend the capacity of network, and update the routers in the bottleneck network sections. However, as long as the network is accessed at such a low cost ("free"), no matter how the network bandwidth is extended, it will be fully consumed immediately — "This is the classic problem of the commons" [8].

Another measure to control the congestion of the Internet and to improve the efficiency of the internet utilization is pricing the internet [8]. From April 1995, commercialized internet network service providers (e.g., SPRINT, MCI, AT&T, etc.) are making their effort to provide their network service to their customers [11]. Therefore, the Internet is becoming the biggest computational economy involving various countries and users all over the world.

The benefit of pricing the internet over free access policy is described in [9] in the form of net benefit of the service supplier and the waiting time of packets. The economic issues of pricing the internet are detailed in [8]. Both of these two papers tried to prove theoretically that pricing is a good idea. Edell et al. [7] proposed an operational structure of billing users and pricing for TCP traffic, showing that pricing and billing users is practical for implementation.

On the other hand, in order to optimize the benefit of the internet utilization, the IP routers, the network routing service providers, should provide prioritized service and a diversity of service preference (like security) to satisfy different user needs.

However, the issues of how to achieve a more optimal global resource allocation and how to achieve a fair and rational resource allocation and scheduling (RAS) locally are not addressed in those papers. In MAS, there is some research in the optimization of task and resource allocation [1], [2], [3], [4], [5]. But the research in the relationship between the price and the resource allocation and scheduling scheme can be rarely found in the current market research literature.

The goal of the paper is to explore the application of Multi-agent systems (MAS) and Distributed Artificial Intelligence (DAI), especially the Market model, in the implementation of the rational IP routers on the priced Internet, and investigate some issues that are not addressed in the field, especially, the RAS strategies for dealing with dynamically arrived tasks with various priorities. The paper is organized as follows. Section 2 describes the problem domain of the internet economy. Section 3 presents the task negotiation model among the IP router, a user or the user's agent, and the agent on behalf of the user's organization. Section 4 proposes the global and local resource allocation strategies, followed by the pricing strategies for IP routers in Section 5. The consumer (user) strategy is discussed in Section 5. Section 6 concludes the paper.

2 Domain Problem Description

The IP Router as the Routing Service Supplier on the Priced Internet. Just like the post office, the Internet providing various services can simplify the procedure and improve the effectiveness of interactions involved in different people. People can send information requests and requested information through the internet. The advantage is obvious using the internet as the general purpose post office. People, instead of going to the local post office, can just sit in front of their computer to send their information requests or products (limiting to information products). Through the Internet, companies can communicate with their customers more easily.

In this post-office metaphor, the internet routers are routing service providers for various users. They acts as gateways for consumers to communicate with each other by routing and transmitting their messages, results, and requests.

Task (or service) preferences. When a consumer sends a request to the Internet (just like a person sends a mail through a post office), he/she may have some preference of the service, or type of service settings, such as the priority of transmission (corresponding to the speed, or delay; e.g., express vs. regular mail), reliability (like registered vs. regular mail); he/she may request to send a large quantity of data (like bulk mail). Besides, on the Internet, some customers may have security requirements for their information transmission, since they may not want the information exposed to their competitors or some malicious entities during the midway.

Various service preferences (types of service) may incur various processing costs, and may affect other requests differently. Therefore, they should be priced differently (detailed in Section 5).

The Internet, task sharing, and payment models. An Internet topology can be represented as a graph: $G = < V, E >$, where V denotes a set of vertices of hosts and gateways, and E represents network links connecting vertices in G (see Fig. 1). Suppose the weight c_{ij} of a link $(< v_i, v_j >)$ in the graph represents the cost of transferring a packet with unit size. For an Internet sending task $T(x, y)$

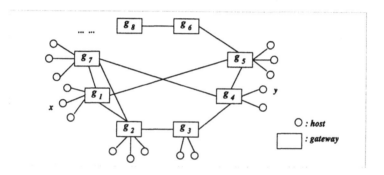

Fig. 1. The Internet topology model

to send the associated packets from source host x to destination host y, there are some alternative routes from x to y. For example, in Fig. 1, a task $T(x, y)$ has the following alternative problem solving paths: $x \to g_1 \to g_2 \to g_3 \to g_4 \to y$; $x \to g_1 \to g_2 \to g_7 \to g_4 \to y$; $x \to g_1 \to g_5 \to g_4 \to y$; $x \to g_1 \to g_7 \to g_4 \to y$; $x \to g_1 \to g_7 \to g_2 \to g_3 \to g_4 \to y$.

Generally, suppose the route for conducting $T(x, y)$ is $x \to g_1 \to g_2, \cdots, \to g_{m-1} \to g_m \to y$, where $g_1, g_2, \cdots, g_m$ are a group of billing gateways (IP routers) between them. Then task T (i.e., sending a packet from x to y) can be regarded as a set of subtasks $\{ST_0, ST_1, ST_2, \cdots, ST_m\}$, where ST_0 represents the subtask of routing packets from x to gateway g_1, and a subtask ST_i for $(i = 1, \cdots, m-1)$ represents a subtask of routing packets from gateway g_i to g_{i+1}, and ST_m is the subtask of routing packets from g_m to y. We can use the following formula to represent the process of task composition and task sharing:

$$T_i = \begin{cases} \{ST_0, ST_1, \cdots, ST_m\} & \text{for } i = 0 \\ T_{i-1} - ST_{i-1} & \text{for } i = 1, \cdots, m \end{cases}$$

The task allocation solution for $ST_0, ST_1, \cdots, ST_m$ is achieved as follows. A user c in the host x originates a sending task T to send a packet to y. Firstly, host x forwards the task request to gateway g_1 (i.e., the subtask ST_0 is completed by host x). Then the gateway g_1 agrees to accept task $T_1 = T_0 - ST_0$, and the user c agrees to pay the cost for the task $T_1(g_1 \rightarrow y)$ (detailed in Section 3). The cost of $x \rightarrow g_1$ is not of interest of ours and is ignored. The reason is just like the post office metaphor. The cost that a person sends his/her mail to the nearby post office, or the cost that he/she puts it to the nearby mail pickup box, is not included in the postage of the mail.

The gateway g_1 decomposes the task T_1 into ST_1 and $T_2 = T_1 - ST_1$. Because g_1 can conduct ST_1, and can not conduct T_2, it subcontracts the remaining task T_2 to gateway g_2, and pays[3] g_2 for the task $T_2(g_2 \rightarrow y)$, and so on; until g_{m-1} subcontracts task $T_m = T_{m-1} - ST_{m-1}$ to g_m, and pays it for $T_m(g_m \rightarrow y)$. As gateway g_m is in the same network as y, it can finish the task T_m or subtask ST_m itself. Suppose the price for conducting $T_1, T_2, \cdots, T_m$ are $e_1, e_2, \cdots, e_m$. Then except that g_m earns e_m, each other gateway g_i, for conducting ST_i, earns the total revenue $(e_i - e_{i+1})$, which covers the total cost of and the profit for the service.

The negotiation model described in the next section explains how user tasks are accepted or rejected by the billing gateways, and how the authorized tasks are shared by gateways.

3 Negotiation Model

User authentication and verification on the priced internet is an important phase before an IP router agrees to serve a user. When a sending task request from a user arrives at the first billing gateway (IP router), in order for the gateway to protect its own interest and avoid being hurt by malicious users or agents, it needs to negotiate with the user about task acception, authenticate and verify the user's eligibility for the requested service. The requirement for a secure task negotiation is not addressed in the original Contract Net Protocol [1]. Sandholm et al. [3] extended the CNP to accommodate the payment information in a contract, yet still leaving the issue of authentication unaddressed.

A user's account is associated with an organization, such as a university, a company, a government, or a commercialized service provider. For the organization to which a user belongs, it has an Access Control Agent (ACA) who will control the user access to the Internet, and disable unauthorized access to the valuable internet resources. All requests from its users will be checked to determine whether the request is allowed.

---

[3] The IP can support this payment scheme. In the IP header [12], there is an option field called Record Route. The IP router adds its address in the Record Route option field when it forwards a packet. When the next gateway receives a packet, it checks the option field to get the address of the previous gateway by which the packet was just routed, then it can record the price and cost information regarding this task.

Therefore, the task negotiation involves three parties: the user (or the user's Personal Assistant Agent (PAA) which can assist the user in negotiation), the Access Control Agent on behalf of the user's organization, and the IP router. The negotiation process (Fig. 2) is described below.

(a) The user application sends a sending task request (which corresponds to a TCP connection request) from host machine x. When this request arrives at the first IP router, the IP router will need to interact with the user and the ACA. For the IP router, the interaction has three goals: (i) to authenticate the user, (ii) to verify the user's willingness to pay, and (iii) to ask the user about his/her service preference. The IP router asks ACA to get the above information, and then waits for reply.

(b) The ACA contacts the User Identification Daemon (Useridd, a user-level process) to identify the user.

(c) If the user is not an authorized one, the ACA sends a "no" message to the IP router. If this request is from an authorized user, the ACA checks whether the request is from a user who has the permission to request such type of information. The ACA maintains an access control list determining (i) who (a user or user group) is given access to a local or remote computer system network (i.e., IP routing resources), and whether the access can be free of charge for this user (the cost may be paid by the organization in a certain form); and (ii) what and how much information (resources) someone can receive.

(d) If the sender has the permission, then the ACA asks the User Name Server to locate the user's Personal Assistant Agent (PAA). Otherwise, a "no" message will be sent to the IP router.

(e) The ACA asks the PAA to verify the user's willingness to pay, and other service preference.

(f) The PAA, either through interaction with the user, or automatically on behalf of the user, obtains the information about the willingness to pay and the service preference. The information is sent back to the ACA.

(g) If the sender (or his/her PAA) responds with the willingness to pay, or otherwise the sender is eligible for free service, the ACA will respond the gateway with a "yes" message along with the service preference. Otherwise, a "no" message is sent to the IP router.

(h) If the IP router receives a "yes" message, then the negotiation is successful. The IP router will accept the sending task originated from the user. Otherwise, the negotiation fails.

If the negotiation succeeds, the IP router will create a connection table entry for this sending task. The entry is uniquely identified by (Source(address, port), Destination(address, port)). The priority and other service preference information is stored in the entry.

After the connection table entry is created, the subsequent data(grams) arrived for this sending task will be scheduled, routed, and forwarded to the next gateway according to the priority (see Section 4.2) and other service preference stored in the entry without involvement of the user. The metering traffic for the associated connection table entry is updated afterwards for each sending call.

Before the entry is dropped (e.g., after the sending task is finished), the entry and its content will be written to a stable storage (called a log) for the purpose of accounting and billing. This information in the log is processed by the IP price/accounting agent (see Fig. 2), which will send the bill to the sender at the proper time.

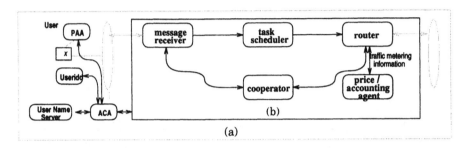

Fig. 2. The negotiation model (a) and components of the IP router (b)

Gateway to Gateway. Having described the task composition and allocation for a sending task in Section 2, we know how a task is shared by a set of gateways. After the packet arrives at the next gateway g_{i+1}, g_{i+1} records the address and metering traffic information, and routes and forwards the packet according to its priority to the next gateway g_{i+2}; or if y is in the same local network, forwards it to y.

4 Resource Allocation Strategies of IP Routers

For a sending task T with source address s and destination address d, it is composed of a set of subtasks $ST_1, ST_2, \cdots, ST_m$. The problem is that in an open environment like the Internet, various tasks come frequently over time, how to allocate resources to optimize the cost of resource utilization, and how to schedule and route different types of tasks fairly. The resource allocation problem is divided into two levels: the global-level resource allocation and the local-level resource allocation and scheduling. The global resource allocation problem is about how to optimize the total cost for a task; the local resource allocation and scheduling (RAS) problem is about how to allocate the local resource to various task optimally and schedule these tasks fairly.

Resource allocation is important, and a problem solving for a task can be regarded as a resource allocation problem. In DAI and MAS, some researchers use contract net protocol (CNP) to achieve a resource allocation solution [1], [3], some use constraint satisfaction approach [2], [6], and some others use the microeconomics or market approach [4], [5]. This paper will use DAI and MAS techniques to optimize the global resource allocation, and will specially concentrate on how a local optimal and fair resource allocation and schedule solution can be achieved for different task classes through careful design and proper strategies.

4.1 Global Resource Allocation among IP Routers

As we have described in Section 2, a task T of sending a packet from source s to destination d may have many alternative problem solving paths in the Internet modeled by a graph G. As the weight of a link in the graph represents the cost of transferring a packet with unit size, then for T, the shortest path (using Dijkstra algorithm, see any text book about graph theory) $s \rightarrow g_1 \rightarrow g_2 \rightarrow \cdots \rightarrow g_m \rightarrow d$ from s to d denotes an optimal problem solving path for task T in terms of the total cost (minimal).

However, although this is optimal theoretically for a single task T, it may not be the case when considering the dynamic load of links and gateways between these two endpoints. If at time t, this route is quite heavily loaded, then it may not be a good idea to still use this route. For example, if the queue of gateway g_{i+1} is full when this packet arrives, then this packet will have to be discarded. In order to reduce the discarding rate of packets, and also to achieve a more optimal global resource allocation, the following strategies can be applied.

Firstly, an IP implementation close to the Internet protocol [12] provides a way to a more optimal task allocation. For a gateway g_i, in its route table, it has a current best gateway address g_{i+1} for sending tasks with source s and destination d. That means when such a task (packet routing) arrives, g_i will route the packet to gateway g_{i+1}. The path is currently optimal to the knowledge of the gateway g_i, and it can be updated to g_k if gateway g_{i+1} informs g_i by an ICMP message [14] that another gateway g_k is better for destination d (due to dynamics of the network topology, links failure, etc.).

Secondly, we can use MAS/DAI technology to achieve a better task allocation scheme for a sending task T. Focused addressing [1], [3] is used as a heuristic to reduce the messages required in Contract Net Protocol. It suggests that when a supplier g_l is idle, it can advertise its status by informing a set of associated suppliers, such that if a supplier g_i sees this advertisement, and it knows that the next gateway g_{i+1} in its routing table does not advertise its status (which means it keeps busy), g_i can choose to send the packet to g_l instead of g_{i+1}. Furthermore, if g_i receives several such type of messages, it can choose the best one according to its knowledge of network topology. Both the sender and gateway g_{i+1} will be better off if the load can be shared by a light loaded gateway, or when a better gateway can be found.

A gateway has a message receiver (see Fig. 2 (b)). When the receiver recognizes an advertisement message, it sends it to the cooperator, who collects such messages, destroys them when they get expired (an advertisement message will expire after a certain time), and decides which gateway is the best for tasks with the same destination. Otherwise, if the receiver receives a sending task, it forwards it to the task scheduler which schedules tasks according to their priorities. The router, when routing a packet (associated with task T), checks the cooperator which gateway is the current best gateway, and then sends the packet to that gateway.

In this context, the decomposition and allocation for a task is done dynamically in response to the gateway load, and will be subject to change when some links fail. This real world case enriches most of the DAI research in which the task decomposition scheme for a task is fixed and done beforehand.

4.2 Local Resource Allocation and Scheduling Strategies

The optimization of resource allocation and scheduling (RAS) for a set of tasks locally is regarded as a NP-hard problem [2]. Some researchers [2], [4] cast the RAS problem as a constraint satisfaction problem, and proposed some strategies to deal with some special cases of the problem. However, their papers did not deal with the problem in which tasks are associated with different priorities, and tasks dynamically arrive at the system while previous tasks are being processed. As high priority tasks have a higher price, resource allocation and scheduling should favor them, and process them first. But if we always process tasks with high priorities first no matter when they arrive, it may cause the starvation of lower priority tasks. Therefore, proper resource allocation and scheduling strategies and implementations should be used to fairly process different priority tasks.

This section discusses the RAS strategies for an IP router, which provides various priority service classes for different sending tasks[4]. In IPv4[5] header, the precedence field has 3 bits with 000 indicating the lowest priority (free service) and 111 the highest priority.

With proper priority resource allocation and scheduling strategies and price strategies (discussed in Section 5), both users and IP routers can benefit from the priority service. To be fair, the following conditions must be satisfied:

(i) Priority scheduling and routing. When two packets arrive at the same time, the higher priority packet (i.e., task) should be scheduled and routed first. This paper only discusses non-preemptive priority scheduling and routing, which means, if a packet with lower priority is out of queue, and is being processed, then the late-coming higher priority packet can not preempt it, causing it to be put back to the queue.

(ii) First come, first served. Packets with the same priority should be scheduled and routed in a first come, first served manner.

(iii) No starvation. Packets with lower priority should not wait indefinitely for the routing resources, while the resources are continuously used by the higher priority packets.

We will discuss the RAS in two priority service algorithms using priority queue implementation: single priority queue (SPQ) and multiple priority queue (MPQ). This paper addresses the single server model for both of these two schemes.

(1) Single Priority Queue/Single Server.
Only one priority queue (Q) is used for all packets with different priorities.

---

[4] The sending tasks in the context of IP routing are packets waiting for routing resources. In the paper, the term packet means a routing task.

[5] IPv4 means IP version 4 [12], and IPv6 is IP version 6 [13].

The IP router, in order to process packets fairly, considers their original priority and their waiting time in its queue. It indicates a local priority $(p_i(t))$ for a new inserted packet, and updates the local priority of a packet whenever it is scheduled behind a packet which arrived later than it (i.e., this late-coming packet is inserted before it). Intuitively, when a task waits too long, in order to be fair (i.e., to avoid starvation), its local priority should be increased.

We say a packet z_2 is "priority scheduled" over another packet z_1 at time t by an IP router if the arrival time of z_1 is earlier than that of z_2, but z_2 is inserted before z_1 in the queue by the IP router, because the local priority of z_2 is larger than that of z_1 at time t.

The following operations are undertaken when a packet, with original priority p_i specified in its IP header, arrives at the IP router:

- If the queue is full, the packet is discarded (the strategy of how to reduce the discarding rate of packets is discussed in the previous global resource allocation.) Otherwise, the IP router first transforms the priority p_i into a local priority number, $p_i(t)$, by multiplying it with a number ξ.
- Then the packet is inserted into a proper position of the queue, such that the local priority of packets from the queue head to the tail is in the non-increasing order.
- For each packet with lower local priority staying behind this packet, their local priority $p_j(t)$ is increased by a certain amount ϵ_j respectively.

At time t, the local priority $(p_i(t))$ of a packet with original priority p_i can be computed as follows:

$$p_i(t) = \begin{cases} \xi p_i + \epsilon_i m; & (p_i(t) < p_{max}) \\ p_{max}; & \text{otherwise} \end{cases} \tag{1}$$

where m is the number of packets that have been "priority scheduled" over it by time t, and ϵ_i is a priority related parameter, denoting the local priority updating degree of a packet with priority p_i each time some other packet is "priority scheduled" over it. For simplicity of analysis, we set $\epsilon_i = 1$ for all $p_i = 0, 1, \cdots, 7$. However, if ϵ_i is adjusted carefully, we can achieve a more optimal use of resources. This priority adjustment formula satisfies all of the fairness conditions. Specifically, it ensures no starvation, as the local priority of a packet is increased whenever another packet is "priority scheduled" over it.

The interpacket spacing (defined as the time interval between the starting times of routing for two adjacent packets in the queue) is denoted by τ (see Fig. 3(a)). For the convenience of analysis, we assume that τ is a constant for all packets.

Generally, if we allow 8 priorities, p_0 to p_7, then $p_{max} = \xi \times p_7 = 7\xi$. Then the maximal number of packets that can be "priority scheduled" over a packet with priority p_i is $(p_{max} - \xi p_i)$. Let W_{p_i} represent the upper bound of waiting time of priority class p_i. Then W_{p_i} is computed as:

$$W_{p_i} = \tau(L_Q + \xi(p_7 - p_i)). \tag{2}$$

Therefore, *in SPQ scheme, the upper bound of the waiting time of a packet at an IP router is dependent on the length of Q, the coefficient ξ as well as the processing speed of the router, τ.*

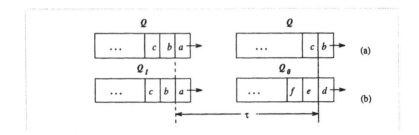

Fig. 3. The meaning of notation τ

(2) Multiple Priority Queues/Single Server.

The second approach is to implement multiple priority queues, say $Q_0, Q_1,$ $\cdots, Q_7$. Each queue Q_i only accommodates packets of priority p_i. In this scheme, the local priority $p_i(t)$ remains the same as p_i.

In a simple MPQ resource allocation and scheduling scheme, an IP router may first check if Q_7 is empty. If not, it processes packets in Q_7; otherwise, processes packets in Q_6, and so on. Only when all Q_7 to Q_{i+1} are empty, packets in Q_i can be scheduled and routed. This simple scheme may bring the problem of starvation of lower priority packets; i.e., they may wait for resources indefinitely.

A fair RAS scheme in MPQ should abide by the following rule: the lengths of priority queues and the resource allocation percentages should be set and adjusted such that (a) the upper bound of waiting time of packets with higher priority should be smaller than that of packets with lower priority, and (b) no starvation. Let L_{Q_i} denote the length of Q_i. Then the problem is how to estimate the upper bound of waiting time, W_{p_i}, of a packet with priority p_i.

To avoid starvation, we need to allocate resources to each of the service class, and use reasonable scheduling scheme. For example, suppose the following resource allocation percentage scheme is used: $\theta_7(10), \theta_6(25), \theta_5(20),$ $\theta_4(15),$ $\theta_3(10), \theta_2(10), \theta_1(5), \theta_0(5)$, where $\theta_i(j)$ means that j percent of routing resource is allocated to p_i. Then a fair scheduling sequence can be as follows:

$$77, 66666, 5555, 444, 33, 22, 1, 0, 77, 6...$$

where $77, 6666, ...$ means two packets with priority 7 are first routed, followed by five packets with priority 6, and so on. In this scheduling scheme, no starvation will occur.

To satisfy rule (a), we need to analyze the relationships among the lengths of different queues, and the percentages of resource allocated to them. We start from two priority queues, Q_0 and Q_1, which have lengths L_{Q_0} and L_{Q_1}.

For simplicity, we assume that the interpacket spacing between the top packet in Q_1 (e.g., packet a in Q_1 in Fig. 3 (b)) and the first top packet in Q_0 (e.g., packet d in Q_0 in Fig. 3 (b)) is τ, the same as the interpacket spacing τ between two adjacent packets in the same queue without switching to another queue (defined in the single queue scheme; see Fig. 3 (a)).

We claim that for n (here $n = 8$) service classes, *in MPQ scheme, if the* *resource allocation percentages satisfy $\theta_i = \beta\theta_{i-1}$, then to satisfy $W_{p_i} < W_{p_{i-1}}$, their queue lengths should satisfy $L_{Q_i} < \beta L_{Q_{i-1}}$. Here $\theta_0 + \theta_1 + \cdots + \theta_{n-1} = 1$.*

We give a brief proof for the case of 3 priority queues, Q_0, Q_1, Q_2. Other cases can be extended easily. Suppose the resource allocation percentages for these three queues satisfy: $\theta_1 = \beta\theta_0$; and $\theta_2 = \alpha\theta_1 = \alpha\beta\theta_0$.

Look at the case when $\alpha \geq 1$ and $\beta \geq 1$, and they are positive numbers. Other cases can be examined similarly. Let the scheduling sequence be:

$$\underbrace{2, 2, \cdots, 2}_{\alpha\beta}, \underbrace{1, 1, \cdots, 1}_{\beta}, 0, \underbrace{2, 2, \cdots, 2}_{\alpha\beta}, \underbrace{1, 1, \cdots, 1}_{\beta}, 0, 2, \ldots$$

Then

$$W_{p_2} = \tau(L_{Q_2} + \alpha L_{Q_2}/\beta + L_{Q_2}/\beta);$$
$$W_{p_1} = \tau(L_{Q_1} + \alpha L_{Q_1}/\beta + L_{Q_1}/\alpha);$$
$$W_{p_0} = \tau(L_{Q_0} + \alpha L_{Q_0} + \beta L_{Q_0}). \tag{3}$$

Therefore, in order to satisfy $W_{p_2} < W_{p_1} < W_{p_0}$, we get:

$$L_{Q_2} < \alpha L_{Q_1}; \text{ and } L_{Q_1} < \beta L_{Q_0}. \tag{4}$$

Strategies of improving the response time. *In order to improve the response time for a certain priority service class p_i, (i.e., a smaller upper bound), two measures can be taken: (i) to increase the percentage of resource allocation to this priority task class by increasing the local priority update degree ϵ_i in the SPQ scheme, or by increasing its resource allocation percentage θ_i; or/and (ii) to cut the length of the priority queue for the priority service class, i.e., to cut the length of Q in the SPQ scheme, or to cut the length of L_{Q_i} in the MPQ scheme.*

Adaptability. To be adaptable to the changing demand or traffic situations, the IP router can adjust its resource allocation percentages and queue lengths. For example, during night time, the demand of lower priority services can be expected to increase, so IP router can allocate more resources to lower priority packets. While during the daytime, higher priority packets should have more share of IP routing resource.

5 Price Strategies of IP Routers

Price in a market functions as a strong link between suppliers and consumers. Suppliers set and adjust the prices for their services or goods in order to maximize their goal, e.g., the profit, which is the revenue less the cost. The revenue from a service is computed as its price times the quantity of the service. The consumers select service classes or commodity brands according to their preference and their needs, and compare the prices of similar services provided by different suppliers. Their goal is to maximize their utilities (e.g., the level of satisfaction) under their budget constraints.

Some market research in DAI assumes that the suppliers are price-takers [5]. So the price setting issue is not discussed. However, when a new type of service is produced (like the priced internet services), the suppliers must consider how to set rational prices for different services. This section will explore the price setting and adjusting issues.

5.1 Price setting

The internal factors determine the price setting strategies [10]. The internal factors include the costs and the objectives of the suppliers (here, the IP routers). The objectives of the network access service suppliers may vary according to whom they provide services to and their corresponding goals. For example, the American NSF first funded NSFNET in order to facilitate the research community to exchange ideas and results more conveniently, thus the internet access for the community is "free". However, the commercialized service providers, such as MCI and AT&T, two biggest American telecommunication companies, have different goals and different price strategies toward different customer sections.

In this section, we will investigate the relationship among the priority queue lengths, the resource allocation percentages and the price for different priority service classes based on the MPQ scheme.

We begin with the discussion of the cost factors involved. Cost factors in this context include the resource consumption and the social delay cost for servicing different tasks.

The higher priority service class (p_i) deserves a higher price due to its higher social delay cost (denoted by Δ_{p_i}) — it delays the packets with the same priority and packets with lower priority in the current network. We do not have special links for different priority packets. Therefore, various packets have to compete with each other for the shared resources.

The delay cost Δ_{p_i} depends on the following factors:

- How much resource (or, θ_i) is allocated to the associated priority service class p_i? The higher θ_i is, the longer delay it causes to other packets. Therefore, the price P_{p_i} should be a strictly increasing function of θ_i.
- How many packets may be delayed by packets of this service class? Prioritization of service implies the sequence of scheduling and routing packets: higher priority packets are always scheduled and routed first when their allocated resources are not used out, or become available again. In the multiple priority queue scheme, the maximal number of packets that can be delayed by priority class p_i is the total of the packets waiting in the lower priority queues: $\sum_{j=0}^{i-1} L_{Q_j}$.
- The time (τ_i) required to route a packet with priority p_i of unit size (corresponding to the interpacket spacing). The longer it takes for an IP router to route such a packet, the longer delay the packet causes to other packets.

Let $\gamma_i = \lambda_i \tau_i$ where λ_i is a coefficient. Then we give the following formula:

$$\Delta_{p_i} = \lambda_i \tau_i \theta_i \sum_{j=0}^{i-1} L_{Q_j}. \tag{5}$$

Previously, we have assumed that $\tau_i = \tau_j = \tau$ for all $i, j = 0, 1, \cdots, 7$.

The price for priority class p_i, P_{p_i} is a strict increasing function f of Δ_{p_i}, or

$$P_{p_i} = f(\Delta_{p_i}) = f(\lambda_i \tau_i \theta_i \sum_{j=0}^{i-1} L_{Q_j}). \tag{6}$$

Another cost factor is due to the security option, which may have different levels [15]. Let $P_{p_i}(\kappa_j)$ represent the price of service with priority class p_i and security level κ_j. The higher κ_j is, the more secure the data transmission, the more processing resources it may requires, and thus the higher its price.

5.2   Price adjustment

The price should be adjusted when external factors change. One of the external factors is the consumer demand for services [10].

In the case of the Internet, the access demand varies with different times of a day, and different days of a week. For example, the maximal and median delays by time of day in New York and east coast of the US are plotted in [8] showing a large delay at 4 pm and small delay at 4 am Eastern Standard time.

In order to improve the efficiency of internet utilization, the price of the access service should be adjusted to achieve a more balanced traffic and higher transmission reliability. During the heavy traffic time, the price should be set high so that some non-urgent requests may be sent during the light traffic time instead, and some low value traffic may be avoided.

The frequency of price adjustment is an important issue. In one scheme, price is adjusted rapidly in response to the traffic. Kuwabara and Ishida give such a price adjustment function in [4]. Another scheme is that price is adjusted according to the time of day, (e.g., day time and night time) and is different from weekdays and weekends. The second scheme is easy to implement, and is more convenient for users to estimate the expected expense of their sending requests. As a result, the interaction process between the billing gateway and the user (described in Section 3) may become faster. We believe that the later is a more practical for implementation.

6   Consumer Strategy

Agents belonging to different organizations and different people can interact through the internet with the development of electronic commerce. Such agents are rational and self-interested [3]. For example, consumers are rational entities to satisfy their goal of either (i) maximizing the quantity of the service (denoted by χ) under certain amount of money, or (ii) maximizing the quality class of service (denoted by ϱ). In this context, the quality of service have two factors: the priority of service, p_i, and the security level κ_j. We use this simple formula to denote the relationship: $\varrho = a_1 p_i + a_2 \kappa_j$, where a_1 and a_2 denote the relative importance of speed and security from a certain user's personal point of view.

The consumers' strategy for selecting the priority and price for their service requests is largely dependent upon their goal and budget constraint.

Let I denote the maximal money that a consumer would like to pay for his request, which represents his budget limit. Then a consumer's goal can be represented as:

$$Max[\chi], \; s.t. \; P_{p_i}(\kappa_j) \cdot \chi \leq I, \; goal(i);$$
$$Max[\varrho], \; s.t. \; P_{p_i}(k_j) \cdot \chi \leq I, \; goal(ii). \tag{7}$$

The Personal Assistant Agent of the user may present a dialog box, ask the user the maximal money I he would like to spend, and the service preference (priority, security, etc.) he would like to set. If the user's preference setting can be satisfied given the money limit, the PAA displays OK to the user in the dialog box. Otherwise, it presents the estimated money when satisfying all the specified preference, or the best service possiblly satisfiable under the money limit. The user can select among them.

The PAA can be more intelligent so that it can do the above task automatically on behalf of the user. This can also shorten the service selection process.

7 Conclusion

Pricing and prioritizing the Internet access can be one of the potential measures to improve the efficiency of the Internet utilization and control the Internet congestion. This paper explored the application of DAI and MAS, especially the market model in the implementation of the rational IP routers on the priced Internet. The main issues addressed in this paper include the following:

- The negotiation model for task decomposition and allocation and the payment model for interaction between users and gateways, and between gateways and gateways for conducting internet routing tasks.
- The application of MAS/DAI in the optimization of global resource allocation among gateways, and the strategies of achieving a rational and fair resource allocation and scheduling locally inside an IP router for various priority service classes it provides. Some strategies for IP router to improve the response time for a certain priority service class, and strategies to improve their adaptability to the changing demand were also proposed.
- The strategies and factors in the setting and adjustment of prices for different priority service classes for the IP routers. The price setting for different service classes is closely related to the implementation of priority queues: the queue lengths of and the percentage of resources allocated to different priority services.
- The consumer strategies. Consumers' strategy is dependent upon their goals and their budget constraints. The intelligent agent technology can facilitate consumers in selecting from different strategies.

There are some issues that are beyond the computational world, and can be classified as social issues on the priced internet. For instance, the payment policy and enhancement issues include: what if a user does not pay IP routers, how to deal with cheating behaviors of IP routers, and so on. The solutions to these problems are largely dependent upon the agreement among these three parties: users, the organizations users belong to, and the IP routers.

Our future research will be oriented to the generalization of the negotiation and RAS models, and testing these models.

References

1. Davis R. and Smith R., "Negotiation as a Metaphor for Distributed Problem Solving", *Artificial Intelligence*, Vol. 20, no. 1, pp. 63-109, 1983.
2. Liu J. and Sycara K., "Distributed Constraint Satisfaction through Constraint Partition and Coordination Reaction", in *Proc. of the 12th International Workshop on Distributed Artificial Intelligence*, Pennsylvania, pp. 263-279, May 1993.
3. Sandholm T. and Lesser V., "Issues in Automated Negotiation and Electronic Commerce: Extending the Contract Net Framework", in *Proc. of the First International Conference on Multi-Agent Systems*, MIT Press, pp. 328-335, 1995.
4. Kuwabara K. and Ishida T., "Equilibratory Approach to Distributed Resource Allocation: Toward Coordinated Balancing", in Castelfranchi C. and Werner E., eds., *Artificial Social Systems, 4th European Workshop on Modelling Autonomous Agents in a Multi-Agent World, MAAAMAW'92*", Spring-Verlag, Italy, pp.133-146, 1992.
5. Wellman M. P, "A Market-Oriented Programming Environment and its Application to Distributed Multicommodity Flow Problems", *Journal of Artificial Intelligence Research*, 1, 1-23, 1993.
6. S. E. Conry, K. Kuwabara, V. R. Lesser and R. A. Meyer, "Multistage Negotiation for Distributed Constraint Satisfaction", *IEEE Trans. Syst. Man., Cybern.*, Vol. SMC-21, No. 6, pp. 1462 - 1477, 1991.
7. Richard J. Edell, Nick McKeown and Pravin P. Varaiya, "Billing Users and Pricing for TCP", to appear in *IEEE Journal on Selected Areas in Communications*, 1995.
8. J. K. Mackie-Mason and H. Varian, "Some Economics of the Internet", Technical report, Department of Economics, University of Michigan, Nov., 1993.
9. A. Gupta, D. O. Stahl, and A. B. Whinston, "Pricing of Services on The Internet", in *IMPACT: How ICC Research Affects Public Policy and Business Markets: A Volume in Honor of G. Kozmetsky*, Fred Phillips and W.W. Cooper eds., Quorum Book, CT, forthcoming.
10. Kotler P., Chandler P., Gibbs R., and McColl R., *Marketing in Australia*, Second Edition, Prentice Hall, 1989
11. H-W Braun and K. Claffy, "Post-NSFNET Statistics Collection", in *Proc. INET'95*, 1995.
12. "Internet Protocol – DARPA Internet Program Protocol Specification", RFC-791, by Information Sciences Institute, University of Southern California, 1981.
13. S. Deering and R. Hinden, "Internet Protocol, Version 6 (IPv6) Specification", RFC-1883, Dec., 1995.
14. J. Postel, "Internet Control Message Protocol – DARPA Internet Program Protocol Specification", RFC-792, Sept. 1981.
15. R. Atkinson, "Security Architecture for the Internet Protocol", RFC-1825, August 1955.

A Sentinel Approach to Fault Handling in Multi-Agent Systems

Staffan Hägg

Department of Computer Science
University of Karlskrona/Ronneby, Sweden
Staffan.Hagg@ide.hk-r.se
http://www.sikt.hk-r.se/~staffanh

Abstract

Fault handling in Multi-Agent Systems (MAS) is not much addressed in current research. Normally, it is considered difficult to address in detail and often well covered by traditional methods, relying on the underlying communication and operating system. In this paper it is shown that this is not necessarily true, at least not with the assumptions on applications we have made. These assumptions are a massive distribution of computing components, a heterogeneous underlying infrastructure (in terms of hardware, software and communication methods), an emerging configuration, possibly different parties in control of sub-systems, and real-time demands in parts of the system.

The key problem is that while a MAS is modular and therefore should be a good platform for building fault tolerant systems, it is also non-deterministic, making it difficult to guarantee a specific behaviour, especially in fault situations. Our proposal is to introduce *sentinels* to guard certain functionality and to protect from undesired states. The sentinels form a control structure to the MAS, and through the *semantic addressing* scheme they can monitor communication, build models of other agents, and intervene according to given guidelines.

As sentinels are agents themselves, they interact with other agents through agent communication. The sentinel approach allows system developers to first implement the functionality (by programming the agents) and then add on a control system (the sentinels). The control system can be modified on the fly with no or minimal disturbance to the rest of the system.

The present work is conducted in cooperation with Sydkraft, a major Swedish power distribution company. Examples are taken from that venture, and it is shown how problems can be solved by programming DA-SoC agents, developed here.

Keywords

Multi-Agent Systems, Fault Tolerance, Semantic Addressing, Sentinel

1 Introduction

Fault handling in Multi-Agent Systems

When discussing fault handling in multi-agent systems (MAS) there are often two opposite positions. The first says that a MAS is inherently fault tolerant by its modular nature; faults can be isolated and generally do not spread. The other says that a MAS is inherently insecure, as control is distributed. It is non-deterministic, and a specific behaviour is hard to guarantee, especially in fault situations.

The Societies of Computation (SoC) Research Project

The background to this paper is a research project, the Societies of Computation (SoC) [5][10], at the University of Karlskrona/Ronneby in Sweden. In a joint effort with Sydkraft, a major Swedish power distribution company, technologies for automating the power distribution process are studied. The goal is to make the distribution process flexible and robust to load changes, re-configurations, faults, etc. (Distribution Automation - DA), and to offer new services to customers, such as the choice between different levels of service and even between different suppliers (Demand Side Management - DSM). Furthermore, and perhaps the most challenging goal is to exploit a new infrastructure for Home Automation (HA), integrated with the DA/DSM system. The physical electric grid is used for communication, and small and simple pieces of hardware are plugged into wall-sockets and lamp-sockets, operating as interfaces to appliances, or are integrated within them. Basic techniques for this is in the process of being standardized. Our challenge is therefore to develop methods for using this infrastructure in terms of computation and communication, thus creating truly plug-in software. Computation in this environment is thus distributed *en masse*, and changes are unpredictable; there exists no generic way of describing the total system at any one point in time.

The first phase of the joint project, called DA-SoC [7], takes an agent-oriented approach to distributed computing, and it includes the definition of an agent architecture, an agent language, and a programmable model of interaction. The second phase, part of which is described here, is called Test Site Ronneby (TSR). Our goal is to create a full scale test environment in the city of Ronneby for DA/DSM and HA, as described above, and doing this, one essential aspect, not covered in the initial work, is to make the running system tolerant to a number of fault situations.

Outline of the Paper

We start with a short outline of how fault tolerance is traditionally addressed in industrial systems and in other MAS research. Then we try to identify what the core problems are when a MAS approach is used. We give an short description of the DA-SoC agent architecture, and then we introduce the concept of sentinels in this context. Two examples of sentinels in a MAS are given: in negotiation and in inconsistency detection. With the conclusions we also sketch how the concept of sentinels may be generalized for other purposes than robustness.

2 Fault Tolerant Systems

First we identify that the applications we have in mind have some common properties:

- a massive distribution of computing components,
- a heterogeneous underlying infrastructure (in terms of hardware, software and communication methods),
- an emerging configuration,
- possibly different parties in control of sub-systems, and
- real-time demands in parts of the system.

Fault tolerance is especially well studied for real-time systems. From that work we take some important definitions as a background to our study. Here, we mainly follow a standard textbook on real-time systems (Burns and Wellings [2]).

The sources of faults

According to Burns and Wellings there are four main sources of faults:

(1) Inadequate specification of software
(2) Software design error
(3) Processor failure
(4) Communication error

where the former two sources are unanticipated (in terms of their consequences). The latter two sources, on the other hand, can be considered in the design of the system.

The consequences of faults

If the occurrence of a fault results in the system not being able to conform to the specification of the system's behaviour, there is a *system failure*. If, on the other hand, the system can handle the fault situation, it is called *fault tolerant*. Even if all possible measures are taken to prevent faults, the former two sources above imply the difficulty in building fault-free systems. This emphasizes the need for fault tolerance.

Degrees of fault tolerance

We observe the important notion of levels or degrees of fault tolerance:

- *Full fault tolerance*, where the system continues to operate without significant loss of functionality or performance even in the presence of faults.
- *Graceful degradation*, where the system maintains operation with some loss of functionality or performance.
- *Fail-safe*, where vital functions are preserved while others may fail.

Methods for building fault tolerant systems

Perhaps, the most basic principle behind building fault tolerant systems is that of modularity. First, it lets the designers give structure to the system, helping in data modelling, implementation, and testing. Second, for the running system, it makes it possible to isolate a fault as it appears, sometimes referred to as *firewalling* against faulty components. Third, it is a basis for other principles, such as information hiding, checkpointing, and redundancy.

Redundancy refers to techniques where several modules are given the same functionality. These can be identical, e.g. mirroring storage systems, or modules backing up the running module in case of fault. There can also be one or more differing modules taking over functionality from a faulty one, though with loss of performance. A somewhat different approach is the concept of N-version programming, proposed by Chen and Avizienis [3]. Here, N individuals or groups independently develop a module from the same specification. Then at run-time, all N modules execute in parallel, and the results are compared and the final result is voted for. This addresses fault sources (1) and (2) above.

The third principle is the choice of implementation language. The language should traditionally allow the system's behaviour to be determined from the code. This demand for *determinism* disregards such features as dynamic binding and operator overloading.

The problem of inconsistency

One approach to handle inconsistency is using formal methods for describing the system. This can be made in the specification phase with specification languages, such as Z, or for the running system, modelling the whole or parts of the system as a Truth Maintenance System. The problem is that all experience say that if the system is of any considerable size or complexity, inconsistencies *will* appear. This is especially the case when, from physical or other reasons, parts of the system is distributed (as is assumed here). Therefore, if it is important to avoid inconsistency entering the system, it is even more important being able to handle inconsistency as it appears (i.e., a fault tolerant system[1]).

Fault Handling Approaches in Multi-Agent Systems Research

Fault handling is not much addressed in MAS or DAI research. Generally, agents are thought of as being both benevolent and fault-free. Some research has addressed non-benevolent agents or agents with conflicting goals, but agent theories and architectures usually avoid the problem with faulty agents. The matter of inconsistency is especially difficult. It is discussed by Boman and Ekenberg [1], and they call a "global inconsistency over a finite number of locally consistent structures ... a *paraconsistency*." However, our use of inconsistency is more restricted than theirs: we do not consider a formal system where inconsistencies automatically can be detected; an inconsistency is defined from the system design as a global state that should not occur, and if it occurs, it is caused by any one of the four sources of faults mentioned above.

---

1. Here we consider an inconsistency being a consequence of one of the four sources of faults mentioned earlier, and hence, the inconsistency is considered a fault. Another notion for this could be a defect, but for reason of simplicity, we do not distinguish between the two in this paper.

For agent based systems that have been used commercially, fault handling is not much considered, and mostly it takes traditional approaches. For example, in ARCHON [13] (a project with partly the same objectives as ours), the problem of global coordination and coherence is addressed. It is determined to be part of the acquaintance model (and hereby it shows some likeness to our approach), but the issue of fault handling is not given much attention as a problem in its own right. In the PRS system [9] which is used for a number of commercial applications, there is no explicit fault handling techniques. Fault handling is taken care of by the underlying communication and operating system. In case of faults generated in the specification, design, or implementation phase of the system, normal debugging and testing procedures are used.

The conclusion is that for MAS, fault handling is considered difficult to address in detail. It is often only addressed by traditional methods for avoiding design and programming errors and then relying on standard fault handling techniques for communication and hardware faults. In the following it is shown that it may be desirable to explicitly address fault handling in a running system, especially with the assumptions on applications we have made.

3 Identifying the Problem

We started with stating that there are two opposite positions to fault handling in MAS, one saying that a MAS is inherently fault tolerant and the other saying that it is difficult to make a MAS fault tolerant. This is easy to understand, given the background of the previous section. The agent paradigm perfectly conforms to one of the basic principles for building fault tolerant systems, namely modularity. At the same time it corresponds very poorly to another of these principles, namely that an implementation language (or, more generally, an implementation model) should be deterministic.

Figure 1 illustrates the relationship between different programming paradigms and the matter of control. Orthodox real-time systems are totally *deterministic*; the behaviour of the system can, at least in principal, be determined from the program code. Object-oriented systems have introduced some dynamic features, such as dynamic binding of modules and operator overloading. These systems were initially criticised but are today widely used for real-time applications (e.g., in the telecommunication area and for making computer operating systems). Multi-agent systems represent the other extreme. There is no inherent mechanism for synchronization or control; the system is inherently *non-deterministic*. If we shall guarantee a specific behaviour, especially in the presence of faults, then we must find a way to deal with the non-deterministic property of the MAS. The method proposed in this paper does exactly that. Sentinels introduce a supervising and control model for the operating MAS.

4 The DA-SoC Agent Architecture

Before we introduce the concept of sentinels we will shortly outline the DA-SoC agent architecture and interaction model. It is not possible to show all details of the architecture, the language, etc. This is further described in [7].

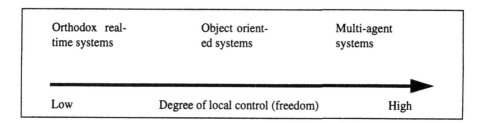

Figure 1. Comparison of local control (freedom) between some types of system.

A DA-SoC agent is procedural and goal-driven, and it holds a world model in declarative form. Its most elaborate feature is a programmable model of interaction, that lets the user tailor its interactive behaviour. A simplified picture of the agent head is shown in Figure 2. The world model consists of a set of beliefs. The reasoner holds agent plans and a goal queue, letting the user program the agent in an event driven fashion. The programmable Model of Interaction (MoI) is realized through a set of interaction plans that are matched and, eventually, executed when a message comes in. By programming the MoI, the user can give agents specific roles in the society.

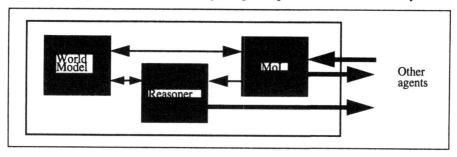

Figure 2. Structure of the DA-SoC agent head

The basic communication mechanism in DA-SoC is a broadcast message passing scheme[1]. When a message is sent by one agent, all other agents receive it, and every agent tries to match it with an interaction plan. The declaration part of an interaction plan has an agent name as the receiver's address and a pattern for what message contents it will accept. Both the agent name (the address) in the message and the message contents must therefore match the declaration part of an interaction plan. Upon a successful match, the plan is executed. During execution, the agent's world model may be altered. There can also be set an internal goal. In this case, the goal is matched with agent plans and, eventually, an agent plan is executed, during which the world model can be altered, goals can be set, and messages can be sent. A special feature is that one agent can hold an interaction plan with the name of another agent as the receiver's

---

1. Fisher discusses in [4] the impact of broadcast communication in MAS.

address. This enables one agent to play the role of another agent within the society with respect to the types of messages that are defined by that interaction plan.

Semantic addressing

Let us call our plans methods, accessible by other agents. Then the broadcast mechanism, the MoI, and agent plans form consecutive steps in an access model which we call *semantic addressing* (Figure 3). (1) shows an agent executing an agent plan. During execution, a message "request ..." is broadcast (2). The receiving agents try to match the incoming message with interaction plan declarations (3), and in (4) we see that agents 2 and 4 execute successfully matched interaction plans, while agents 1 and 3 failed in matching the message. Finally, (5) shows that agent 2 set a goal during execution of the interaction plan, and the matched agent plan is now executed. Here, agent 4 either did not set a goal or failed in matching the goal with an agent plan.

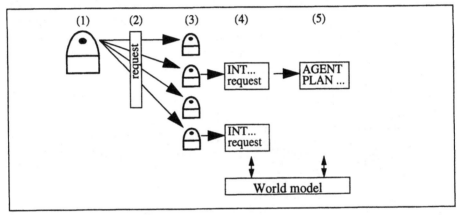

Figure 3. Semantic addressing in DA-SoC

Semantic addressing allows agents to access methods within other agents in the society without knowing where they should be found. But moreover, a method is accessed wherever it is semantically meaningful according to the application definitions, and where it is consistent with the agent's world model (which can change). The world model may be altered due to changes in the surrounding world or in agents' capabilities. Thus, the next time the same message is sent, there may be a goal set and a plan executed within another agent than the first time.

Semantic addressing is outlined in length in [8]. There it is shown how this access scheme allows for agents to play different roles in a society (e.g., backing up each other, or adapting communication patterns to changes in the environment). Here we lay down semantic addressing as a basis for the concept of sentinels.

5 Sentinels in a Multi-Agent System

In our approach we first conclude that if the total system is of considerable size and complexity, involving unreliable communication media, a fully fault tolerant system is not realistic. Therefore, the designer must decide on which functions are most vital for the system's integrity. The system must also have good support for both fault handling and fault reporting. Second, the technique we choose, actually decreases the freedom for agents where it is necessary for preserving the system's integrity[1]. And third, this control must be easy to maintain and change (e.g., in case of version changes, during repair of faulty components, or as the system emerges over time).

Sentinels

A sentinel is an agent, and its mission is to guard specific functions or to guard against specific states in the society of agents. The sentinel does not partake in domain problem solving, but it can intervene if necessary, choosing alternative problem solving methods for agents, excluding faulty agents, altering parameters for agents, and reporting to human operators.

Being an agent, the sentinel interacts with other agents using semantic addressing. Thereby it can, by monitoring agent communication and by interaction (asking), build models of other agents. It can also use timers to detect crashed agents (or a faulty communication link).

Checkpoints

Given a set of agents that cooperate in realizing a system function, a sentinel is set to guard the operation of that function. The sentinel now maintains models of these agents, as mentioned above. Some items in such a model (expressed as beliefs) are directly copied from the world model of the agent in concern, becoming parts of the world model of the sentinel. We call these items *checkpoints* (Figure 4). These check-

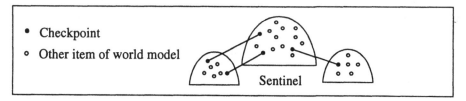

- Checkpoint
- Other item of world model

Sentinel

Figure 4. Checkpoints and world models

points let sentinels judge on the status of an agent, not only from its behaviour, but from its internal state. This is a means for early detection of a faulty agent and of inconsistency between agents (which is considered a system fault).

System development

The DA-SoC architecture supports incremental system development. In a typical development process, the developer iterates between design and implementation (and even back to specification). With DA-SoC, some agents, realizing a certain function,

---

1. This may be a controversial result. Many researchers prefer to view agents as totally independent. We find it, however, essential to impose this kind of restriction to agents freedom in order to cope with the non-determinism, mentioned earlier. This is further discussed in the conclusions of the paper.

may be implemented and the function can be tested. Other agents can thereafter be entered to the running system, and the total system emerges over time.

For our purpose this means that the whole system can be developed and its operation can be tested before the control system (the sentinels) is put on top of the fully operating system, Figure 5. The decision on checkpoints can be made as the sentinels are designed, as well as communication between the sentinels and between sentinels and operator terminals. It also means that the control system can be modified later without disturbing the running system.

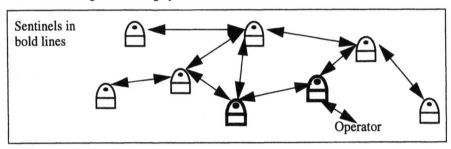

Figure 5. Sentinels in a society of agents

6 Example: Sentinels in Negotiation

Hägg and Ygge [7] present an example where DA-SoC agents are used for *load balancing* in power distribution. Distributor and customers operate on a spot market, where power is sold and bought[1]. The goal is to optimize the utilization of distribution lines, reducing load peaks, and avoiding overload in bottlenecks. Customers and distributor are represented by agents, negotiating about prices and the amount of power to sell. Suppose a customer's agent constantly underbids in negotiations, winning all contracts and thereby undertaking to reduce its power consumption more and more.

We now enter a sentinel who's task is to monitor agent communication, maintain models of the negotiating parties, and protect the negotiation process according to given guidelines. Soon it will detect that there is something wrong with the overly generous customer's agent. Depending on the guidelines, the sentinel may raise an alarm to an operator, or it can tell the distributor's agents to disregard that customer's agent for the moment.

Monitoring agent communication is quite simple using the semantic addressing scheme. Suppose the agents send bid messages on the following format[2]

```
(bid(<distributor agent> <bid time> sell(<amount> <price>
<duration>)))
```

If the sentinel now has the following interaction plan as part of its MoI

---

1. A customer "sells" power if he offers to use less power than previously agreed upon in long term contracts.
2. The expressions and plans should be quite intuitive to read, but see [7] for a full outline of the language.

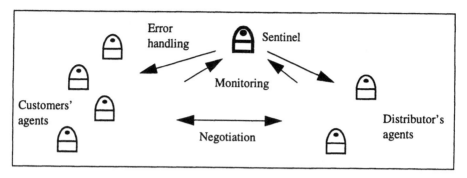

Figure 6. A sentinel supervising negotiation

```
INTERACTION PLAN bid($VOID $time $$fact)
        BEL(SENDER $time $$fact)
```

it will pick up all bid messages in the society, and soon it will have a number of items of its world model as negotiation goes on:

```
BEL(c_ag_1 time_1 sell(am_1 pr_1 dur_1)
BEL(c_ag_2 time_2 sell(am_2 pr_2 dur_2)
BEL(c_ag_3 time_3 sell(am_3 pr_3 dur_3)
...
BEL(c_ag_n time_n sell(am_n pr_n dur_n)
BEL(c_ag_1 time_(n+1) sell(am_(n+1) pr_(n+1) dur_(n+1))
BEL(c_ag_2 time_(n+2) sell(am_(n+2) pr_(n+2) dur_(n+2))
...
```

These items become parts of the sentinels models of the customers' agents, and from them the sentinel can analyse the behaviour of those agents. A simple procedure for detecting underbids is the following agent plan:

```
AGENT PLAN ME check_for_underbids()
BEGIN
      ?BEL(ME $VOID price_limit($lower_limit
              $upper_limit)) // get limit values
      ?BEL($agent $time sell($amount $price
              $duration) // get list of monitored
                    // beliefs
      CHOOSE(MIN($price)) // choose belief with
                    // minimum price
      IF($price<$lower_limit) THEN // price is too low
      BEGIN
           SACT(start_error_check($agent NOW
               price_limit($lower_limit
               $upper_limit))) // ask the agent
                    // to start error checking
           BEL($agent $time underbid($amount $price
                    $duration)) // catalogue the event
           ~BEL($agent $time sell($amount $price
```

```
                              $duration)) // remove the bid
                 GOAL(ME NOW check_for_underbids())
                              // check for more underbids
        END
        ELSE // there is no price that is too low
        BEGIN
               ?BEL(ME $VOID check_interval($interval))
                       // get the time interval for checking
               GOAL(ME LATER(NOW $interval)
                       check_for_underbids()) // set next goal
        END
   END
```

While the interaction plan picks up all bids and maintains models of bidding agents, the agent plan periodically checks for underbids, initiates error checking procedures, and catalogues error events. There can of course be other plans (e.g., checking for other limit transgressions)[1].

There are at least two important reasons for not integrating this control function with the distributor's agents. First, supervising the negotiation process is a strategic matter that aims at protecting the system's integrity. If strategies change, the sentinel can be given new guidelines without disturbing the normal operation. Second, normal operation would perform poorer if these and similar decisions should be taken into account during negotiation[2].

7 Example: Sentinels in Inconsistency Detection

Another example from power distribution is shown in Figure 7. The secondary substa-

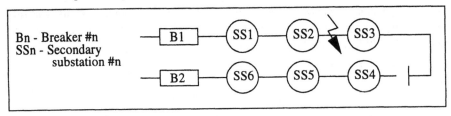

Figure 7. A short circuit between two secondary sub-stations.

tions, SS1 - SS4, get voltage through breaker B1 or breaker B2, depending on where the circuit is open. If, in the example, there is a short circuit between SS2 and SS3, B1 will automatically open and SS1 - SS3 will be without voltage. Agents representing

---

1. If the sentinel should calculate more elaborately on the retrieved information, it would be nice to have access to, for example, a spreadsheet or a database program. The DA-SoC architecture is designed for this purpose; an agent's body is defined to be any program that can communicate with the agent head using a well defined protocol. To our testbed [7] we have ready made interfaces to MS Excel, Borland C++, and MS Visual Basic, allowing us to create body programs for virtually any purpose.

2. This may be implementation dependent.

the breakers and the secondary substations will now try to solve the problem, resulting in SS2 and SS3 opening local breakers to disconnect from the faulty line, SS3 and SS4 closing local breakers to supply SS3 with electricity from SS4, and B1 closing to supply SS1 and SS2. This is called *grid restoration*, and so far the agents solved the problem (see [6] how it is solved), and the grid has now changed to the situation in Figure 8.

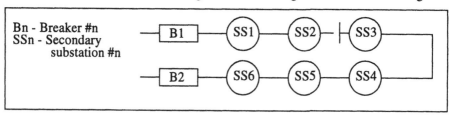

Figure 8. After grid restoration.

Suppose now that after these operations, $Agent_{SS3}$ in its world model holds the belief that its local breaker to SS4 is closed (which it should be) and the belief that its voltage level is high (which it also should be). At the same time $Agent_{SS4}$ believes that its local breaker to SS3 is open (which it should not be). Obviously there is something wrong. Either SS4 has a faulty sensor incorrectly indicating an open breaker to SS3, or SS4's breaker did not really close during the restoration and at the same time SS3 has a faulty sensor incorrectly indicating a high voltage level (or possibly a third explanation, maybe a programming error).

The problem is that neither $Agent_{SS3}$ nor $Agent_{SS4}$ has the information needed to detect the fault, less the nature of the fault; there is an inconsistency between the agents that requires global information to detect. If the second explanation is correct, SS3 is out of voltage, and customers will eventually call the distributor about it. According to the first explanation (and perhaps the most likely from what we know), the grid is operating correctly, but SS4's faulty sensor may cause failures later.

Observe the two levels of fault handling: Restoring the grid is the normal operation of the MAS, while taking care of the inconsistency is to make the restoration system fault tolerant. If we introduce a sentinel to the MAS and let it through agent communication use essential beliefs of the other agents as checkpoints, it can detect inconsistencies of this kind.

If the sentinel through monitoring, as in the previous example, or through direct agent communication, has the following items of its world model

```
BEL(SS3 time_1 local_breaker(SS4 closed))
BEL(SS3 time_2 voltage(high))
BEL(ME time_3 voltage_from(SS3 SS4)
```

but not the item

```
BEL(SS4 time_4 local_breaker(SS3 closed))
```

then the following agent plan will detect the inconsistency and start the error handling procedure.

```
AGENT PLAN ME check_local_breaker($source $dependant)
         // testing $source's local breaker to $dependant
BEGIN
      ?BEL(ME $VOID voltage_from($dependant $source))
               // does $dependant get
               // voltage from $source?
      IF SUCCESS THEN // yes
      BEGIN
            ?BEL($dependant $VOID voltage(high) // has
                  // $dependant a high voltage level?
            IF SUCCESS THEN // yes
            BEGIN
                  ?BEL($source $VOID local_breaker(
                     $dependant closed)) // is the
                              // breaker closed?
                  IF NOT SUCCESS THEN // no
                     GOAL(ME NOW error_local_breaker(
                        $source $dependant)) // start
                              // error handling
            END
      END
END
```

The plan is invoked by the goal

```
GOAL(ME <time> check_local_breaker(SS4 SS3))
```

to check for the correctness of SS4's local breaker to SS3. This should be done periodically, and for all local breakers. Possibly the error handling procedure can, by retrieving more information, identify the nature of the fault, make the involved agents
observant of it, and, in any case, report it.

The arguments for not letting the operating agents do the consistency checking
themselves are the same as in the previous example. Yet another argument is that it
would surely take more computing and communication resources to use distributed
algorithms for this.

8 Conclusions and Future Activities

Conclusions

We have already stated that the problem of fault handling in MAS concerns the question of determinism. If a MAS should be tolerant to faults, the inherent property of
non-determinism must be restricted. The philosophical question, indicated earlier,
whether this restriction not violates the very concept of agenthood builds, as we see it,
on a misconception: Agents' freedom and non-determinism from a system's perspective is an architectural issue. Even DA-SoC agents are modelled independently, and
there are no limitations within the architecture that prevent agents from changing its
behaviour or taking new roles in the society from time to time. On the other hand, the
restrictions laid upon agents is a structural (or design) issue. By imposing a certain

structure onto the agent society, some specific behaviour can be guaranteed, and other behaviour can be prevented from.

Distributed AI often takes its metaphors from social sciences. Many human activities require cooperation. If the cooperation by any reason goes wrong, some "fault handling routines" must be executed. If the society is of any size, it is necessary to have some control structure, rules, etc. and supervisors to secure it. Here, the supervisors execute the "fault handling routines". This does not conflict with the concept of humanness (perhaps with the exception of extreme dictatorship). On the contrary, it is natural to humans, and it actually helps them in fulfilling their common tasks.

A similar discussion is that of centralized vs. decentralized control in distributed computer systems. It is sometimes assumed that decentralized control makes the system more flexible. It is, however, often difficult to find decentralized solutions that are both efficient and fault tolerant (Tanenbaum [12], pp. 27-29). In this respect, our sentinel approach means that we enter a centralized control structure. But, again, there are limitations on the centralized aspects: agents can change roles, and the control system may change over time.

The sentinel approach to fault handling indicate that total control of possible fault situations and global consistency are not always realistic. For the applications we consider, it would be far too expensive in terms of computation and communication, if achievable at all. Sentinels are a means for designers to guarantee partial consistency and graceful degradation in case of faults, given the priorities of the application.

Our approach allows the system implementer to program the functionality of the MAS and then design and implement the control system. The control system can also be changed with minimal disturbance to the application.

Abstraction levels

Finally, we will very briefly generalize the sentinel concept from mere fault handling to a generic way of entering abstraction levels in a MAS. This is subject for future research, but it is a natural extrapolation of the present work. Figure 9 shows five groups of agents. Each group can be defined from its global role (e.g., representing a certain functionality). Agent group C, D, and E may realize different operational proc-

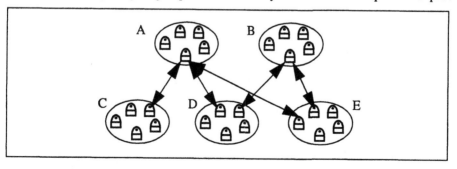

Figure 9. Five groups of agents representing abstraction levels

esses, while groups A and B may realize strategic functions, setting limits for the operational groups. If the application is telecommunication management, the operational groups can control communication lines. Group A can be responsible for economic transactions, and group B can handle customer demands. There may also be other groups taking care of fault handling, security, etc. There may also be additional levels in the MAS. A similar approach is shown by Somers [11], developing HYBRID, a Multi-Agent System for telecommunication management.

Using the agent-oriented approach, these groups, as well as individual agents, may be developed or modified on the fly, with no or minimal disturbance to the rest of the system. With DA-SoC agents, programs written in traditional languages, or even legacy programs, can be used to realize basic functionality, glued together with the interaction of agent heads.

References

[1] Boman M., and Ekenberg L., Eliminating Paraconsistencies in 4-valued Cooperative Deductive Multidatabase Systems with Classical Negation, in *Proceedings of the Second International Working Conference on Cooperating Knowledge Based Systems*, University of Keele, England, June 1994, ISBN 0-952-17892-3.

[2] Burns A., and Wellings A., *Real-Time Systems and Their Programming Languages*, Addison-Wesley, 1990, ISBN 0-201-17529-0.

[3] Chen L., and Avizienis A., N-version programming: a fault-tolerance approach to reliability of software operation. In *Digest of Papers, The Eight Annual International Conference on Fault-Tolerant Computing*, Toulouse, France, 1978.

[4] Fisher M., Representing and Executing Agent-Based Systems, *Proceedings of the ECAI'94 Workshop on Agent Theories, Architectures, and Languages*, August 8-12, 1994, Amsterdam, The Netherlands.

[5] Gustavsson R., Akkermans H., Hägg S., Ygge F., Kozbe B., Lundberg C., and Carlsson B., *Societies of Computation (SoC) - A Framework for Open Distributed Systems, Phase II: 1995-98*, University of Karlskrona/Ronneby, Research Report 8/95, ISSN 1103-1581.

[6] Hägg S., and Ygge F., An Architecture for Agent-Oriented Programming with a Programmable Model of Interaction, in *Proceedings of the Seventh Annual Conference on AI and Cognitive Science '94*, Trinity College, Dublin, Ireland, September 8 - 9, 1994.

[7] Hägg S., and Ygge F., *Agent-Oriented Programming in Power Distribution Automation - An Architecture, a Language, and their Applicability*, Ph.L. Thesis, LUNFD6/(NFCS-3094)/1-180/(1995), Lund University, Sweden, May 1995.

[8] Hägg S., Adaptation in a Multi-Agent System through Semantic Addressing, in *Proceedings of the Workshop on Decentralized Intelligent and Multi-Agent Systems (DIMAS'95)*, Krakow, Poland, November 1995.

[9] Ingrand F. F., and Georgeff M., *Procedural Reasoning System, User Guide*, 1991, available from the Australian Artificial Intelligence Institute, 1 Grattan Street, Carlton, Victoria 3053, Australia.

[10] Societies of Computation (SoC), *Internet Home Page*, http://www.sikt.hk-r.se/~soc.

[11] Somers F., Intelligent Agents for High-Speed Network Management, in *Proceedings of The First International Conference and Exhibition on The Practical Application of Intelligent Agents and Multi-Agent Technology (PAAM'96)*, London, England, April 22 - 24, 1996.

[12] Tanenbaum A. S., *Distributed Operating Systems*, Prentice-Hall, 1995, ISBN 0-13-143934-0.

[13] Wittig T., ed., *ARCHON an architecture for multi-agent systems*, Ellis Horwood, 1992, ISBN 0-13-044462-6.

Springer
and the
environment

At Springer we firmly believe that an
international science publisher has a
special obligation to the environment,
and our corporate policies consistently
reflect this conviction.

We also expect our business partners –
paper mills, printers, packaging
manufacturers, etc. – to commit
themselves to using materials and
production processes that do not harm
the environment. The paper in this
book is made from low- or no-chlorine
pulp and is acid free, in conformance
with international standards for paper
permanency.

 Springer

Lecture Notes in Artificial Intelligence (LNAI)

Lecture Notes in Computer Science